Equity Now

Equity Now

Justice, Repair, and Belonging in Schools

Tyrone C. Howard

FOR INFORMATION:

Corwin

A SAGE Company

2455 Teller Road

Thousand Oaks, California 91320

(800) 233-9936

www.corwin.com

SAGE Publications Ltd.

1 Oliver's Yard

55 City Road

London EC1Y 1SP

United Kingdom

SAGE Publications India Pvt. Ltd.

Unit No 323-333, Third Floor, F-Block

International Trade Tower Nehru Place

New Delhi 110 019

India

SAGE Publications Asia-Pacific Pte. Ltd.

18 Cross Street #10-10/11/12

China Square Central

Singapore 048423

Vice President and
  Editorial Director: Monica Eckman

Program Director and Publisher: Dan Alpert

Acquisitions Editor: Megan Bedell

Content Development Editor: Mia Rodriguez

Content Development Manager: Lucas Schleicher

Senior Editorial Assistant: Natalie Delpino

Project Editor: Amy Schroller

Copy Editor: Melinda Masson

Typesetter: C&M Digitals (P) Ltd.

Proofreader: Lawrence Baker

Indexer: Integra

Cover Designer: Candice Harmann

Marketing Manager: Melissa Duclos

Cover concept by Maria Muhammad

Printed in the United States of America

Library of Congress Cataloging-in-Publication Data

Names: Howard, Tyrone C. (Tyrone Caldwell), author.

Title: Equity now : justice, repair, and belonging in schools / Tyrone C. Howard.

Description: Thousand Oaks, California : Corwin, [2024] | Includes bibliographical references and index.

Identifiers: LCCN 2023051428 | ISBN 9781071926383 (paperback) | ISBN 9781071926406 (epub) | ISBN 9781071926413 (epub) | ISBN 9781071926437 (pdf)

Subjects: LCSH: Educational equalization—United States. | Belonging (Social psychology)—United States. | Social justice and education—United States. | Discrimination in education—United States. | Students with social disabilities—Education—United States.

Classification: LCC LC213.2 .H66 2024 | DDC 379.2/60973—dc23/20231130

LC record available at https://lccn.loc.gov/2023051428

This book is printed on acid-free paper.

24 25 26 27 28 10 9 8 7 6 5 4 3 2 1

Contents

Publisher's Acknowledgments

Corwin gratefully acknowledges the contributions of the following reviewers:

Elizabeth Alvarez
Superintendent
Forest Park District 91
Forest Park, IL

Sydney Chaffee
Humanities Teacher and Instructional Coach
Codman Academy Charter Public School
Boston, MA

Lisa Graham
Director, Early Childhood Education
Douglas County School District
Douglas County, CO

Gerald Luke
Director of Access and Equity, African American Student
    Achievement
Palmdale School District
Palmdale, CA

Latish Reed
Executive Leadership Consultant and Coach
Derute Consulting Cooperative
Milwaukee, WI

About the Author

Tyrone C. Howard is the Pritzker Family Endowed Chair in the School of Education and Information Studies at the University of California, Los Angeles. Dr. Howard is the co-director of the UCLA Pritzker Center for Strengthening Children and Families. He also is the co-director of the UCLA Center for the Transformation of Schools. Dr. Howard has published over 100 scholarly journal articles, book chapters, policy briefs, and technical reports. He is the author of six books. Dr. Howard is the president and a Fellow of the American Educational Research Association, which is the world's largest educational research organization. In 2021, Dr. Howard was elected as a member of the National Academy of Education. His work has been highlighted by the *New York Times*, the *Los Angeles Times*, and the *Washington Post*. He is regularly featured on National Public Radio and many other media outlets. Dr. Howard is considered one of the nation's foremost thinkers and change agents on issues tied to racial inequality in education.

Dedicated to my grandchildren
Jaye Simari, my joy, and Harlem Rashaad, my angel.

Introduction

Why Equity Matters

May 2024 will mark the 70th anniversary of the historic *Brown v. Board of Education* ruling. At the time, the *Brown* decision was hailed as a landmark judicial decision that would address one of the most stubborn and complex realities of U.S. life: unequal education. Core to the idea of equal education for all students was a dismantling of racial inequities that have plagued non-white students for centuries in the United States. *Brown*, at the time, in all its hubris sought to end racial inequality in U.S. schools and, in the eyes of many, was thought to be a potential catalyst for how racial equality in other aspects of U.S. society could be achieved. The idea was that if the nation could do better by its young people and schools, the rest of the country would soon follow suit. In almost three-quarters of a century since the *Brown* decision was rendered, the dreams, hopes, and wishes of a country built on freedom, justice, and equal opportunity have been deferred for many and outright denied for others. In the words of Dr. Martin Luther King Jr., in his famous March on Washington speech of 1963:

> In a sense we've come to our nation's capital to cash a check. . . . It is obvious today that America has defaulted on this promissory note insofar as her citizens of color are concerned. Instead of honoring this sacred obligation, America has given the Negro people a bad check, a check which has come back marked "insufficient funds."

How can schools, and the United States, honor the request of Dr. King to hold our nation, and its schools, to the promise of fairness, justice, and the pursuit of happiness? In many ways, schools have served as an experimental site for the wider United States when it comes to racial justice, hope, and opportunity. How can U.S. schools deliver on the promissory note that Dr. King talked about when it comes to a basic and fundamental right such as education? Many in this country are hopeful for a first-rate education for their children, yet it remains elusive for too many—desperately desired, but for so many unattainable. Families move across district, city, and state lines; immigrant families make tremendous sacrifices across borders and oceans; working families work multiple jobs; and parents and caregivers spend massive amounts of their income, all with the hope of getting their children a good education. So, questions remain. Can we achieve racial equity in schools? Can education be the proverbial equalizer for social mobility, racial harmony, and societal cohesion? The idea is that if schools can serve as harbingers of justice and spaces of integration, opportunity, and access, other aspects of the nation will follow in creating the type of democratic society that abides by its lofty ideals and principles. Educational researcher Rosalyn Mickelson wrote a compelling research article in 1990 called "The Attitude-Achievement Paradox Among Black Adolescents." What she found is that despite ongoing obstacles to equal education, poor performance, and less-than-ideal supports in schools, education was still highly valued by Black youth, Black families, and Black communities. She reported that Black youth have positive attitudes about education and believe in the power of education as a vehicle for social mobility. Yet, seven decades after the *Brown* ruling, many of the stubborn educational inequities that fall along racial and socioeconomic lines have not diminished. Why do those whom the nation has gone to great lengths to deny education still believe in the power that it has?

In a moment when our nation is becoming increasingly diverse along racial and ethnic lines, the reality is that those on the margins of society still hold a firm desire and belief that with a good education there is no limit to how far one can go. I am often reminded of the comments my father, who grew up in the segregated South in the '40s and '50s, would make to my brother and me when it came to education. He frequently said, "Take your education seriously. Get as much of it as you can, because once you get it, no one can ever take it from you." Those words have resonated with me for a lifetime, and it is a sentiment that countless other adults heard growing up and a message that many young people continue to hear from parents, caregivers, and other family members today. In short, the message was then, and is today, loud and clear: education matters. At a time when new economies and emerging technologies continue to emerge and creative, diverse, cross-collaborative citizens are in an increasingly interdependent world essential, education still matters, but opportunities to learn have remained stubbornly intact for many students. Notable progress cannot be denied for the education of BIPOC (Black, Indigenous, people of color) students in the nation's schools over the past several generations. However, what remains painfully clear with almost any examination of P-20 systems is that educational justice and equality in education remain elusive. Derek Bell (2004), a noted legal scholar, says of *Brown* that the justices tried to solve a social problem with a legal remedy. In essence, Bell wondered, can you legislate hearts and minds when it comes to educational opportunity? In many ways, race, gender, socioeconomic status, language, and ability all remain considerable points of contention when it comes to who receives educational access and opportunity in the United States. Why does race continue to plague educational opportunity? Why do anti-Black racism, anti-Asian hate, and xenophobia remain a reality in far too many schools across the country? Why has a student's zip code continued to be a reliable predictor of school opportunity and success? Why has *Brown* not reached its lofty goals? What does our science tell us about educational opportunity? Why do so many aspects of educational research, policy, and practice omit examinations of race and racism? How have we addressed gender inequities in schools? As educational leaders, thinkers, practitioners, scholars, researchers, and policymakers, it is essential for our community to start and sustain a national and international dialogue about opportunity and education for all students comprehensively and collaboratively. It is vital to create an intersectional lens to how and why we do the work that we do. Why has our quest for equality been so elusive? Are we okay with certain students not getting the type of education that all students deserve? The purpose of this book is to focus squarely on a term that has been used excessively in education over the past two decades—*equity*. We need equity now. Not next week, not next month, not next year, but in a much more urgent fashion, as in now. We need a hard reset on educational equity and racial justice in schools. Many thought that the reopening of schools postpandemic would provide us an opportunity to reimagine schools and to think bold and creatively about education. Unfortunately, we have largely gone back to business as usual. Our children need and deserve more equitable practices and more equitable schools. But more importantly, what does equity look like in action? I have had the honor of working with hundreds of schools and thousands of teachers and leaders over the past two decades, and what I have consistently heard is that there is a clearer sense of what the term *equity* means, but less clarity about what it looks like in action. This book seeks to address the gap between how we understand equity conceptually and what equity looks like in practice. Equity in action rests on the idea that large segments of today's student population are not receiving the type of education that they deserve; moreover, the overwhelming number of students who come from racially diverse and low-income backgrounds are among those most in need of better educational opportunities. Students who are among our most vulnerable need something different in today's schools.

The 2020s will be seen through a historical lens as one of the most monumental decades when it comes to society's challenges. The quest for racial reckoning, an unstable economy, and intense climate change are all major realities in this decade. Also looming large over the entire decade will be COVID-19 and its impact on everyone. In many ways, the COVID-19 pandemic and its residual effects could likely result in one of the biggest detractors to educational equity since racially segregated schools. Disparate outcomes in educational experiences became even wider in the face of school closures, disproportionate death, and grief in particular communities, and ongoing debates about masks, vaccinations, and virtual learning will reverberate for years to come. Increasing data points continue to emerge, highlighting how much all students regressed academically during the pandemic but that those who were already on the fringes suffered even further erosion in academic gains. The mantra of education as the proverbial equalizer has come into serious question over the past three years. In many ways, COVID-19 exposed deep-seated inequities that have plagued the nation for decades, and at a time when the nation's schools are more racially and culturally diverse than ever before, the consequences have national ramifications for the largest segments of the student population (low-income, English learners, students of color), and this is why we need equity now. Furthermore, having students of color, a disproportionate number of whom happen to be low-income, has major implications for the future of the nation. The issues faced in education today are not Black problems, white problems, Latinx problems, or poor people's problems. They are American problems and will require a national effort to get this done right—to close opportunity gaps, increase equity in schools, and ensure that every student has access to a high-quality education. With issues such as climate change, polarizing politics, a volatile yet new economy, inflation, and increased homelessness and hopelessness all becoming relevant in this moment, we need something different. We need a hard reset to seriously contemplate how we create the schools that our students need and deserve. We need a deep reflective state as a nation to better understand, in a moment of increasing diversity, that the students who are most diverse often face the most social and academic challenges. We must recognize the toxicity that the nation and its schools face from centuries of racism, classism, sexism, and ableism (Benjamin, 2022).

This book makes a call for us not to prioritize equity as our goal but for equity to be our pathway to achieve equality, with all its aims and aspirational focus. However, to achieve educational equity requires a bold, courageous, and unapologetic commitment to advocating for our most vulnerable students. I make the contention that, if you are serious about doing the work of equity, you recognize that this is not for the faint of heart, it is not for the thin-skinned, and it is not for those easily shaken by criticism. If you are doing the work of transformative equity, you must be prepared to be ostracized, denounced, demoted, excluded, and seen as someone who is a problem. Doing the work for those on the margins is not easy. Though it should be lauded, it is the hardest work to do, because the rugged individualism mantra we have been socialized with teaches us to think that people's failures or shortcomings are a result of their own lack of effort, hard work, and decision making. This book operates from the standpoint that systems and structures, not only individual efforts, are the primary explanations for today's widening disparities. Yes, local acts can go a long way in dismantling systems and structures of disadvantage. Thus, it is important to be bold, courageous, and brave when doing equity work. I have often suggested that in doing equity work it is vital for us to make a fundamental shift in our approach to doing this work. It is important for us to move from safe spaces to brave spaces. A *safe space* is ideally one that does not incite judgment based on identity or experience, where the expression of both can exist and be affirmed without fear of repercussion and without the pressure to educate. While learning may occur in these spaces, the ultimate goal is to provide support. Safe spaces are vital because they require respect, cordiality, and decency. The challenge is that we have often remained in the safe space too long. Many people are conflict averse and do not want to have hard conversations about why students fail in schools every year. Our willingness to stay safe and play nice is making us complicit in student failure. If we want equity now, we need to make a move to a bolder, more necessary space, or what I refer to as a brave space. A *brave space* encourages honest, sustained, and critical dialogue. Such dialogue requires recognizing our differences and holding ourselves, and each person, accountable to do the work of sharing experiences and coming to new understandings about our current realities in schools—a feat that's often hard and typically uncomfortable. Brave spaces are hard because they require vulnerability, self-reflection, and ultimately action. Brave spaces also require us to have hard discussions with people who we work with, and may even like, but who we see inflicting harm on students. Figure I.1 lists the elements of both safe and brave spaces. One of the key elements of equity in action is that school leaders, board members, superintendents, classroom teachers, and other school personnel must be prepared to have challenging dialogues about the attitudes, values, and beliefs that serve as barriers to creating educational equity. The discussions that are needed must be centered on root causes of why disparities persist and, most importantly, what role we all can play in creating welcoming, affirming, responsive, and rigorous classrooms and schools. This book seeks to be solutions oriented about what can be done to make equity a reality.

FIGURE I.1 ● The Elements of Safe and Brave Spaces

SAFE SPACES	BRAVE SPACES
Cordial, respectful, congenial	Respectful, but challenging at times
Avoid confrontation	Encourage respectful differences of opinions
Evade difficult conversations	Lean into difficult conversations
Comfort is priority	Discomfort creates opportunity for growth and transformation
Goal is support	Goal is to create equitable spaces

This book asks readers to lean into brave spaces to create the schools that so many of our students desperately need. We need equity now. Creating brave spaces in schools means that we cannot avoid topics about institutional and individual acts of racism that occur in schools and create irreparable harm for many students of color. It also means that we cannot avoid uneasy discussions about gender inequities, homophobia, and transphobia that are often rampant in certain schools and classrooms. The same thing can be said about deficit-based beliefs and behaviors that are directed toward students who are growing up in poverty that only center on what those students cannot do, and what they do not have, and fail to see their promise and potential. Schools cannot improve and become equity centered until brave spaces become a normal part of school culture. Adults have to become comfortable being uncomfortable in certain spaces if we are to attain equity-centered schools. Frequently, adult comfort supersedes students' well-being.

If we cannot be uncomfortable when discussing ways that we may be reinjuring students, then we have larger challenges. I often ask, "What is our fear in being uncomfortable?" Why can't we experience what is so common for countless students in our schools? The reality is that many students are uncomfortable in our schools every day and have been so for years. They are uncomfortable because of their race, gender identity, language, ability, sexual orientation, socioeconomic status, and other identities that we have not affirmed, or because we have not created schools that will support them for their unique identities. Hence, adult discomfort to create greater student comfort and inclusion is the least that we can do if we are focused on getting this work done. In many schools today, adult comfort supersedes students' well-being, which is unacceptable. We can and must do better. All of us. Every educator has room for growth and the ability to better support students. The work is difficult and challenging at times, but the outcomes can be immensely rewarding, and the potential transformation and results are well worth the sacrifice.

MOVING EQUITY FORWARD FROM THEORY TO PRACTICE

This book makes the call that equity-based approaches need to be embedded in all of our efforts as educators at all levels. We need equity now. Our students deserve it, and I believe that we can create and sustain equity-centered schools. The book seeks to lay out ideas, practices, policies, and strategies that can help us to obtain that goal. In Chapter 1, I lay out a call of what equity is, and why it matters. I offer definitional delineations between equity and equality and make a case that equity is in line with core democratic values, such as righteousness, fairness, and inclusion, which we purport to live by in a free and fair society. I also discuss the equity framework that will guide this book and be referenced throughout, the importance of justice, acknowledging and repairing past harms, and inclusivity. In Chapter 2, I make a case for what districtwide equity can look like. When considering equity at what I call the 30,000-foot aerial view, it is essential to examine structural factors such as per-pupil funding, hiring practices, promotional opportunities, policies and procedures, and leadership structures that set the tone for the entire district. In Chapter 2, I also lay out core questions and considerations that superintendents, board members, and district leaders should be continuously asking. I frequently am asked to come and talk to various school districts about equity-related concerns. I typically hear from teachers and staff: "This is a training that our leaders at the district need," or "Why aren't our board members and the superintendent's team here for this?" In short, school districts cannot maximize their impact on students unless all hands are on deck, and it starts with those at the top, namely district leadership, which must embody equity if it is to be enacted at the school level. Chapter 3 will detail what schoolwide equity can look like now. Similar to the work of districts, there are efforts that school-level leaders can take when it comes to creating equitable outcomes. School personnel with an equity-based focus need to think about how they inspire each other, how they can create conditions for equitable practices to flourish, and how they can engage in real courageous conversations with colleagues about diversity, equity, and inclusion. Moreover, equity-based leaders need to also think about how they can work with their staffs to become more culturally responsive with their practices, and how to build an equity-centered culture at the school and be intentional about engaging families and caregivers in an equitable fashion. Chapter 4 will lay out approaches that specifically address what role school leaders can play in achieving equity. Leaders provide an important foundation for teachers and students to be successful. Building leaders are vital in setting a tone, building a culture, and creating the type of environments for everyone to thrive. To that end, how can leaders be instructional leaders, building managers, and innovative leaders with equity at the center of all their efforts? In Chapter 4, I lay out important characteristics of equity-based leadership that can prove valuable for all school- and building-level leaders. In Chapter 5, I talk about equity at the classroom level. Even if the school- and district-level efforts fall short in creating an ecosystem that allows equity to thrive, teachers can still be instrumental in creating equitable learning opportunities in their classroom. While acknowledging the challenges that come when schools are not right, teachers still have significant power when it comes to relationships, expectations, curriculum, instruction, assessment, and classroom climate that can help or harm students. In Chapter 5, I also identify essential practices, strategies, and resources that teachers can think about and implement. Chapter 6 speaks to one of the more important yet overlooked aspects of equity, which is family and parent/caregiver engagement in schools. Parents/caregivers are essential partners in the educational enterprise for students, and as a result, schools need to rethink how to engage parents and caregivers. Among the issues addressed in this chapter is being mindful of who our parents and caregivers are. What do parents/caregivers want most from schools and teachers? How can schools move beyond superficial aspects of parent/caregiver involvement to a more robust engagement with them that sees them as knowledgeable, resourceful, and equal partners in the education of young people? Finally, in Chapter 7, I discuss equity-based ways to examine, analyze, and understand data with an equity lens. Given the fact that districts are being provided access to more data than ever before, what are rubrics or templates that leaders and teachers can use to make the most sense of the data to inform their practices, policies, and procedures? Data-informed decision making continues to be a hot topic for educators at all levels. But whose data and what data counts? However, without an equity lens to make meaning of data, such efforts can only reify current practices that disrupt equity efforts.

There will be three key important theoretical anchors that guide the work of equity now. I will address them more in detail in Chapter 1, but those anchors are (1) justice, (2) recognizing and repairing harm, and (3) belonging. Each chapter will identify ways to address these three anchor points in education policy and practice. Each chapter will conclude with seven questions that can be used for deeper learning in small learning communities. The purpose of the seven questions is to help practitioners, leaders, and parents/caregivers reflect on policies and practices that are most relevant to them as they engage in equity work. The purpose of these questions is also to lead small learning communities, teacher and leader professional development, or just individual introspection. Please use the questions as a guide and a gauge of where you and your school or district are with the work of equity. Finally, each chapter will conclude with seven additional resources and readings that can be used for deepening the knowledge on key concepts for that chapter. The primary audience for this book is school leaders and practitioners. However, the book also has relevance for school board members, district superintendents, school counselors, paraprofessionals, and other school personnel who are focused on achieving educational equity. It is also my intent to not make this book highly prescriptive. I often cringe when asked by people to tell me five things to do to be more equity-minded. I lay out suggestions, strategies, and resources in this book. But I try to stay away from step-by-step "how to" approaches. I do not think equity is achieved that way; every district, every school, and every classroom has its own culture, makeup, and complexities. It is my hope that readers can use this book and apply the information to their unique ecosystem. This book is designed to encourage participation, disagreement, reflection, inquiry, and discussion of educators on important topics that play out in schools every day yet are not often discussed in small learning communities, in staff meetings, or at the district level. It is my hope that this book serves as a guide for resources, supports, knowledge, and strategies that will help educators with their equity walk. It is essential to remember that not everyone is at the same place along their equity journey. Our goal is not to push those away who are not where we think they should be or where we are in the journey. To the contrary, our schools are better when we call everyone in to be leaders in their equity journey.

CHAPTER 1

Equality Versus Equity

Delineating Definitions

For years, there have been discussions around how to create the types of schools that all students need and deserve. For years, we have heard the mantra of educational equality. This idea emanates from the perspective that as a society that promotes democratic ideals of fairness, justice, and equality, it only makes sense that our schools would serve as spaces that embody these same principles, and that we would socialize students to value and uphold these principles. However, what is clear is that from the beginning of the United States as a nation-state, there has always been a distinction between who has access to schooling and who does not. The work of Joel Spring (2016) is important here, because he documents how, since the 17th century, the idea of formal schooling was only afforded to the sons of wealthy, white landowners. Hence, girls, poor whites, Indigenous peoples, and subsequently enslaved Africans were not deemed worthy of having access to education. Accordingly, when we talk about equity as opposed to equality, we must understand that at the outset of formal education in the United States not everyone was provided the same opportunity, and there has been an incessant game of catch-up ever since. Thus, for decades, schools served as spaces that provided education in literacy, numeracy, science, leadership, love of country, government, and other approaches to being learned to only a select few, while others were excluded from such spaces. From the outset, inequities were essentially baked into our nation's educational DNA. An example that I frequently use is a 100-yard race. If one participant can start at the 50-yard mark while others are at the starting line, we cannot ignore the significant head-start advantage that one of the runners has over the others. The runners at the starting line can run with the same amount of effort, stride, and form, but it will not matter; they will still lose the race. The significant head start given to the head-start runner means that this runner will win every time. And we will continue to tell those who do not win that they have to work harder, improve their form, train harder, and run with more grit and focus if they want to win. In many ways, that is the way that we must think about educational equality in the United States. For centuries, girls, Indigenous peoples, enslaved Africans, and other colonized populations were denied access to education. During this time, the sons of wealthy, white land-owners were able to develop the reading, writing, numeracy, and thinking skills that afforded them to acquire, build, and transfer wealth and educational opportunity that would serve as the foundational building blocks of the United States. Hence, when looking at any type of academic data today, it should come as no surprise that Black, Indigenous, Latinx, and Asian Pacific Islander students are consistently behind their white counterparts. The same groups have been behind for centuries in a never-ending game of catch-up. As we have made efforts to close achievement and opportunity gaps, there have been narratives that center on the need for students to work harder, be more focused, and make better choices and for families to adopt better values. Yet, missing from many of these narratives is a focus on larger structural and historical inequities, which shows how educational disparities have existed since America's first days and have endured ever since. Angela Duckworth (2016) has talked about the need for students to develop more grit (perseverance and persistence) to be successful. I personally take major exception to such asks because they essentially place pressure on students to try harder in a system that sets up many of them to lose from the outset. I think we need to demonstrate grit to fix the systems that do not serve all children well. I think we need to demonstrate grit to dismantle inequality in our communities and schools. I think we need to demonstrate grit to eliminate racism, misogyny, exploitation, transphobia, and homophobia in our society. Our essential, fundamental questions must be these: When will we stop blaming students and families and start blaming systems and structures that do not serve them well? How can we provide more supports, resources, time, attention, and advocacy for those groups that have been historically disadvantaged to create more equal schooling opportunities?

AN EQUITY FRAMEWORK

There have been an endless number of books, articles, and reports on educational equity. Yet, we still seem to not be able to get it right and create the types of schools that all students deserve. So what makes this book different? Well, this book seeks to place an emphasis on some of the historical issues that have led us here but, more importantly, seeks to identify resources, strategies, *and practices* that can have an impact on students in schools in the here and now. Moreover, this book seeks to talk to all stakeholders involved in the education of students. Simply stated, if our work is not having a meaningful impact on our students, we must ask why we continue to engage in such efforts. Attaining educational equity to have meaningful impact for all students is one of the primary goals of this book. The framework for equity in this book is centered on three core principles (see Figure 1.1): *justice, recognizing and repairing past harms*, and *belonging*. Each of the principles has core relevance to how I think about creating equity-based schools, and should be thought about by all school personnel involved in the work of educating today's student population. The principles in my equity framework need to be understood, analyzed, studied, critiqued, and implemented by all stakeholders in today's educational enterprise and will be referenced throughout this book.

Justice is rooted in the fundamental idea of recognizing and doing what is right. The concept of justice is rooted in the notion of moral righteousness that is afforded to all people. The justice construct is anchored in the context of recognizing each person's humanity and providing the basic necessities that allow each person to be seen, heard, valued, and recognized. Justice is also connected to the idea of what education scholar Maisha Winn (2018) calls a paradigm shift that anchors justice as not just an idea, theory, or abstract concept but a way of being that informs our thoughts and actions in everyday practice. When I was younger, my mother would always tell my brother and me that while she wanted us to get good grades in school, she was more concerned with us being "good people" who would be "productive in the world." My mother would also say that the key to being a good person is to "just do what is right." I have always held that mantra close to my heart, to try my best to always do what is right. Whether helping those in need, speaking out against injustice, having hard conversations with peers and colleagues, or making challenging decisions in my current work, I frequently come back to my mother's charge about doing what is right. One of the ways that we can attain equity in schools is to commit ourselves to doing what is right by students. Moreover, justice seeks a level of reciprocity, respect, and affirmation of the human condition, where people are treated with the honorable and principled decency that should be afforded to everyone in a democratic society (Winn & Winn, 2021). Every student in our schools deserves to have access to adults who will always do right by them. This is a core element of justice in this work—putting students first. Why justice, one might ask? Simply stated, justice serves as the foundation of a civilized and humane society. Ruha Benjamin (2022) calls for what she refers to as *viral justice*, which

> orients us differently towards small-scale, often localized actions. It invites us to witness how an idea of actions that sprouts in one place may be adopted, adapted, and diffused elsewhere. But it also counters the assumptions "scaling up" should always be the goal. (p. 19)

Every student in our schools deserves to have access to adults who will always do right by them. This is a core element of justice in this work—putting students first.

It is the localized actions that matter most for educators when it comes to equity. We may not be able to change systems immediately, but local acts and loving practices can happen every day and help us to achieve justice in meaningful and empowering ways. Cornel West (2008) advises us to "never forget justice is what love looks like in public" (p. 14). Educators must always think about what our love looks like in classrooms, in hallways, and in schools. Do students see, feel, and hear love in their daily activities? Do our practices demonstrate justice? Societies (and schools) without justice tend to be harsh, exclusionary, unloving, and unfair, often leading to deprivation and conflict as people fight for what they believe they are worthy of: equal treatment under the law. We hold up the rule of law and the ideal of justice as being blind to social status, wealth, or anything else. When it comes to justice in education, each day every person dedicated to the uplift and well-being of students should ask, "Am I being just to all of my students?" "Do I love the students that I teach?" "Are the policies in place just to all families?" "Do my students feel like this is a just and fair learning environment?" and "If not, what modifications am I willing to make in my school, classroom, or district for students to feel like justice is embedded in all we do?"

I remember teaching fifth graders in Compton, California, where I was a classroom teacher, and one of the things that I did daily was to greet my students at the door with a smile and a warm greeting and ask, "How are you doing today?" While that might seem like a small act, the action was rooted in justice by affirming the students' humanity to let them know that they were worthy of a smile and a greeting from their teachers every day. My students would come back to me years later and say that those daily greetings made them feel seen, valued, and cared for. Sometimes justice is rooted in the simplest and smallest acts.

Do students see, feel, and hear love in their daily activities?

I was fortunate enough to grow up in a household where both of my parents stressed the importance of doing right, and in the case of my father, he was keen on helping those in greatest need. I can recall Saturdays when my dad would awaken my brother and me early in the morning to go cut the grass in our yard, rake the leaves of neighbors with disabilities, or visit older or sick family members who lived alone or in nursing homes. We often brought food to those individuals who suffered from food insecurities. My father also told us to never look down on those who were unhoused or had mental health challenges, because we did not know their stories and with the slightest change of circumstances we could be one of them. My father would often tell us that in our working-class neighborhood of Compton, these were some of the hardest workers, and while they often did not get far, they never complained. Deeply embedded in my father's message was to help those who were greatest in need. He regularly talked to strangers on the street who were struggling, to make them feel humanized. He would easily reach for change in his pocket to help a struggling individual. Every summer, my father would send my brother and me to his tiny, rural hometown in Louisiana because he wanted us to be immersed in a community where people had very little but were proud, caring, loving, and hardworking; gave their last to others if they needed to; and always saw a connection between themselves and others. The values of giving, caring, hard work, loving, and helping others have remained etched in my mind and heart and shape so much of who I am and what I do today. In so many ways, this book is rooted in those ideas of justice that my parents instilled in my brother and me—to try to always do what is right and to always be mindful of those in greatest need. That is the conception of justice that anchors this book that is desperately needed in schools today. *Do right by all students but pay particular attention to those in greatest need.*

Do right by all students but pay particular attention to those in greatest need.

The second foundational principle of the equity framework is *recognizing and repairing past harms.* A closer look at the groups today who need more equity-centered practice reveals their ties to a larger history of oppression, locally and globally. Take, for example, Indigenous children, who are consistently shown to be behind virtually all students when it comes to academic outcomes and who are frequently omitted from discussions around marginalized student populations because of their small numbers relative to other groups. To examine the realities of Indigenous children in isolation would ignore the atrocities that have been inflicted on Indigenous populations for centuries in this country (Lomawaima & Ostler, 2018). An equity-focused approach does not mean that teachers have the individual or collective power to undo what has been done to Indigenous communities or any other group, but it does mean they must recognize that today's conditions for them are connected to a larger history that cannot be ignored—a history that is rooted in genocide, deculturalization, and miseducation by way of Indian boarding schools (Pember, 2019). The recognition ideally should spark a paradigmatic shift in how we see student outcomes to a view that does not see students, their families, and their communities as the problem but sees what has been done to them as the problem. Such a paradigm shift then should help educators see themselves as partners with students, families, and communities to use education as a tool to repair harm through what education scholar Patrick Camangian (2019) calls "humanizing pedagogy" where teachers center three core ideas—(1) knowledge of self, (2) solidarity, and (3) self-determination—in their classrooms. This shift also asks teachers to not blame students for a history of exclusion, discrimination, inferior education, and displacement of communities. Similar to what many nations have done recently with atonement commissions, an equity-centered school focuses on recognizing and repairing past harms. Thus, there is less of a focus on punishment and discipline, and an intentionality on restoration and healing. A truth commission, also known as a truth and reconciliation commission or truth and justice commission, is tasked with discovering and revealing past wrongdoing by a government in the hope of resolving conflict left over from the past. South Africa and Canada are examples of countries that have recognized the atrocities inflicted upon certain native populations, acknowledged wrongdoing, and made a collective commitment to undo and repair the harms and injustices of the past. But the acknowledgement is only one part, so it must be accompanied with certain actions, efforts, resources, or services to help make people whole. This is where schools come in; an equity-based education can play a vital role in helping to amend the past by providing education and not schooling. Education researcher Mwalimu Shujaa (1994) makes this distinction between education and schooling:

> Education is our means of providing for the intergenerational transmission of values, beliefs, customs, rituals, and sensibilities along with the knowledge of why these things must be sustained . . . the schooling process is designed to provide an ample supply of people who are loyal to the nation-state and who have learned the skills needed to perform the work that is necessary to maintain the dominance of the European-American elite in its social order. (p. 10)

Education that repairs past harms ensures that schools recognize the way many students' cultural, racial, gendered, and linguistic identities are often under assault explicitly and implicitly through school curriculum, policies, and practices. Equity-centered schools not only acknowledge the harm done to minoritized students, but they also actively seek to disrupt and repair the harm that schools have done to certain populations. Moreover, educators in equity-centered schools see the disparate outcomes of minoritized students not as being solely due to effort, achievement, and intelligence but as occurring within a larger historical context. Education scholar Gloria Ladson-Billings (2006) says that "our focus on the achievement gap is akin to a focus on the budget deficit, but what is happening to African American and Latina/o students is more like the national debt. We do not have an achievement gap; we have an education debt" (p. 5). The debt that Ladson-Billings refers to is what we must pay attention to in today's schools. Recognizing and repairing past harms requires being aware of the education debt faced by many students and structuring schools in a manner that seeks to eliminate gaps. Because past injustices have often left long-lasting harms on people, communities, and students, recognition of past harm is vital to achieving real equity in schools. Repair addresses:

- The survivor's need for healing. Survivors heal through the encounter and its outcomes.

- The offender's need to make amends, as offenders must atone for wrongdoing and work to regain good standing in a particular community. Encounters empower offenders to make amends directly to survivors and potentially community members.

- The community's need for relational health and safety. Family, friends, and others support survivors and offenders as they heal and reintegrate into the community.

Who are the offenders and who are the survivors when it comes to educational equity? It is important for school officials to acknowledge and be aware that, beyond their control, schools have been one of the biggest sources of harm to many marginalized communities. In many ways, school practices, policies, and personnel have been and continue to be the offenders. And unfortunately, many educators are often guilty by association, though they may not have been active participants in that harm. Minoritized populations are the survivors of harm done intentionally and unintentionally by schools. Hence, school personnel must understand that much of the angst, anger, distrust, and dislike that some students have toward school is rooted in a historical memory of stories, episodes, acts of exclusion, and experiences of miseducation that have been shared by parents, grandparents, elders, community members, and survivors or that young people have witnessed firsthand. For schools to make equity a reality, a full reckoning of how to repair and redress harm is essential and will be discussed throughout this book.

Strategies that educators might take to heal students include:

- Words of affirmation
- Acknowledging effort
- Being willing to apologize
- Identifying and verbalizing students' academic and social strengths
- Building healthy student–teacher relationships

The third foundational principle of the equity framework, the concept of *belonging*, is centered on the idea that equity should be more than an ideal—you must meet people where they are for them to get where they need to be. People want and need to be included, seen, heard, and valued. Our students want to feel like they belong. Often schools consciously and unconsciously cater to the middle or the center of where we think most students are situated. Think of the typical bell curve where we frequently have outliers on both ends. A belonging framework is quite mindful of those on the margins or the tail ends of the bell curve and seeks to structure beliefs, practices, and policies that are always mindful of how our actions affect those on the margins. Belonging is predicated on the idea that no one is left behind, excluded, overlooked, or rendered invisible. Equity is not possible without belonging. Belonging cannot be attained without equity. Belonging is rooted in the idea that an individual has a persistent feeling of security and support, and that there is a sense of acceptance or membership in a group or community. Belonging tells students that they matter, and truly belonging means that students feel a sense of belonging that is unwavering and not only recognizes but affirms their identities and contributions toward being a part of something bigger than themselves.

We cannot create equitable schools without being ever mindful of how we ensure that all students have access to opportunities and resources that they might otherwise be excluded from, such as students who come from low socioeconomic backgrounds, students of color, students who are linguistically gifted (multilingual learners), students who are gender nonconforming, and LGBTQ+ students, as well as students with physical or intellectual disabilities and members of other minority groups. Belonging would be mindful of the exclusion of Muslim students in schools in various ways. In practical terms, in everything that I seek to lay out in this book, readers should be thinking, "Who might be excluded?" "Are we including all stakeholders?" "Does this policy make it harder for certain populations of students and their families?" "Who has been historically excluded?" "Does every family feel like they belong as part of a school community?" "Is this fair to everyone?" Belonging seeks to make sure that there are no discriminatory practices and there is a concerted effort to remove barriers that prevent anyone from full participation in school opportunities. Belonging would speak out against and put an end to the surveillance, criminalization, and punishment of disproportionate numbers of Black and Brown students; these same students are disproportionately suspended and expelled from schools—actions that are catalysts for the school-to-prison pipeline in our country. Belonging would repudiate acts of antisemitism. An authentic approach to equity is about making schools welcoming places for all students, regardless of their differences. Education scholar Jeff Duncan-Andrade (2022) states that equity "is what is fair and right" (p. 16).

FIGURE 1.1 ● Equity Framework

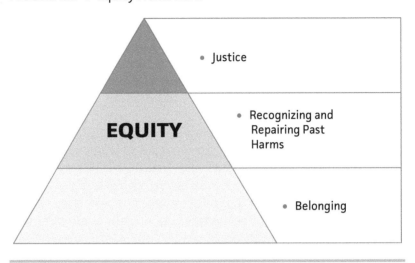

Equality says provide everyone the same thing. Equity says meet people where they are.

EQUITY NOW AND WHY IT MATTERS

For the purposes of this book, equity is defined as providing the necessary supports, interventions, and actions to correct past wrongs with the goal of justice and belonging for all students. Moreover, here equity is defined as the approaches, actions, or ideals of being just, impartial, and fair to create equal opportunity for all students. Simply stated, equality is our goal, and equity is the mechanism or process that we use to get there. We need equity now. We are losing too many students to inequitable schooling policies and practices. We need to act with an intense, unapologetic, and intentional sense of urgency to create equitable schools. Our students need it; our students deserve it. As mentioned in the framework, equity is synonymous with fairness and justice. It is rooted in the idea that past harms and actions have created inequities that require additional, and at times compensatory, actions. Equity also operates from the standpoint that we need to meet people where they are to get them where they want and need to be, and one of the essential ways of doing that is through belonging. Moreover, it is helpful to think of equity as not simply a desired state of affairs or a lofty value. To create equity in schools and classrooms we must think about it as more of a structural and systemic concept. There have been countless numbers of books about equity. What makes this book different, one might ask? Many of the books written about equity have been largely conceptual and theoretical, which leaves many leaders and practitioners wanting more clarity. I frequently have had school practitioners ask me, "But what does equity look like in the classroom?" I have had school leaders ask, "But can you give me examples of what equity looks like in a school?" This book seeks to answer those questions and more. This book will provide examples and strategies of what equity looks like in classrooms and in schools. This book seeks to be much more practical than most other books about equity. This book seeks to identify those educational structures, policies, practices, and procedures that work to either dismantle inequity or uphold it. Equity cannot and should not be thought about as simple acts or lessons that are done on a given day. Equity at its core must be seen as a way of being, integral to our core values—our thoughts, acts, or ideas that emanate in how we live our daily lives. Another way of thinking about equity is in how we might parent our own children. For many parents/caregivers, we may recognize that our children have different needs. Equality would suggest that we give all our children the same thing, but that often does not work. I have four children (who are all grown now), but having three sons and one daughter, I would frequently observe how different they were in so many ways. My oldest and youngest son frequently needed little attention from my wife and me. They were introverts by nature, very much kept to themselves, and did not socialize a lot unless prompted. My middle son and daughter were quite to the contrary. Much more social and extroverted, they thrived on social interactions, were social butterflies, could light up rooms, and had very different social needs. If my approach as a parent were to ask all four of my children to talk more, socialize more, and be more extroverted, that would not have worked for two of my sons, because that is not what they needed. Equity says to observe, listen, and learn from our students, then meet them where they are; it is unfair to ask students to be something that they are not, or to demonstrate mastery of skills that they were never taught, but to be nimble and flexible in meetings. In short, equity matters for many reasons, seven of which will be woven throughout this book:

- Students deserve equity now.
- Diversity demands equitable education.
- Equity is rooted in justice.
- Equity seeks to address past harms and injuries.
- Equity challenges us to do education, not schooling.
- Belonging is vital to create equitable schools.
- Equity is the just and right thing to do.

Equity cannot and should not be thought about as simple acts or lessons that are done on a given day. Equity at its core must be seen as a way of being, integral to our core values—our thoughts, acts, or ideas that emanate in how we live our daily lives.

UNPACKING EQUALITY

In this book I make the stance that equality should be our goal as educators, yet equity can and should be our pathway to achieve equality. Equity involves trying to understand and give people what they need to enjoy full, healthy, and fulfilling lives. Equality, in contrast, aims to ensure that everyone gets the same things to enjoy full, healthy lives. If we were all the same, perhaps achieving equality would not be so elusive. Yet as students become increasingly diverse in our nation's schools, a one-size-fits-all approach simply will not work, much in the same way that it would not have worked for my four children. Nearly every educator wants their students to be successful, healthy, and thriving in all aspects of their lives, and few can argue against equality as an end goal. But equality can only promote fairness and justice if everyone starts from the same place and needs the same things. Unfortunately, that is simply not the case. The Kirwan Institute for the Study of Race and Ethnicity (2013) defines equity as

> the intentional belonging of everyone in society. Equity is achieved when systemic, institutional, and historical barriers based on race, gender, sexual orientation and other identities are dismantled and no longer determine socioeconomic, education and health outcomes.

In schools, students arrive with a diverse set of strengths, skills, and abilities, but also with diverse needs. One of the reasons why teaching is one of the most demanding and intellectually and emotionally exhausting jobs is that educators have to assess students' strengths and needs on a daily basis. As mentioned before, if equality is our goal and equity is our pathway to get there, it requires a mindset shift of adults who serve students every day. I will talk more about why a mindset shift is required later in this book. Another example that I frequently use involves restrooms in public spaces. I have more than once been with my wife at a concert or sporting event where we both take a bathroom break. My wife always laments about how long the women's restroom line is compared to the men's. I frequently go in and come out in no time flat while my wife waits in line with 20–25 women in front of her. When we see these long lines for women's restrooms, we do not say, "If women just worked harder, their lines would not be so long." We would never say that if women demonstrated greater grit while in their stalls, there would no lines. We do not suggest that men just work harder or a smarter, and that is why they do not have long lines. We recognize that when it comes to restrooms in most public spaces, the needs of men are different than the needs of women. Hence, a *one restroom for men–one restroom for women* approach (equality) does not work for women. While the restrooms available are equal, such an approach does not consider the unique needs of one group compared to the other. The women are not the problem; the structure of available restrooms is the problem. So, what if we had four restrooms for women and one restroom for men? It would not be equal, but it would respond more to the needs of women. Perhaps, the greater goal is to create gender-neutral restrooms where no one waits in line or everyone waits in line in equal ways. But what if we used a similar approach with our students and said it is not the students' lack of effort and grit that explains inequalities; what if the structures are the problem? What if it is the mindsets, attitudes, beliefs, practices, policies, and pedagogies in schools that are the problem? And what if we sought to change them as opposed to changing students? Such a very different approach would require very different approaches to address the problem.

Understanding the root causes of educational disparities in outcomes for today's students is essential. While many practitioners ask why root causes are necessary, it is important to note that our understanding of root causes usually informs our reaction or response to the current-day disparities. If a teacher notices that a student appears disengaged and attributes the student's behavior to a lack of care about their education, it could easily be met with an amount of indifference from the teacher, such as the typical "If the student doesn't care, then why should I?" However, if that teacher approaches the same student and asks why she does not seem to be engaged in doing work today, and the student responds by saying that she has been having a hard time focusing because she and her family have been experiencing homelessness and have been living in her mom's car the last few days, the teacher's response may be different. Again, root causes matter. In today's increasingly diverse context for young people, it is crucial to recognize that an equity-based focus on teaching and learning requires an understanding of who students are, the circumstances that they are currently dealing with, and the people in their lives who are helping (or not) to navigate those circumstances.

Much of what happens in many schools today, especially with students of color and students from low-income backgrounds, is that a deficit-based mentality exists that sees students and their families as the reasons for their own less-than-ideal circumstances. Hence, the effort that is dedicated to students is muted because the idea is that people need to make better choices, need better values, or lack a sound work ethic and motivation.

ALL HANDS ON DECK

A critical concept of this book is that everyone can play a role in the creation and maintenance of equity-based schooling. Doing equity-based work is not a function of one's title, one's credentialing, one's years of experience in the field, or one's pay scale. Individuals at the district level, at the schoolhouse, in the classroom, on the playground, at the bus stop, or in the cafeteria; school counselors; and persons in the front office or at after-school programs can all play a role. Custodial staff can be just as impactful as classroom teachers. The school nurse can be equally as supportive of students as the principal. Bus drivers, cafeteria workers, instructional aides, paraprofessionals, and front-office staff all have the potential to be change agents for students, and many do that every day in schools across the country. This book seeks to highlight the collective and collaborative nature of how equity can and should work for all students. One of the reasons why many equity efforts fall short is that such efforts are often taken up by a small cadre of individuals, while others assume that it is not their responsibility or duty. To be clear, creating equitable schools is everyone's responsibility or duty. Recently, a number of districts have hired equity coordinators, or diversity, equity, and inclusion (DEI) directors who are tasked with the work of equity. It is also important to note that many DEI efforts are under attack in cities and states across the country. Many states have banned DEI trainings and workshops because they are viewed as divisive to some. Such positions are important and can play an important role in school transformation. However, frequently, these positions have little power or authority and limited resources, and the district places what should be an organizational effort on the shoulders of one person or office. Efforts such as these often result in burnout of the lone DEI champion and are frequently doomed to fail. They almost invariably have limited impact, because they are typically seen as outside of the structure of schools, as opposed to being an integral part of how an entire district or school operates. Jamila Dugan (2021) writes about what she calls "equity traps and tropes" that provide an excellent overview of what many schools must be aware of when engaging this work.

- **"Doing" Equity:** Sometimes educators treat equity as a series of tools, strategies, and compliance tasks versus a whole-person, whole-system change process linked to culture, identity, and healing.

- **Siloing Equity:** Look at the strategic plans of many organizations and schools working toward equity. You will likely find a policy, a new "equity" vision statement, or a newly formed task force designed to increase equitable outcomes.

- **The Equity Warrior:** The Equity Warrior is an incredible educator, often treated as a martyr to the work. This person is eager to push their colleagues and school forward and willing to take on significant additional work to bring the team along. Unfortunately, the Equity Warrior can easily become the default holder of the school or system's vision for equity, allowing colleagues to opt out, stay inside their comfort zones, or refuse to invest in their own equity learning, which is critical to the change effort

- **Spray-and-Pray Equity:** Many school leaders are convinced that if they just get the right trainer, everything will be "fixed." The staff will become more equity centered. A common refrain we (as trainers ourselves) hear is "If we just train our teachers around their implicit biases, then they will treat students better."

- **Superficial Equity:** Superficial equity essentially amounts to grasping any equity-centered practice with little understanding of its origins, its purpose, and how to engage in it with depth and authenticity

- **Boomerang Equity:** Boomerang equity may be one of the hardest traps of all to disrupt. It feeds itself back to the econometric, test-driven education frame we seek to dismantle.

Do any of these traps and tropes sound familiar? Are they playing out in your school or district? If so, it's time to reconsider your efforts. It is never too late to take an honest inventory of your individual practice or the policies and practices of your building or system in the interest of addressing a simple but fundamental question: *How can we be better?* Similarly, we must have the courage to confront both the quantitative and qualitative data that tell the story of who is benefiting and who is not. Education scholar H. Rich Milner (2020) says it best: "Start where you are, but don't stay there" (p. 5).

WHO ARE WE SERVING TODAY?
THE DIVERSITY–EQUITY REALITY

In doing the work of equity it is essential to understand the diverse makeup of our clientele—students. Equity is about tailoring our efforts based on the needs, complexities, and identities of students who enter schools. Today's schools are becoming more diverse with each passing day, and this dramatic transformation will have an impact on schools and ultimately our society for decades to come. In short, diversity is here to stay, and this is precisely why equity must be front and center in our work in schools. To be clear, equity is not a one-size-fits-all approach; what works in one district, classroom, or school may not work in another. Yet, at the same time, there are core practices that will have utility for all students. The work of equity is complex, complicated, and challenging. So, let's start with a snapshot of who our students are in 2021–2022. In fall 2021, close to 50 million students were enrolled in public schools in prekindergarten to Grade 12 across the United States (National Center for Education Statistics [NCES], 2022). Of the 49.4 million public school students, consider a snapshot of who they are:

- 32.6 million attended prekindergarten to Grade 8.
- 15.4 million attended Grades 9 to 12.

It should be noted that these numbers refer to students enrolled in public schools only in the United States (including charters). In fall 2019, approximately 5.5 million students attended private schools (NCES, 2022). This estimate includes prekindergarten enrollment in schools that offer kindergarten or a higher grade. When we disaggregate these data by racial/ethnic groups, we quickly see that today's schools are more diverse than ever in our nation's history; of the 49.4 million students enrolled in public schools from prekindergarten through Grade 12 in 2020–2021:

- 22.4 million were White (45%)
- 14.1 million were Latinx (Hispanic) (28%)
- 7.4 million were Black (14%)
- 2.7 million were Asian American (5%)
- 2.3 million were of two or more races (4.6%)
- 0.5 million were American Indian/Alaska Native students (1%)
- 0.2 million were Pacific Islander students (0.5%)

Many of today's conversations tied to equity have an explicit focus on improving the educational experiences and outcomes of students of color and, in particular, Native American, African American, Pacific Islander, and Latinx students (T. C. Howard, 2020). Given the fact that students of color now make up a majority of students in U.S. public schools, a deep analysis and understanding about how schools respond to increasingly racial, ethnic, cultural, and linguistic diversity is essential. I will discuss the reality of today's racial and ethnic demographics throughout the book.

STUDENTS WITH DISABILITIES

When discussing equity, one of the largest student groups that must be served includes students with disabilities. Enacted in 1975, the Individuals with Disabilities Education Act (IDEA), formerly known as the Education for All Handicapped Children Act, mandates the provision of a free and appropriate public school education for eligible students ages 3–21. Eligible students are those identified by a team of professionals as having a disability that adversely affects academic performance and as being in need of special education and related services. Data collection activities to monitor compliance with IDEA began in 1976. From school years 2009–2010 through 2020–2021, the number of students ages 3–21 who received special education services under IDEA increased from 6.5 million, or 13% of total public school enrollment, to 7.2 million, or 15% of total public school enrollment. It is important to note that a number of scholars have raised important questions and brought considerable attention to the overrepresentation of students of color who are identified with disabilities and special educational referrals (Harry & Klinger, 2014). Schools cannot have an equity focus if there are not authentic considerations for students with disabilities.

LANGUAGE LEARNERS

Students who are identified as English learners (ELs) can participate in language assistance programs in schools to help ensure that they attain English proficiency and meet the academic content and achievement standards expected of all students. Participation in language programs can play a vital role in improving students' English language proficiency, which can increase equitable outcomes for students whose first language is not English, which in turn has been associated with improved educational outcomes. The percentage of public school students in the United States who were ELs or linguistically gifted increased between fall 2010 (9.2%, or 4.5 million students) and fall 2019 (10.4%, or 5.1 million students). Spanish was the home language of 3.9 million EL public school students in fall 2019, representing 75.7% percent of all EL students and 7.9% of all public school students. Arabic was the second most reported home language (spoken by 131,600 students). English was the third most common home language for EL students (105,300 students), which may reflect students who live in multilingual households or students adopted from other countries who were raised speaking another language but currently live in households where English is spoken. Chinese (100,100 students), Vietnamese (75,600 students), Portuguese (44,800 students), Russian (39,700 students), Haitian (31,500 students), Hmong (30,800 students), and Korean (25,800 students) were the next most reported home languages of EL students in fall 2019. Language is an essential part of culture and students' identities, and some programs are designed to be *subtractive*, meaning their goal is to replace students' home languages with English without any effort to preserve and strengthen the home language. Students who are asked to suppress, change, or dismiss their native language are placed at significant risk for school failure (Martinez, 2018). The United States also continues to see a massive influx of immigrant students who have complex language and learning needs that districts and schools must respond to in an equity-based manner (Suarez-Orozco & Michikiyan, 2016). Given the growing numbers of students who come from linguistically diverse backgrounds, any equity focus that districts and schools take must be serious about a robust engagement of programs and interventions to support linguistically gifted students.

STUDENTS LIVING IN POVERTY

Poverty continues to be one of the biggest challenges to equity in our nation. Growing up in poverty is one of the greatest threats to healthy child development and academic success (Milner, 2015). The effects of economic hardship, particularly deep and persistent poverty, can disrupt children's cognitive development, physical and mental health, educational success, and other life outcomes (Gorski, 2018). These impacts reverberate throughout adulthood. Child poverty, calculated by the Supplemental Poverty Measure (SPM), fell to its lowest recorded level in 2021, declining 46% from 9.7% in 2020 to 5.2% in 2021, according to the U.S. Census Bureau (Creamer et al., 2022). However, now childhood poverty is on the rise. The recent elimination of the Child Tax Credit (CTC) program has caused the number of children living in poverty to spike to 12.4% or approximately 9 million children. Young people need to have their basic needs met to be healthy and whole when they enter school. The official poverty measure, on the other hand, is based on pretax cash income. In 2021, the official poverty level was $27,479 for a family of two adults and two children. Families can earn well over this amount and still struggle to meet their basic needs, especially in high-cost areas such as Los Angeles, San Francisco, Miami, and New York. Though there have been downturns in childhood poverty over the last few years, there is a disproportionate number of youth of color who continue to live in poverty compared to white students. Consider the following statistics from 2021:

- 8.2% of white families lived in poverty.
- 17.0% of Latinx families lived in poverty.
- 19.5% of Black families lived in poverty.
- 8.1% of Asian families lived in poverty.
- 24.3% of Native American/Alaska Native families lived in poverty.

It is also worth noting that while poverty affects millions of students every day in this country, the condensed and segregated nature of students growing up in poverty cannot be understated. Gary Orfield (2022) has documented how racial segregation in the nation's schools is just as prevalent today as it was in the 1960s and has important implications for students of color and access to higher education. Moreover, current data highlight that for many schools and districts across the United States, there has been persistent, generational poverty. It is not uncommon to find students today who attend the same schools that their parents, grandparents, or even great grandparents attended decades earlier, especially in urban and rural communities. For example, the percentage of students who attended high-poverty schools was highest for Black students (45%), followed by Latinx (Hispanic) students (43%), Native American/Alaska Native students (37% percent), Pacific Islander students (25%), students of two or more races (17%), Asian students (14%), and white students (8%). At the other end of the school poverty spectrum, a nearly opposite pattern is evident. The percentage of students who attended low-poverty schools was highest for Asian students (40%), followed by white students (30%), students of two or more races (24%), Pacific Islander students (12%), Native American/Alaska Native students (8%), Latinx (Hispanic) students (8% percent), and Black students (7%).

Equity efforts must be prepared to address the complexities of today's students' realities. Perhaps no issue is more prevalent in this fight than childhood poverty. The ramifications for students are deep and wide, and significant investments are required at the local, county, state, and national levels to dismantle the seemingly insurmountable obstacles that poverty presents for millions of children in this country. There is also a need for equity to take an intersectional lens to recognize particular groups are at even greater disadvantages compared to others. Legal scholar Kimberlé Crenshaw (1991) has talked about intersections as a layered and cumulative way that the effects of different forms of discrimination combine or overlap. In other words, her contention is that we cannot look at identities in narrow and discrete categories and fully understand them (e.g., white women, Black men). She contends that different forms of discrimination and systems of oppression do not exist in a vacuum: For those who embody different marginalized identities, they often overlap and amplify each other to create a unique experience of discrimination that is more than just the sum of its parts. Therefore, when talking about poverty, an intersectional framing asks us to think about what poverty means for a young girl who is a Latina immigrant, who may have a disability, and who may not have been raised in an English-speaking home. How and why would her lived experiences be fundamentally different from the experiences of, say, a white male who is growing up in poverty? The complexity of intersecting identities cannot be stressed enough.

Educators should be aware of how these identities and corresponding systems of oppression intersect in the lives of students. Reflect, for a moment, on how schooling may play out in the life of a white male who is poor and experiencing homelessness. Now contrast this experience with that of a young mixed-race girl who is transgender and living in an affluent community. As we learn to frame our own and our students' experiences through an equity lens, we fine-tune our understanding of how these layers of identity and their corresponding systems of oppression impact the experience of school, and we further appreciate why a one-size approach cannot work—whether in a large comprehensive public school district or a small, private, or independent school. Our approach must be measured, tailored, mindful of historical disadvantages and current realities, aware of the nature of generational poverty, conscious of racial disparities and the multiple identities our students possess, and committed to recognizing that assisting the most vulnerable students helps support all students. At the end of each chapter, I will lay out the equity framework of justice, repairing harm, and belonging to offer tips to generate ideas, lead discussions, or offer practical strategies that can become actionable for individuals or organizations.

THE CURRENT POLITICAL MOMENT

I would be remiss if I did not mention that I am writing this book at a time that the United States continues to become increasingly polarized. The partisan politics in our society that have permeated schools have made the political climate in education an unhealthy one for many students. From bans on discussions of DEI, limiting teaching in classrooms about race and racism, to denying students' rights to self-define and honor their gender, schools are quickly becoming unsafe places for countless numbers of young people. This book calls for equity now because schools are supposed to be places where students are encouraged to laugh, learn, explore, be affirmed, experience joy, experiment, be creative, imagine, dream, meet and learn about people from diverse backgrounds, and grow academically, socially, emotionally, and psychologically. However, the current political climate in schools in many ways is infringing on students' rights to know the country's true history, and it is allowing the vocal minority to show up at school boards and dictate an agenda that affects all students. In many ways, the current educational terrain is frightening and outright harmful for students. At a time when students' mental health, psychosocial well-being, and sense of self are becoming increasingly fragile, the current political moment is contributing to higher levels of stress, depression, anger, and anxiety for many students. Equity now is needed because we need bold leadership, courageous adults, and caring individuals to stand up to the current political moment to say that students should always be first. *Students should always be first.* All that is done in schools should be done with students being the number-one priority. I understand many adults want what they believe is best for their children and adolescents. And I respect the rights of parents/caregivers. But this current moment should call on all adults to be introspective; to be respectful of different viewpoints, perspectives, and lived realities; and to listen to young people. We may not always understand and agree with what young people are saying, but they are growing up in times that we as adults did not. Equity now is needed because we are witnessing the most intelligent, creative, and compassionate group of young people the world has known. They care deeply about the climate, they are more accepting of differences, and they desire a world that respects their right to self-expression, voice, and choice. Let us not be the adults who douse their burning flames to create a better world. Let's do equity now so that all students can live to reach their highest potential.

Equity now is needed because we need bold leadership, courageous adults, and caring individuals to stand up to the current political moment to say that students should always be first.

Equity Now Charts

To make the equity principles accessible to education leaders and practitioners, the *equity now* charts offer ways for readers to identify and demonstrate how justice, repairing harm, and belonging (the three theoretical anchors of the book) can be embedded in the ideals, practices, and policies in districts, schools, classrooms, and communities. The aim of these charts is to provide educators with actionable items that can be used to create equity now. The charts also provide a template for what parents/caregivers and school personnel can use to analyze to what degree school districts and individual school sites are enacting equity. The practices and policies in the charts are not meant to be prescriptive but are offered as general principles to be applied with the given context to create more equitable schools.

JUSTICE	REPAIR	BELONGING
• Recognizing the changing ethnic, racial, and cultural demographics in a school or district	• Acknowledging that low performances of racial/ethnic groups are rooted in historical trauma and disadvantage	• Creating curriculum and instructional strategies that reflect diverse ways of knowing, thinking, and communicating
• Providing more resources (human and fiscal) to schools and districts that have a larger number of students from low-income backgrounds	• Providing students from low-income backgrounds with the strongest and most skilled teachers • Avoiding placing inexperienced or ineffective teachers with students who are behind academically	• Consistently changing the narrative in schools about what students from low-income backgrounds do not have to what they do have • Moving from deficit discourse and practice to asset-based discourse and practice

JUSTICE	REPAIR	BELONGING
• Accurately identifying students who are language learners	• Affirming and maintaining students' native tongue • Providing adequate support to English learners • Reclassifying regularly and providing rigor in courses that are taught in students' home language	• Ensuring that classroom and school walls have a diversity of languages displayed • Honoring and celebrating languages other than English throughout the school

Questions for Consideration

1. Has my district started discussions or taken steps toward developing and implementing an equity plan?

2. How have the demographics changed in my district and community over the last five years?

3. Who are the student groups in greatest need of more equitable supports and services?

4. What additional supports are in place in my district for students living in poverty?

5. What evidence do we have to suggest whether the current supports are working?

6. How, if at all, have stakeholder groups been a part of our equity efforts?

7. Why might there be resistance to discussions and actions connected to equity?

Recommendations for Reading and Resources

1. Milner, H. R. (2020) 2nd ed. *Start where you are, but don't stay there*. Harvard Education Press.

2. Frey, W. (2018). *Diversity explosion: How new racial demographics are remaking America*. Brookings Institution.

3. Spring, J. (2022). *Deculturalization and the struggle for equability* (9th ed.). Routledge.

4. Muhammad, G. (2020). *Awakening the genius: An equity framework for culturally and historically responsive literacy*. Scholastic.

5. Duncan-Andrade, J. M. R. (2022). *Equality or equity*. Harvard Education Press.

6. Winn, M. (2018). *Justice on both sides*. Harvard Education Press.

7. Morris, M. (2018). *Pushout: The criminalization of Black girls in schools*. New Press.

Districtwide Equity

Responding to the COVID-19 Effect and Beyond

When discussing equity in education, I would be remiss to not discuss the biggest challenge that public education and schools have faced perhaps in over 100 years—COVID-19. In this chapter, I will examine the ongoing fallout from the pandemic and why districts should be mindful of moving forward; then I will address five key equity steps that districts can take to deal with the aftermath of the pandemic. Finally, I will conclude Chapter 2 with why an intentional focus on mental health is necessary in this moment and how community schools have the potential to become centers for transformation postpandemic.

During the COVID-19 pandemic, arguably nothing was turned more upside down than schools. Without a doubt, 2020 will go down undeniably as one of the most titanic, disruptive, and trying years in U.S. history. The coronavirus—which claimed the lives of approximately 7 million people worldwide, including over 1 million Americans—altered the entire educational landscape perhaps forever. The sudden, although temporary, end to in-person classes affected the entre education spectrum, and no child was untouched by the ripple effects of nationwide school closures. Many of today's contemporary challenges in school districts are to respond to a litany of effects of COVID-19 and the loss of educational opportunity for millions of students nationwide.

During the 2020–2021 and 2021–2022 academic years, countless numbers of students endured the loss of loved ones due to COVID-19; were disconnected from teachers and peers; experienced isolation, exasperation, and anxiety; lived through a profound economic downturn; and felt great uncertainty about the future. All these COVID-19 pressures were compounded by racist violence during the summer of 2020 with the deaths of George Floyd and Breonna Taylor and by ethnic hostility, political turmoil, and even armed insurrection at the start of 2021 at the U.S. Capitol. But to be clear, the pandemic was certainly the tsunami that education could least afford to experience. The pandemic had a terribly disproportionate impact on low-income families and communities of color. In particular, Indigenous, Latinx, Black, and Pacific Islander communities experienced a range of severe impacts of COVID-19 (D. J. Davis et al., 2020; Horsford et al., 2021; J. R. Howard, 2023), including higher fatality rates. People of color have been more likely to contract, be hospitalized from, and die from the virus compared to their white counterparts (Hill & Artiga, 2022; Monte & Perez-Lopez, 2021).

The beginning of the pandemic, in March 2020, saw an unprecedented and unparalleled reality in the United States—the closure of public schools for safety concerns related to the virus. Within a matter of days upon recognizing the highly transmissible rate of the virus, close to 50 million students who attended public schools in the United States were required to learn remotely due to the closing of schools—indefinitely. Without much notice or any significant advanced communication, schools were required to radically transform the way they delivered educational services to students. Schools across the United States have inadequately served millions of low-income students and students of color for many decades, if not longer (T. C. Howard, 2020). So, it goes without saying that the academic gaps that were already glaring and apparent between students of color and their peers became even wider during the pandemic (U.S. Department of Education Office for Civil Rights, 2021). A recent national analysis from scholars at Harvard shows that when schools went remote, achievement growth was lower for all subgroups but especially for students attending high-poverty schools (Goldhaber et al., 2022). Data from the U.S. Department of Education demonstrated that the gaps that many predicted did indeed occur. Consider the following:

- Data showed an average decline of 5 points in reading and 7 points in math for 9-year-old students compared to 2020, which is the largest decline in reading scores since 1990 and the first ever decline in math scores on the National Assessment of Educational Progress (NAEP) long-term trend reading and math assessments for 9-year-old students.

- Declines were present regardless of achievement level, still widening the gap between the lowest and highest performers. In the past few years, the gaps in NAEP scores between the lowest and highest performers were widening because of the highest performers staying stagnant or improving, while the lowest performers sporadically increased or declined. However, the COVID-19 pandemic led even the highest performers' scores to decline. The gap widened instead because the lowest performers declined at a steeper rate than their counterparts.

- When looking at scores broken out by race and ethnicity, white, Black, and Latinx students experienced the same 6-point decline in reading scores from 2020 to 2022. However, math scores for Black students declined 13 points compared to 8 points for Latinx students and 5 points for white students.

Educators will be responding to and addressing the fallout of the pandemic in classrooms for years to come. Researchers will continue to analyze academic trends that emerge in the immediate future. Policymakers will assess where and how school systems could have served certain students better. The increasing declines of outcomes and widening academic disparities in schools have frequently been framed around lack of access to education for some students, or what education scholar H. Rich Milner (2020) refers to as "opportunity gaps." Opportunities to learn and have access to education became one of the biggest challenges at the onset of the pandemic, and there were clear socioeconomic and racial ramifications. One of the first obstacles for students in March 2020 in the immediacy of school closing was access to sufficient technological devices to access teachers, schools, and curriculum (Darling-Hammond et al., 2021). Much in the way that opportunity gaps have existed in schools, technology gaps proved to be just as stubborn and persistent, as countless numbers of students did not possess Chromebooks, laptops, iPads, or iPhones to log on to learning platforms (Gallagher & Cottingham, 2020). Nationwide, millions of residents from low-income backgrounds were disconnected from school learning platforms, and many depended on unstable smartphones, which provided insufficient connections for such tasks as schoolwork or attending class online (Galperin & Le, 2021). One report found that an estimated 16.9 million students across the nation did not have adequate internet access. Even those students who had the access to devices were not always able to access schools and classrooms, as large swaths of areas in urban and rural communities sorely lacked the necessary hotspots that would allow connectivity to occur (Gross & Opalka, 2020). During the first months of the pandemic, educational inequity was on display in gross and disturbing ways. As a result, schools provided millions of devices to students and pressed for delivery of Wi-Fi hotspots to tens of thousands of areas across the country, merely for students to log on to see their teachers, get access to content, interact with their peers, and approximate some semblance of learning. Yet, while some students struggled to gain access to learning opportunities, more affluent communities pooled resources, and many created learning pods and teaching co-ops to ensure that their students did not miss a beat; this is how gaps widened. Such acts only exacerbated inequality and created the need for equity in this moment. Though challenging and hectic at times, the pandemic demonstrated what a collective effort could look like to support our most vulnerable students. Not only were devices and hotspots delivered but in many cities in states across the country, school districts provided meals to families by the tens of millions to make sure that children and their families had access to basic food needs. We truly witnessed a mass, collective effort to help those who were in need. In many ways, equity-based efforts were on full display. Mass efforts were being put in place to assist our most vulnerable children and families in a time of crisis; that is one of the essential core pillars of equity—justice in the name of doing what is right.

The rollout in the early days, weeks, and months of the pandemic for technology was uneven and inconsistent, as many students went through extended periods without access to technology, missing out on valuable instructional time (Willis & Fensterwald, 2021). Teachers, many of whom had never delivered content via technological platforms, struggled to connect and engage students (Gandolfi et al., 2021). Many of the most disenfranchised students, a disproportionate number of whom are low-income students of color, had parents and caregivers who served as essential workers and thus did not have the luxury of working remotely (Novoa & Jessen-Howard, 2020). The unfortunate reality was that many students were required to do school at home alone and some had to monitor the learning of younger siblings, along with their own learning. Beyond such collateral damage to K–12 education was the real threat of the seriousness of COVID-19 to society at large. In the initial months of the virus, there were still many unknowns. How is it transmitted? How long would a vaccine take to develop? Who was at most risk? Were adults safe? Were children susceptible to the virus? Were masks and gloves protective in the spread? To be clear, all students were affected in some way by the closing of schools. However, the most vulnerable student populations, mainly low-income students and students of color, suffered terribly between 2020 and 2023, and the ramifications will be long lasting. The manifestations of trauma and the way millions of young people and adults struggle with mental health issues because of the pandemic are, and will continue to be, significant. Moreover, the lack of foundational supports offered by schools, districts, counties, and states may very well have contributed to irreparable academic harm for millions of students, severely compromising their life chances.

The manifestations of trauma and the way millions of young people and adults struggle with mental health issues because of the pandemic are, and will continue to be, significant. Moreover, the lack of foundational supports offered by schools, districts, counties, and states may very well have contributed to irreparable academic harm for millions of students, severely compromising their life chances.

It should be noted that even though students are back in schools now, there are still hybrid teaching and learning models in place. A closer examination of the data on in-person versus remote learning offers insightful realities that have important implications for districts. Consider that at the end of the 2020–2021 academic school year, just 14% of white students were still learning remotely, compared to 35% of Black students, 28% of Latinx students, and more than half of Asian American students. Moreover, during the same school year, over 60% of Black, Latinx, and Asian families said they preferred remote learning compared to only 34% of white families (Zamarro & Camp, 2021).

The loss of instructional time has been proven to increase academic gaps and has potentially devastating outcomes (Goldhaber et al., 2022; S. L. Johnson et al., 2021). For example, students with major learning disparities are less likely to graduate from high school; individuals without a high school diploma or equivalent have greater likelihood of experiencing homelessness, becoming incarcerated at some point in their lives, and needing greater social and economic safety nets; are less politically active; and will have significantly lower lifetime earnings (Chetty et al., 2016, 2020).

To be clear, in-person learning and instruction works for most students. An overwhelming number of students missed out on essential academic and social–emotional learning, formative relationships with peers and adults, and opportunities to play, share, run, explore, laugh, learn, and engage in other developmental necessities when they were kept at home. Children living in poverty, students of color, English learners, children with diagnosed disabilities, and young children faced severe losses. This current moment requires an equity-based approach to respond to the growing gaps that are occurring with millions of students across the country.

POSTPANDEMIC, WHAT CAN DISTRICTS DO TO ATTAIN EDUCATIONAL EQUITY?

To think about systemwide transformation with an equity-minded approach postpandemic, school districts need to be committed to the long-haul work of creating equitable outcomes. Equity-centered educators cannot be afraid of taking bold steps that were needed prior to the pandemic and have become even more relevant since the pandemic. Such topics could include engaging in serious discussions about important topics that could very well result in massive pushback. The political moment that we live in has created tension, division, finger-pointing, deep-seated hate, and even violence. Racism, homophobia, transphobia, and anti-immigration are each hotly discussed topics in schools today, and the political climate has made them even more polarizing. These topics will be discussed at greater length later in this chapter, but, for now, I would argue that the following conditions increase the odds of success for equity-driven change efforts:

1. An authentic and sustained commitment to equity

2. Equity-focused school board leadership and budget

3. Enrichment programs with a punch

4. The willingness to move beyond a "lone ranger" equity officer

AN AUTHENTIC AND SUSTAINED COMMITMENT TO EQUITY

An authentic and sustained commitment to equity is centered on the idea that equity work is not done in a single day, a single week, or a single month, and in many instances ongoing results are not accomplished after a year's work. The commitment to equity must rest on a recognition of the historical and structural challenges that particular communities have faced for centuries (Love, 2023). Hence, for district leaders, a systemwide approach works to disrupt deficit mindsets that manifest as blaming families or take the form of deficit-based depictions of families not valuing education or children not being motivated to do well in schools. To the contrary, a sustained commitment to equity requires an asset-based approach, which recognizes, for example, that families that live in poverty often are among the hardest workers, maintain multiple jobs, and do some of the most physically intensive work in our society. Moreover, an authentic and sustained commitment to equity requires district leaders to engage in deep-seated reflection and analysis about who will be charged with this work. Equity work is not for everyone because many do not see its value, others are afraid to push for districtwide change, and others would rather blame people than systems and structures. Even those who are motivated to undertake the work will not be able to succeed without the support of structures and systems that readily identify the most vulnerable students and have the capacity to create and implement customized interventions for targeted groups. The commitment to being better and equity-focused means giving ourselves permission to do what Jamila Dugan (2022) says is "radical dreaming," in this moment where we recognize that

> the dreams of students are alive and well, but if we focus solely on what we believe they've lost, we may miss another opportunity for transformation. Leading with fear and hyper-focusing on our students' perceived deficits and loss will not lead us to a better future. (p. 59)

An authentic and sustained commitment to being equity-focused comes with the realization that we have an opportunity during what has been a chaotic time to be better, do better, think outside the box, and imagine a different way of how schools can best serve students. In doing so we must commit ourselves to recognizing and repairing past harms. Therefore, the message that must consistently emanate from the district leadership is one that explicitly states the goal is to help all students to be the best that they can—but doing so with a recognition of the root causes that have placed students in a state of disadvantage from the outset. The sustained commitment requires us to keep our eyes on the future of helping students to be their best while being mindful of past actions that have shaped our current reality, which means that along the way there will be setbacks and pitfalls. Admittedly, the journey can be fraught with obstacles, but we cannot allow the temporary frustrations keep us from what we want with permanent hope and possibility. When we think about repairing past harms, for example, that means having the courage and conviction to tell families and students that missteps have been made when individualized education plans (IEPs) have not been as effective as thought. It also means acknowledging that school police may create more anxiety and do more harm on campuses where Black and

Brown students attend schools—and that instead of ensuring safety, they have caused hurt and suffering to some unfairly. A commitment to equity requires the bold step of saying "we were wrong," "we erred," or "our actions or policies were hurtful and need to be amended."

EQUITY-FOCUSED SCHOOL BOARD LEADERSHIP AND BUDGET

Two core areas that can demonstrate important insight into a district's commitment to equity are its school board leadership and budget. A closer look at the composition of a school board can provide great insight into its commitment to equity. Frequently, many school boards are comprised of individuals from ethnic and racial backgrounds that are dramatically different than the demographics of the students they serve. This does not mean that those individuals cannot serve those students well, but it does beg the question about why there is not greater representation from those who live in the community and send their children to local schools. Or frequently, the composition of the board is made up of mostly or all male members, with little to no gender diversity. Representation matters, and it is more than fair to ask why the board does not mirror the community that it serves. Nuance also matters: We cannot assume that being a member of a marginalized group automatically predisposes an individual to equity leadership. It is also important to note that over the past several years, a growing number of individuals and organizations with harmful political agendas have sought school board positions to implement divisive policies. Equity is centered on not allowing the voices of a vocal minority overshadow what is in the best interest of the collective body. Often such individuals can be the biggest resistors to school transformation and equity-centered schools.

An additional step that school boards have taken lately is to adopt diversity or equity statements. The purpose of such statements has been to provide a forward-facing declaration that articulates that one of the core goals of a district is to embrace and celebrate diversity and equity. While symbolically important, it is critical to note that over the past few years, various statements have come under considerable scrutiny, as many parents and concerned community members have taken exception to some of the content in such statements. Resistance to diversity, equity, and inclusion (DEI) efforts have intensified over the past several years. In an ideal world, such statements should make an affirmation about equity. However, a number of districts across the country have gotten into contested debates about how to speak to equity in the face of intense resistance, when many parents/caregivers and community members do not believe in the value of equity (Gorski, 2019) or feel that affirmation and support of the LGBTQ+ community should not be a focus of the district. Others suggest that language about being anti-racist is problematic and should not be in a statement. Each of these points of resistance speaks to the work of equity and why it is challenging. Equity statements should be ideals and core values that all members of a given community can stand behind and be proud about. The better equity statements that I have seen typically highlight the following:

- No acceptance for disrespect, discrimination, or hateful language to anyone
- Recognition of the value and importance of diversity
- Denouncement of all forms of racism
- Affirmation of all ethnic and racial groups
- Celebration of students with diverse gender identities
- Affirmation of members from the LGBTQ+ community
- Recognition of harm and injury to historically marginalized groups
- Creation of spaces that recognize the diversity of abilities
- Commitment to create just, inclusive, and affirming school experiences for all students

Some statements go as far as to commit to anti-racism as well as challenging and dismantling homophobia and transphobia. Equity seeks to be inclusive as the framework outlines. Therefore, all statements that are developed should seek to create democratic, fair, and just schools that respect all students and families. To be clear, while statements are essential and offer core ideals that the district believes matter, some statements, no matter how eloquent, are strictly performative. Ultimately, the day-to-day decisions and actions of school leaders, teachers, and other stakeholders are far more important than statements. Some of the most beautifully crafted statements can be found in places that are not safe for Black, Brown, and LGBTQ+ students. Again, the real work is not in the words of our districts but in the actions of the adults who lead our districts (Milner, 2023). It is the job of school boards to create a better sense of belonging and not contribute to the angst seen in many states. In the current political moment, it has been individual board members who have sanctioned efforts that are proving harmful to certain students. Consider that a handful of districts move to expand parental rights by limiting the rights of LGBTQ+ students. California is suing one of its districts as the school board endorses anti-LGBTQ+ policies.

The current school board policy requires schools to notify parents and caregivers when students request to be identified by a name or pronoun or use facilities or participate in a program that does not align with the sex on their official records. Parents will be notified even if they do not have the student's permission. If boards believe in creating belonging schools that do not cause harm, students' rights should be protected.

Budgets matter as well when it comes to equity, because districts must demonstrate a commitment of fiscal resources to address long-standing inequities. This was the intent of Title I— the nation's oldest and largest federally funded program, according to the U.S. Department of Education. But sometimes, good intentions are not enough. Annually, Title I provides over $15.5 billion to school systems across the country for students at risk of failure and living at or near poverty. While well intentioned, the funding per student is quite low, averaging about $500 to $600 a year per student. And there is minimal evidence that the overall program is effective or that its funds are used for effective services and activities. Large proportions of school principals report using Title I funds for teacher professional development, which many studies have shown to be ineffective and which teachers do not find valuable (Darling-Hammond et al., 2017). While the message here is not to move away from professional development but to recognize that teaching is a highly complex and multifaceted endeavor, efforts to provide professional learning should avoid one-and-done approaches that are often checklist oriented and disconnected from the day-to-day work of teachers. Darling-Hammond et al. (2017) report that the most effective professional development for teachers (1) is content focused, (2) incorporates active learning, (3) supports collaboration, (4) uses models of effective practice, (5) provides coaching and expert support, (6) offers feedback and reflection, and (7) is of sustained duration. When done well, helping to expand teacher learning and growth through sustained and responsive professional development can be one of the most essential gateways to creating more equity in schools and classrooms. Research has been consistent for decades that one of the most salient factors in improving student performance is highly trained, culturally competent, and knowledgeable teachers (Darling-Hammond et al., 2017).

Moreover, professional development when done with an equity focus takes on a much different tone and tenor than traditional professional development. As mentioned in Table 2.1, equity-focused professional development is intentional in its emphasis on students' identities, teacher reflections, thinking about differences, and acquiring skills and knowledge focused on student learning.

TABLE 2.1 ● Equity-Focused Versus Traditional Professional Development

EQUITY-FOCUSED PROFESSIONAL DEVELOPMENT	TRADITIONAL PROFESSIONAL DEVELOPMENT
Professional development (PD) is informed by teachers' thoughts, suggestions, recommendations, and ideas.	PD is always determined by the school principal.
PD places an emphasis on helping teachers develop skills and strategies to help all learners but with a particular focus on struggling and advanced learners.	PD places little focus on strategies and skills, and more on programs. Caters to middle and not students on the margins.
PD regularly focuses on difficult issues that affect schooling experiences such as race, culture, mental health, and discrimination.	PD provides little to no attention on issues tied to race, ethnicity, and culture.
PD is centered on setting goals toward future aspirations and fostering collaboration between teachers and families to make plans about achieving them. Works daily toward accomplishing these goals.	Goals remain stagnant. No collaboration between teachers/leaders/families. Goals are rarely mentioned.
Seeks grants. Applies for out-of-school programs to enhance student learning opportunities, when possible.	Relies solely on funding from district.
Seeks help and guidance, when needed, from broader support networks such as peers, family, and trusted adults.	Assumes that schools always know what is best for students, and PD reflects such a belief.
PD stresses taking ownership and accountability after making mistakes, using mistakes as an opportunity to learn and further academic and emotional growth.	Places total blame and responsibility for student failure on parents, families, and communities. No ownership of schools as a factor in underperformance.
Continuously learns about implicit bias, with attention to identifying and challenging your own biases, and identifying and addressing implicit bias in the school community.	Pays no attention to bias.
PD challenges educators to continuously learn about people's multiple identities (e.g., cultures, languages, orientations, abilities, and socioeconomic backgrounds) that are different from their own.	Focus remains solely on flaws, deficiencies, and shortcomings of students and families. No focus on teacher reflection.

Thus, from an equity standpoint, district leaders need to examine how Title I funding is distributed across their respective schools and assess whether a one-size approach is appropriate. Often it is not. In many districts across the country, wide economic disparities exist. In some cases, students from low-income backgrounds attend schools two to three miles away from some of the most affluent neighborhoods, yet funding does not reflect those discrepancies. Moreover, district leaders should be intentional in ensuring that schools with high levels of poverty receive additional supports. Those supports can and should be supplemental programs, academic enrichment, teacher's aides, after-school tutoring, and ongoing outreach and engagement with parents and caregivers. Furthermore, an equity-focused look at the budget examines how resources are allocated and investigates patterns of which teachers, schools, and special programs allow students access to opportunity. Then, equity-focused leaders should brainstorm how to reallocate resources and patterns to help more students achieve. Equity in education, broadly speaking, means that schools provide all students the supports they need to reach their fullest potential. To that end, an intentionality around breakfast and lunch programs should be a must for all students. Likewise, providing consistent resources for after-school programs, tutoring, and supports for English learners should be a staple in high-poverty schools. Even in those schools that are not considered high poverty, inequities are present, and fundamental equity questions still apply. For example, is school funding used to hold assemblies featuring engaging speakers and culturally responsive activities for students of color? Are funds allocated to introduce and expose Black and Brown students to college fairs with an intentionality on Hispanic-serving institutions (HSIs) or historically Black colleges and universities (HBCUs)—all of which are shown to have higher rates of supports and graduation for Black and Brown students?

In this current moment, equity has become a polarizing concept that has been used to split communities, where many people see it as a dividing concept or an idea that suggests resources are being taken from one group of students and given to the other. To be clear, that is not equity, and district leadership must develop strategic communication plans that outline what their given equity plan will look like and underscore that they are not "zero-sum games." Heather McGhee (2022) points out that for many whites, any progress being made by people of color is often seen as coming at the expense of those who have historically had privilege and power. The same applies to equity; advocating for, and supporting our most vulnerable student populations does not mean taking away resources, time and attention away from other students. Districts in many instances should be explicit in reaching out to some of the most disenfranchised groups. Consider the Seattle Public School District, which in 2019, after seeing persistent dismal test scores of Black males, decided to implement the Office of African American Male Achievement. In short, the district believed that the approach of explicitly focusing on improving Black male outcomes would have far-reaching benefits. In short, district leaders believed that if the district could get the education system to work for Black male students, it would work for everyone else. The effort to boost curriculum and teaching strategies to improve academic outcomes and experiences for African American male students in Seattle Public Schools would raise achievement for all students.

District leaders must work to discredit misguided beliefs—for example, stating plainly that equity work doesn't mean teaching critical race theory in K–12 classrooms, nor does it indoctrinate students to become Marxists, nor does it mandate racial equity training that is intended to depict whites as "bad people," and to make "white students feel guilty." Rather, we must be clear and intentional in presenting a powerful counternarrative—that is, that equity is about justice, fairness, belonging, opportunity, and providing access to those students who have been historically disadvantaged. Our budgets must reflect a commitment to evidence-based programs and strategies that are moving the needle in eliminating disparities. Furthermore, the message must be clear, concise, and consistent, that equity benefits all students, because it seeks to have all students reach their fullest potential. Perhaps most importantly, district leaders must convey a clear and consistent message that helping all students does not harm others. In fact, the concept that rising tides lift all boats is appropriate here. Again, there is no place that embodies the idea of zero-sum games like districts and schools, from which students get access to accelerated programs, gifted and talented programs, Advanced Placement (AP) and honors courses, and other prized opportunities. Equity asks questions such as the following:

- Why are students of color underrepresented in gifted and talented programs?
- Why are students of color overrepresented in suspensions and expulsions?
- Why are there so few teachers and administrators of color?
- What supports are in place for multilingual learners?
- Are our practices and policies helping or hurting students who are in special education?

- Why are so few girls in leadership positions at schools or in science, technology, engineering, and math (STEM) classes?

- How are schools responding to the complex needs of children living in poverty and those who are experiencing homeless?

- Why are there a disproportionately high number of students of color in remedial classes?

- Do any students find the school mascot offensive in any way? And if so, why?

- What are we doing to ensure that the identities of our most marginalized students are honored and affirmed?

Perhaps most importantly, district leaders must convey a clear and consistent message that helping all students does not harm others. In fact, the concept that rising tides lift all boats is appropriate here.

There are vital ways to overcome intrenched inequities. Innovative and transformative district leaders are clear about what their data mean and how they define equity, and they are thoughtful in how they build up supporters of the work in their school systems, creating a critical mass of equity advocates to counter the critics who will never buy in. Another strategy is more pragmatic: to make the case that the new policies benefit everyone and that our budgets consistently reflect a commitment to supporting those who have consistently been on the margins.

ENRICHMENT PROGRAMS WITH A PUNCH

To make up ground for students who have long suffered academic disparities, districts and states need to develop short- and long-term strategic plans for how they will respond to the needs of students who have lagged academically. Such plans should have input from multiple stakeholders such as teachers, staff, building administrators, parents/caregivers, and students about how to address the needs of students. One of the most essential ways that schools can repair harm for students is to provide the academic supports to those who have historically been neglected and remain academically behind their peers. Arguably the most important way to make amends for past harms to student groups is to ensure their academic success. Schools should be places of formal and informal learning. To that end, districts may want to ask the following questions to inform their equity-focused strategic plans.

- Who are the students most in need of academic supports? Naming groups is vital in equity-centered approaches (e.g., Black students, English learners, students in special education).

- What programs or interventions are currently in place to support struggling students?

- How do we know that current interventions are working (or not working)? What evidence or data do we have to inform us about the effectiveness of current programs?

- How have stakeholders been involved in the creation of given programs/interventions?

- What resources are we willing to dedicate to assist our most vulnerable students?

- What supports are in place for nonacademic services such as mental health and social–emotional supports?

- What policies protect LGBTQ+ students?

Questions such as these can begin to generate organic discussions about how to develop a strategic plan. However, what is most evident for many students who are behind academically is a need for a robust, sustained, and culturally responsive set of academic interventions that have an emphasis on students acquiring essential basic skills, expanded learning opportunities, acceleration, and critical thinking skills. To that end, the following are some of the steps that districts can take to assist learners to create more equitable outcomes.

- *High-quality summer learning.* The effects of students and the summer slide have been well documented (Atteberry & McEachin, 2016). However, if districts can identify their lowest 10%–15% of schools on the academic continuum and place high-dosage tutoring in those sites, then summer learning can be more beneficial. However, summer learning cannot be framed as a punishment. Intense focus on academic enrichment, coupled with outdoor learning, play, and exploration, can go a long way. At least one study has shown that students who participated in summer programs that included math activities experienced significantly better math achievement outcomes compared to their control group counterparts (Lynch et al., 2022).

- *One-on-one tutoring.* Individualized tutoring has proven for years to be one of the most effective ways to provide students the academic supports they need. Districts that invest in sustained one-on-one and high-dosage tutoring that comes at no cost to students could make a big step in the right direction to close opportunity gaps. Growing research has been placed on the utility of high-dosage tutoring, which is generally seen as one-on-one tutoring or tutoring in very small groups at least three times a week, or for about 50 hours over a semester (Fryer, 2016).

- *After-school programs with an academic focus.* Many schools across the country have after-school programs for students. Yet many of them serve as high-level day-care situations. After-school programs usually offer a much lower adult-to-student ratio, and even an hour of individualized instruction can help enhance academic skills. Programs with a literacy focus are among the best. See the work of Freedom Schools (T. C. Howard, 2016).

- *Academic coaches for teachers.* One of the best ways to support students is by supporting teachers. Academic coaches can provide direct support to teachers by assisting in building their knowledge, skills, and confidence in working in classrooms, supporting diverse learners, and thinking about instructional variety. Coaches can provide customized support based on teachers' need, be it with instruction, planning, classroom management or content, or assistance with particular students.

- *Extended school day.* Many nations have 9- to 10-hour school days. Another option that could be considered is the extending of the U.S. school day. However, this has some obvious risks. Longer days with poor or no instruction will be counterproductive. Also, extracurricular activities may have to be rearranged as well.

- *Saturday schools.* The belonging of another day of learning can be vital for students. In many ethnic communities, Saturday schools are a staple in student learning. Korean Saturday schools and Rites of Passage programs, all of which are used to teach culture, history, and core values, are staples across the nation, with much of the instruction occurring on Saturdays either in a full-day or half-day format.

- *Smaller class size.* There has been extensive research showing that in the primary grades, classes that do not exceed 20 students can provide students with greater opportunity to have more individualized instruction, which improves outcomes (McKee et al., 2015). For students in fourth grade and higher, ideally class sizes would not exceed 30 students. Yet, research by John Hattie (2005, 2008) has highlighted that while reducing class size *can* have a positive impact, it cannot be done in isolation. In particular, if teacher practices are not dynamic, the effects of small class size can be negligent.

- *More instructional aides.* For schools that are unable to reduce class sizes, an important approach that can be taken is to get more adults in the classroom to reduce the adult-to-student ratio. Instructional aides or paraprofessionals often serve as valuable classroom supports, by being able to provide one-on-one attention to particular students, supporting teachers, or working with small groups of students. Moreover, as schools look to diversify their teaching ranks, paraprofessionals can make an important contribution. Many come from similar ethnic/racial and language backgrounds to the students, they often live in the community of the school, and they may have ongoing relationships with parents and caregivers.

- *Reimagining homework.* For years, homework has been seen as a necessary task for many educators but a useless chore for countless students. In schools across the country, homework has become a rudimentary practice with minimal evidence that it improves student learning. Ideally, homework should be for reviewing previously taught material and provide students additional practice with concepts. Yet too often students are given homework on material that they were never introduced to or did not understand if and when they were. Reimagining homework would entail either eliminating it altogether, because many students do not have individuals who can assist with it; significantly scaling down homework requirements; or making time during class to reteach concepts that would otherwise be assigned for homework.

While all these supports can have a positive impact on student achievement, there is arguably no more important approach to helping support student learning than individualized, intensive instruction or tutoring. Such approaches can and should be done in addition to the regular school-day instruction. But the literature on one-on-one tutoring has been extensive for some time now and reports a number of benefits for student learning.

A recent meta-analysis reviewed studies of tutoring interventions that have been evaluated by randomized controlled trials in the past few decades and found that, on average, tutoring increased achievement by roughly an additional 3 to 15 months of learning across grade levels (Dietrichson, 2017). Another review of almost 200 rigorous studies found that high-dosage tutoring—defined as more than three days per week or at a rate of at least 50 hours over 36 weeks—is one of the few school-based interventions with demonstrated large positive effects on both math and reading achievement (J-Pal Evidence Review, 2020). In short, tutoring matters, and it helps to close learning disparities. When setting up or engaging in tutoring, some of the key factors to consider are the following:

- *Session length.* The data are clear that tutoring that is 30–60 minutes in length is optimal for one-on-one sessions. But the quality of the session is more critical than actual minutes of time. Elementary students may benefit from shorter but more frequent sessions (i.e., 20 minutes, five times a week).

- *Frequency.* Tutoring is most likely to be effective when delivered in high doses through tutoring programs with three or more sessions per week or intensive, weeklong, small-group programs taught by individuals with content expertise. In the ideal situation, students would receive tutoring four to five times a week.

- *Setting.* Areas that are free of noise and distractions are ideal for students to make sure they can receive the benefits of tutoring. Settings can include a quiet workplace at school, a relaxed atmosphere outdoors, or even a Zoom arrangement where students might be at home so that parents/caregivers can assess how the session is going.

- *Relationships.* Learning for many students is deeply relational. Thus, working with the same tutor has the likelihood of greater success. Moreover, ensuring students have a consistent tutor over time may facilitate positive tutor–student relationships and a stronger understanding of students' learning needs.

MOVING BEYOND THE "LONE RANGER" EQUITY OFFICER

Across the country, more districts have moved toward developing an office for equity or a DEI department to respond to the needs of students who have been historically marginalized. In the wake of the George Floyd and Breonna Taylor deaths in 2020, many districts recognized the need to look inward to see how they could be better when it came to achieving racial equity in schools. Hence, we have seen an explosion of equity initiatives in districts and states; out of this has come the role of the equity officer. In most districts, those who serve as equity officers or in similar roles are usually experienced, credentialed people of color—in fact, they tend to be women of color. Equity officers are typically hired to change or institute policies and practices that ensure students who have been historically disadvantaged can receive similar supports and opportunities as their more privileged peers. Despite their expertise, equity officers sometimes have their judgment questioned by district leaders and certain school personnel, and it is not uncommon for equity officers to face other forms of workplace hostility, such as resistance, microaggressions, or outright refusal to take their work seriously. Moreover, many of these efforts led by equity officers fall woefully short because they frequently have little to no budget, have no staff, do not have direct reporting to the superintendent, are siloed, and are seen as outside of the "real" functioning of the district. Perhaps the biggest challenge that they face is the intense and persistent resistance, and at times direct hostility, from colleagues, district leaders, and parents. What is key to understanding why equity has become such a boogeyman and divisive concept, and why equity officers have been directly in the line of fire, is the zero-sum fallacy discussed early in the chapter—that is, that many adults feel that equity seeks to take from some and give to others. Writer Heather McGhee (2022) outlines this best when she states that we have to move past the zero-sum game approach to equity. She writes:

> The narrative that white people should see the well-being of people of color as a threat to their own is one of the most powerful subterranean stories in America. Until we destroy the ideas, opponents of progress can always unearth it and use to block any collective action that benefits us all. (p. 15)

The importance here is that *equity* has become a nasty buzzword for many parents/caregivers because it suggests that privileged students will not have the same access to many of the perks and luxuries of public schools such as gifted and talented programs, AP and honors courses, or extracurricular programs that have important cache.

Moving beyond an equity officer calls upon superintendents and school boards to issue a strong and clear message about why such a position is necessary. Moreover, effective DEI efforts need to provide resources such as a robust budget for the equity officer to develop a strategic plan centered on training, coaching, programs, and data analysis of outcomes. In addition, moving beyond an equity officer requires that there be a districtwide effort to equity. Most of the effective efforts typically have an equity representative at each school who works with the equity officer to coordinate and customize the equity efforts at that particular site. Finally, moving beyond the equity officer also means a consistent and strategic communication plan from the district that stays on message with a steady flow of information to the wider community about the work that is being done through the office for equity. And arguably, the biggest step that can be taken is that, in the face of political scrutiny that is sure to come, of having the back of the equity officer and providing them with assurance that no matter the criticism leveled against their efforts, the district is committed to the work of equity in the long run. With that said, the equity officer must also have the awareness and courage to confront a painful truth—that is, that the schools that they serve were never designed to meet the needs of those at the margins. Moreover, over the past year or two, intense attacks on DEI have made the work of equity officers even more challenging. The work is a constant battle for systemwide change. Performative window dressing such as adding slogans and showing a handful of students of color who have won awards or recognition will do little to disrupt an inequitable status quo. Real transformation is impossible without confronting the reality that the policies, curriculum, procedures, and practices that are baked into the fabric of schools failed to consider the needs and realities of students of color and those living in poverty. Thus, changing mindsets is perhaps the most difficult challenge in this work. In many instances, the adults who control budgets, oversee personnel, work in unions, and set polices are often the biggest barriers to creating equitable schools. Why, might one ask? Because equity is impeded by entrenched beliefs, attitudes, and actions that particular students (e.g., students of color, students from low-income families, English learners, students in special education, and LGBTQ+ students) are either incapable or not worthy of real opportunities to learn. A critical question is how to effectively counter resistance that is grounded in such deficit assumptions. When core beliefs are challenged, a natural outcome is discomfort caused by cognitive dissonance. With that said, out of such discomfort comes learning—learning that can lead to positive change. When we identify resistors and show them models of success, we begin to chip away at their deficit-based beliefs. Similarly, when we reveal data points that highlight inequities, resistors are faced with irrefutable evidence that contradicts their beliefs about meritocracy. What about a more direct response such as asking them if, at their core, they *really* care about all students. Even if we do all this, many might argue that "we have done all those things, and nothing has changed." To that end, equity advocates must find ways to collaborate with like-minded individuals and learn to work around the obstacles, and at times to subversively engage in equity-based practices in league with sympathetic parents, caregivers, and concerned community members. Above all, we need to keep a student-centered approach to the work. In short, when the going gets rough, remind yourself that there is a long history of educators and leaders working against the grain to attain educational justice and equity.

Real transformation is impossible without confronting the reality that the policies, curriculum, procedures, and practices that are baked into the fabric of schools failed to consider the needs and realities of students of color and those living in poverty.

BOOK-BANNING NATION: A CAUSE FOR CONCERN

At present, we face another form of resistance—a massive effort to ban books, lessons, and conversations related to race, ethnicity, gender identity, and LGBTQ+ issues. Starting in January 2021, legislators in 44 states have introduced bills or took other steps to limit classroom conversations and staff training on racism and sexism. Eighteen states have passed bans and restrictions through legislation or policies. And between July 2021 and March 2023, book bans—specifically bans on books that have LGBTQ+ characters, feature people of color, and address race and racism—were instituted in 86 school districts across the country, affecting 2 million students, according to PEN America (2022). What may surprise some readers is that in many states across the country, such efforts to put bans on certain types of content are not widely supported by parents and caregivers—even though the bans are often framed as matters of "parental rights."

Removal of books that are about racial injustice, experiences of members in the LGBTQ+ community, social protest, or exclusion of marginalized groups feels quite draconian because it essentially amounts to omitting various life experiences that are all too real for countless adults and children in the United States and beyond. Issues such as racism, sexism, transphobia, and homophobia are unfortunately all too real for countless Americans. Students need to learn about these experiences so that they can learn to fight all forms of discrimination and prejudice. Book banning is proving to be one of the biggest threats to inclusive education that we have seen over the last two decades.

It does not go without saying that groups that are leading the book-banning charge are largely conservative groups that want to paint a romanticized and idealized view of America's past and present. Those who are calling for book bans argue that content is often not age appropriate and deals with sexual orientation and gender identity issues that they think schools should not address, or promotes critical race theories, which they believe are guilt inducing. In many ways, a small minority seems to be attempting to control content for all students in certain states. There appears to be a politically motivated effort to induce fear into parents to believe that schools are indoctrinating students with content not suitable for young learners. However, banning books about the experiences of Black people, other people of color, and members of the LGBTQ+ community denies them being seen in what students learn. Such a view is damaging to students on many levels. One, it denies them the truth about U.S. history. Two, it prevents them from learning about the current realities and experiences of groups who face hardship. And three, it thwarts students' ability to understand the challenges that groups have had to overcome to make our democracy better. Banning books like Amanda Gorman's *The Hill We Climb*, *All Boys Aren't Blue* by George Johnson, and *The Hate U Give* by Angie Thomas (all books that have been banned in Florida) is a direct threat to the American idea of sharing the stories of a diverse and changing America.

A poll in 2022 by the American Federation of Teachers discovered that two-thirds of the 1,500 respondents (588 of whom were parents or caregivers) said that they were not concerned about teachers indoctrinating their children about topics tied to racism, sexism, and gender identity. Thus, efforts to demonize the "woke" agenda are not supported by many parents/caregivers nationally. Moreover, most of the parents surveyed said that the most important priority for them was that schools provide safe and welcoming learning environments that ensure all students, regardless of their backgrounds and identities, be given access to strong fundamental skills in reading, writing, and math and have the ability to develop critical thinking and reasoning skills. In essence, this is the gist of what equity seeks to do. Equity now is centered on belonging and doing the just and righteous thing for all students regardless of their backgrounds and identities.

RESPONDING TO STUDENTS' MENTAL HEALTH AND OTHER NEEDS

The pandemic shined a light on one of the serious issues in our nation's schools today: the reality of children's mental health challenges. There cannot be discussions around equity without an intentional focus on our students' mental health needs. Learning does not take place in a vacuum, and neglecting mental health in schools creates a formidable barrier to student learning. Justice is about helping students to heal, and far too many of our students are hurting. They struggle with real-life challenges in their efforts to be whole and healthy in their pursuit of learning. To be clear, schools have always been mindful about the overall social and emotional development of young people. However, the last decade has seen a significant increase in the focus on the role that schools have to play with mental health and well-being (Craig & Sporleder, 2017). The challenge before schools is that many school personnel are not equipped with the knowledge, skills, and dispositions to accurately identify young people who are suffering from anxiety, depression, and bipolar disorder, among other debilitating conditions. The new normal of schools requires consistent attention to the way students' ability to function academically is profoundly affected by the reality of mental health issues. Many students are still reeling from the effects of being disconnected from peers, caring adults, and the safety and comfort that school provides, because of the pandemic. Although schools have been back in session for several years now, the damage done during the closure of schools cannot be understated. In this moment, understanding the effects and root causes of trauma and well-being is paramount for every educator in schools (M. Howard, 2019). There cannot be a true commitment to equity without understanding how mental health matters continue to be a challenge for countless numbers of students.

There cannot be a true commitment to equity without understanding how mental health matters continue to be a challenge for countless numbers of students.

Over the past decade, our understanding and awareness of childhood trauma has increased, as has the call for trauma-informed approaches, with a focus on how to create teaching practices, school climate, and the delivery of trauma-related in-service and preservice teacher education for practitioners (Cole et al., 2005; Crosby, 2015; Day et al., 2015; Oehlberg, 2008). From an operational standpoint, trauma includes current or past experiences or events that are perceived as harmful, create intense distress, and affect an individual's overall well-being (Substance Abuse and Mental Health Services Administration [SAMHSA], 2014). Complex trauma is the result of persistent, ongoing, or repeated traumatic exposure over an extended period, generally resulting in significant dysfunction or reduced well-being (Wolpow et al., 2009). Research has shown that psychological trauma is commonly experienced by both children and adolescents (Costello et al., 2002). Consider that close to two-thirds of adults have reported experiencing adverse emotional events (i.e., trauma) during childhood (Anda et al., 2006). Research has also shown that such trauma in childhood is associated with impediments in school performance, as social, emotional, cognitive, and even brain development can be significantly impeded by traumatic stress (Perfect et al., 2016). Childhood trauma can negatively affect students' capacity for self-regulation, concentration, memorization, organization, comprehension, and problem solving (Wolpow et al., 2009), affecting them academically and socially throughout their school experiences. So, what are steps that districts can take?

- An increasing number of districts and states are partnering with philanthropic foundations to secure donations that allow them to hire additional psychiatric social workers, therapists, and behavior specialists.

- Some schools are partnering with local colleges and universities that have master's in social work (MSW) programs where individuals are required to do internship (volunteer) hours and work with various schools around counseling and therapy.

- Schools and districts are contracting with community-based mental health programs that offer supports at a significantly reduced rate and offer therapeutic services and supports to students with the highest need.

- A more radical approach that states are taking is providing mental health days for students. Twelve states currently allow for mental health days according to a recent tally by Verywell Mind (Nelson & England, 2023). Ten states have passed legislation for student mental health days that allow students to reset and recharge. Allowing students to take mental health days, which are excused absences, sends the message that mental health is as important as physical health and reduces the stigma that often accompanies efforts to practice self-care in the interest of well-being. A recent poll by the National Alliance on Mental Illness (2023) found that 70% of parents support schools offering mental health days to students.

ANOTHER APPROACH: COMMUNITY SCHOOLS

Considering learning disparities that were in place prior to the pandemic and the fact that they have gotten wider during school shutdowns, what can schools do to forge a path forward to create equitable schools? What are steps that districts can take to be more equity oriented? One of the more promising models that states and districts have taken recently to respond to growing inequality in communities and schools has been the creation of community schools (Maier et al., 2017). Community schools are not new to the education landscape. In fact, they are a century-old idea that recognizes the inseparable link between schools and communities (Saunders et al., 2021).

The arrangement of school–home–community is anchored on core pillars. The pillars of the Community Schools Initiative are the following:

- *Integrated student supports* address out-of-school barriers to learning through partnerships with social and health services agencies. Partnerships may employ social–emotional learning, conflict resolution, and restorative justice practices to support mental health and decrease conflict, bullying, and punitive disciplinary actions.

- *Expanded learning time and opportunities* include after-school, weekend, and summer programs to provide additional academic instruction and support, enrichment activities, and opportunities for real-world learning.

- *Active parent/guardian and community engagement* brings greater parent/caregiver presence into schools as educational partners and makes schools serve as neighborhood hubs for learning and support for students and families.

- *Collaborative leadership and practices* build a culture of professional learning, collective trust, and shared responsibility, wherein families know, are connected to, and communicate consistently with school personnel and service providers.

Community schools are committed to addressing many of the out-of-school factors that students face that impede in-school learning possibilities. Grounded in the concept of bringing community resources to schools in a permanent and sustainable fashion, community schools are centered on the idea that for students to succeed, there must be an investment of nonacademic supports to ensure students have all the tools needed to be successful in schools. Thus, community schools place an emphasis on bringing in community resources such as food banks, mental health programs, vision and dental clinics, legal support teams, and adult job training to actual school campuses. The state of California, for example, has allocated $4.1 billion to develop community schools with the hope that these schools have the potential to transform K–12 education. The plan is to enrich schools in areas that struggle with poverty and other social ills to become neighborhood centers to meet the needs of students and families. In Los Angeles County, the Community Schools Initiative (CSI) launched at 15 school sites in September 2019. The goal of community schools is to serve as hubs for a variety of support services for students and their families. Each of the campuses was provided with a full-time CSI program specialist to coordinate services from participating and local agencies. The sites are also provided with a full-time educational community worker (ECW) to support parent/caregiver engagement with schools. The focus of the CSI is to provide a wraparound set of services that can be located at schools. In many ways, the CSI seeks to establish a one-stop shopping entity to support students and families and is viewed as a conduit to improving school outcomes for students. The areas of primary foci for the CSI are as follows:

- Mental health support
- Basic needs support
- Family engagement
- Physical health and well-being
- Support for special populations
- College and career readiness
- Behavior interventions and supports
- Enrichment and intervention programs

The CSI is centered on the concept of a robust and culturally responsive partnership that provides supports from various service providers to students and families.

EXPECTED OUTCOMES OF THE COMMUNITY SCHOOL INITIATIVE

1. Increase in graduation rates
2. Decrease in chronic absenteeism and dropout rates
3. Reduction in suspensions
4. Increase in family engagement

In studying the impact of the CSI during the 2021–2022 academic year, the UCLA Pritzker Center for Strengthening Children and Families along with the Los Angeles County Department of

Mental Health engaged in a series of listening sessions with various school administrators who are engaged with CSI work. The principals from the 15 sites spoke quite favorably about how their schools and students are benefitting from a whole-school approach. They highlighted the importance of additional support, engagement with parents and caregivers, connections to social and support services, and a greater whole-school approach. One administrator noted:

> A big benefit was lending sustainability to programs: not a consultant or outsider, but someone who knows our community and is there every day . . . it's a school-based program specifically for our school to make decisions and meet with stakeholders. Integrating different portions of the schools with one another. Another set of hands, eyes, and ears in the community. It was like having a general assistant.

Among the other key benefits that the principals mentioned were these:

- Offering resources to students is made visible to teachers, improving the educational ecosystem at schools. Such approaches helped provide teachers and staff with valuable resources, connections, and personnel to support students.

- A growing number of administrators stressed the mental health needs of students increased exponentially during the pandemic. Hence, mental health support, including having mental health specialists in schools and classrooms and establishing a sense of connection between students, was important.

- Physical resources that were dispersed such as free hygiene products, clothes, and school supplies were instrumental for many students. An increasing number of families needed essential resources and basic supplies in the aftermath of the pandemic.

- Administrators stressed that CSI specialists were vital in securing essentials for students and families in need.

- As food insecurity became commonplace in many communities, the need to identify food supports became a big challenge for many students. Administrators stated that education community workers were vital in the effort to combat food insecurity to making connections between students/families and food security sources.

- Connections to free or pro-bono community resources were mentioned by a number of administrators as a valuable benefit of CSI specialists. Several principals said that it was quite helpful for CSI specialists to make phone calls or home visits to students who were chronically absent, in ways that other school staff could not.

- A number of administrators talked about the valuable contributions that CSI specialists made in providing information and support for parents and caregivers, such as helping to identify vouchers for families dealing with housing insecurities, food banks, and other needs. Moreover, administrators said that having CSI specialists was like "having another staff member" to help address various needs at the school.

While community schools are not the panacea to fix all that ails schools, they may play an important part of the elixir that can help to create more equitable schools. Students frequently do poorly in schools because of factors that affect them before they enter schools. Chronic poverty, structural racism, limited resources, environmental factors, and underinvestment in particular communities all limit students' abilities to thrive. Moreover, we know that students of color are more likely to deal with adverse childhood experiences (Noguera et al., 2019) than their white peers. The community schools' effort may provide promising results that districts nationwide may consider.

Equity Now Chart

JUSTICE	REPAIR	BELONGING
• Recognizing that the effects of the COVID-19 pandemic will have consequences for years to come for students academically, socially, and emotionally	• Rethinking traditional metrics of achievement • Providing additional academic and mental health supports to students and teachers	• Providing space for teachers and students to know that mental health challenges are not stigmatized • Offering regular counseling sessions

JUSTICE	REPAIR	BELONGING
• Creating offices(s) of equity that are equipped with permanent resources, adequate staffing, comprehensive budgets, and authority to implement districtwide policy • Reporting directly to superintendent	• Creating districtwide statements on diversity that recognize historically marginalized groups • Developing districtwide strategic plans with culturally responsive metrics dedicated toward improving outcomes for underserved student populations	• Creating equity teams throughout the district • Ensuring districtwide equity teams comprise school personnel (e.g., teachers, instructional aides, front office staff), parents, caregivers, and students (high school) • Conducting ongoing climate surveys and focus groups to all stakeholders, with findings to be shared community wide
• Providing intense one-on-one academic tutoring to students who persistently underperform • Providing additional instructional aides to the lowest-performing schools and classrooms • Placing a priority of putting the most skilled and experienced teachers in the classrooms with students who have the greatest academic challenges	• Providing information sessions to parents/caregivers explaining causes of student underperformance, and district plans to address disparities • Placing intentional focus on the lowest tier of underperforming students (10%) and developing case studies for support and intervention	• Creating clubs and organizations designed to provide peer tutoring • Establishing awards and recognition for students who have demonstrated academic growth, progress, and non-academic excellence (e.g., leadership, volunteering, extracurricular participation)

Questions for School Districts to Consider

1. What special interventions/programs have we designed to assist the most disadvantaged students and communities?

2. What are the indicators or data points that would demonstrate that our interventions are working or having success?

3. How do our fiscal resources reflect a sustained commitment to assisting our most marginalized student populations?

4. How do we communicate with our larger school community about our commitment to equity?

5. How does our school board composition reflect diversity, equity, and belonging in its makeup?

6. What resources do we have for students with mental health needs?

7. What do our intensive tutoring programs look like? Have they been effective?

Recommendations for Reading and Resources

1. Joseph, N. (2022). *Making Black girls count in math education: A Black feminist vision for transformative teaching.* Harvard Education Press.

2. Burks, N. (2018). *The deepest well: Healing long-term effect of childhood adversity.* Houghton Mifflin Harcourt.

3. Craig, S. (2016). *Trauma informed schools.* Teachers College Press.

4. Douglass, S. (2011). *Learning in a burning house: Educational inequality, ideology, and (dis)integration.* Teachers College Press.

5. Noguera, P., Darling-Hammond, L., & Friedlaender, D. (2015). Equal opportunity for deeper learning. Deeper Learning Research Series. *Jobs for the Future.*

6. Ladson-Billings, G. (2006). From the achievement gap to the education debt: Understanding achievement in US schools. *Educational Researcher, 35*(7), 3–12.

7. Francois, A., & Quartz, K. H. (2022). *Preparing and sustaining social justice educators.* Harvard Education Press.

CHAPTER 3

Schoolwide Equity

Centering Our Most Vulnerable Students

W e must remember that equity is about excellence and opportunity. As I have said throughout this book, our students deserve equity now. Moreover, we must keep justice, recognition and repair of past harms, and belonging at the center of our equity efforts. Equity should and must involve getting all students access to excellent teaching and rigorous, culturally responsive, anti-racist learning materials. Furthermore, equity now means helping all students, but with a particular focus on ensuring that our most vulnerable students learn as much as they can, helping them identify their passions, providing opportunities for them to explore the world around them, and meeting their needs along the way. Finally, our focus on equity should not be a one-size-fits-all approach. Standardization is not equity. Every day, students bring diverse and unique skill sets, experiences, interests, and backgrounds to school. Thus, a focus on collaboration and differentiation in instruction is vital. At times this may require consistent and intensive individualized tutoring. In some instances, it may require much larger chunks of time that may be provided in summer-school learning opportunities, after-school programs, or Saturday schools. The bottom line is that an unapologetic equity focus is always about taking deliberate and evidence-based practices to level the playing field for students to be contributing members of society. We all win when our most marginalized students have realistic opportunities to succeed. I come back to my father's sentiment that I discussed in Chapter 1: How are we helping those in greatest need?

In this chapter, I will address why closing equity gaps is best done when there is a districtwide commitment and culture that extends throughout every school in the district. This is when equity works best, when the message comes from on high that this is who we are as a district, this is what we stand for, and our resources, goals, mission, policies, and practices are equity focused. As I discussed earlier, many districts across the nation must have a sense of urgency when it comes to equity. We need equity now. Our students cannot wait, and the stakes are too high to take a complacent approach to their futures. However, the unfortunate reality is that this is not the case for many districts, which makes it quite challenging for schools to uphold equity-based principles. However difficult, schoolwide equity is possible even when the district is not as supportive as it could be. In short, leaders, teachers, staff, and concerned community members cannot throw up their hands and give up when the district is not on board. There can and still needs to be an approach of how individual schools can do this work. In this chapter, I will outline some of the steps that schools can take— even when their efforts are not supported by the central office. Equity is most likely to be achieved when the entire organization has a culture that is built on serving all students but has an intentionality on its most vulnerable students. The importance of school culture is pivotal and has been documented in a number of books and articles (Gruenert & Whitaker, 2015). Culture matters in a school because it sets the tone on core goals, norms, practices, policies, and values that drive everything in the building. Culture is important because it explicitly and implicitly communicates to everyone in the building or organization *who we are*. Gruenert and Whitaker (2015) describe organizational culture as a "social indoctrination of unwritten rules that people learn as they try to fit in a particular group" (p. 7). Culture is important because it can be one of the essential elements of repairing harm. When students enter schools that are equipped with adequate personnel, caring adults, resources, goals, and objectives dedicated to helping students learn, thrive, and grow, harm can be repaired, and healing and growth can occur. Unfortunately, far too many students enter schools without a clear culture, and as a result further harm can, and is, done to students every day. That is why equity now is essential. The following section identifies the most important characteristics that are crucial to building an equity-centered school culture.

STEPS TOWARD BUILDING AN EQUITY-CENTERED SCHOOL CULTURE

While the following components are especially important in creating and sustaining a culture of equity, the list is by no means exhaustive. As you read this section, you are encouraged to add other components to the list.

SHARED GOALS AND VISION

In an equity-centered school, all adults should be working toward the same goal. When individuals are empowered to take ownership of their goals, it can cause a shift in the culture of a school. As individuals learn how to work in alignment with the school's vision and values, new relationship norms are created that have less to do with individuals seeking success for their own class, team, or department and more to do with a shared vision of what can be done collectively to support students. Remember, our goals should always be about doing what is best to support and improve the experiences of students. Justice is always the goal, and students are always the top priority in a culture centered on equity. A key equity-centered question should always ask, "Is this what is best for students?"

COLLABORATION

Teachers often have higher levels of efficacy and belonging in a school when they feel like they are supported by peers and administration. To that end, the goals of a school can be quite diverse. A schoolwide macro goal can be to build a culture of success, implementing culturally responsive practices school-wide, while a grade-level team may have more micro-level goals such as engaging in cycles of inquiry around standards-based learning goals. Are professional learning communities working toward common, equity-centered goals that have been embraced by the school community? Are teams in alignment around these common goals? Working together can build a sense of "we are all in this together." To that end, collaboration is best when it is built on equal status of participants, respect for all members, honesty, acceptance of diversity of thought and problem-solving approaches, and transparency. Collaboration also understands that heathy tension or disagreement is not a bad thing.

CONTINUOUS IMPROVEMENT

Teachers in a positive, equity-centered school culture know that there is always capacity and room for improvement for everyone. Leaders set the tone for improvement by always suggesting that they have room for growth and improvement and outlining steps that they are taking to get better in their leadership journey. Opportunities for learning and development are seen in all aspects of school life regardless of how experienced certain members might be. Therefore, staff are empowered to view themselves as lifelong learners and to help facilitate the learning of others within the school. Learning is seen as a key part of the adult learning journey, enabling individuals to achieve ever-varying degrees of personal and professional maturity.

RESPECT FOR DIVERSITY

A healthy school climate recognizes, respects, and celebrates diversity in all its manifestations. To that end, racial, ethnic, linguistic, and cultural diversities are seen as strengths of students. Moreover, diversity is seen not only through a racial lens but also through cognitive processing, family background, socioeconomic status, ability, gender identity, body type, and native-born/non-native status. Diversity of thought is also encouraged. A healthy respect for diversity is shown not only for students but for teachers and staff as well. The climate also reflects the incorporation of experiences, histories, and stories for people from across the global community in curriculum, on walls with posters and famous quotes, and at various celebrations and events.

PARENT/CAREGIVER ENGAGEMENT

An important reminder: A child's education (and child development, in general) extends well beyond the classroom or schoolhouse walls. Rather, it is enacted in a complex ecosystem that encompasses families, communities, and the broader sociopolitical environment. As I will discuss in greater detail in Chapter 6, equitable schools affirm the critical role of parents and caregivers as partners in the education of students. To that end, schools do not see mere involvement but recognize authentic engagement wherein parents and caregivers have input into decision making, contribute to certain budget and personnel matters, and have a voice in curricular choices and extracurricular offerings at a school. Furthermore, schools need to be willing to think about how to incorporate parents and caregivers who are most often marginalized. Repair is accomplished when those who have been historically omitted from key decision-making processes—for example, those whose first language is not English, individuals who may not have transportation, and families where the adults work multiple jobs, which prohibits the ability to come to school-sanctioned events—are invited in, are given a meaningful seat at the table, and feel a sense of belonging. Schools and school leaders play a pivotal role in ensuring that schools can become more equitable and belonging spaces for students (S. M. Johnson, 2019). The same things must be the case for the adults who care for students.

Again, schools that work to create and sustain a culture of belonging and equity that informs individual and collective decisions and actions can make a significant impact on addressing equity even if they are not supported by the district. Recently, one of the disturbing realities in many schools has been issues tied to racial hate and discrimination by students toward their peers (S. M. Muñoz, 2021). An equity-focused school culture makes it loud and clear that no type of hate is allowed, and this must be echoed by all adults who are part of the school community.

Schools that work to create and sustain a culture of belonging and equity that informs individual and collective decisions and actions can make a significant impact on addressing equity even if they are not supported by the district.

ADDRESSING HATE SPEECH: AN IMPORTANT PART OF POSITIVE SCHOOL CULTURE

An important part of school culture is how an organization addresses matters that harm students. As I have mentioned throughout the book, repairing harm is one of the key pillars of achieving equity now. Over the past several years, an increasing number of incidents have been happening on school campuses, and in classrooms, that involve hate speech (Pérez Huber & Muñoz, 2021). It is difficult for students to learn when they are direct or indirect targets of hate speech. Schools must become hate-speech-free zones. But I want to be clear that just as hate is learned, it can be unlearned. Hate speech is any form of expression through which a person intends to demean, vilify, humiliate, or incite hatred against a group or a class of persons based on race, religion, skin color, sexual identity, gender identity, ethnicity, disability, or national origin. Immediate responses and condemnations to racism, sexism, homophobia, transphobia, and other types of hate speech need to be consistent across the school. Indifference, silence, or confusing messaging in response to hate speech only exacerbates the harm to the receiving party. Moreover, all individuals are watching how adults respond to incidents of hate, and in many ways refusal to acknowledge and repudiate such messages is akin to giving the green light for further hate. It also tells the targeted person that "you are not protected here." I can recall working with a high school in New Jersey, and the principal notified me that they had an incident where someone wrote the N-word on one of the bathroom walls in big, bright red letters. The principal shared with me that he wanted to "get to the bottom" of the incident, find the perpetrators, and address the matter. He explained to me how he met with his team, laid out a plan to investigate the matter, and "took several days" to ultimately respond to the incident. My first thought was that at this school with such a small number of Black students his response was not only inadequate but furthered harm. I explained to him that there was a likelihood that many students had seen the N-word displayed, and the fact that there was no immediate comment or announcement prohibiting this type of behavior sent a powerful message to Black students: You are not protected here. Such a delay of days to act communicates indifference, lack of care, and failure to protect, and cosigns for similar behavior to happen. I shared my thoughts and my deep concern with this principal, and he shared that after not being able to identify the responsible party, he made a statement days later because he "wanted to gather all the facts first." Totally unacceptable. One can only imagine how Black students felt at that school.

I would also make the distinction that hate speech is different from microaggressions, which I discuss in greater detail in Chapter 5. Hate speech is often deliberate and meant to be hurtful, while microaggressions are often more common, subtle everyday slights directed at someone's identity. Microaggressions can be intentional or unintentional, and often perpetrators are unaware of the injury that they may have caused. Hate speech, on the other hand, is usually intentional and a direct attack on some aspect of a person's individual or group identity. Both are problematic at schools and happen far too often, especially to minoritized students. Educators can and must play a role to stop hate speech in schools. Here are some steps that can be taken to address racism and hate speech in schools and classrooms:

1. **Address the issue (do not ignore it!).** Far too often, when teachers hear hate speech, there is a tendency to ignore it because they are not sure how to address it (see the aforementioned principal). Teachers might think, "I am not sure what to say" or "How should I address a racially insensitive word?" or "It wasn't my issue." Whenever hearing hate speech, teachers and leaders should immediately speak out against it, tell students that such talk and actions will not be tolerated, and be firm in such a stance. Silence on these matters is complicity, does not protect students, and only gives license for more hateful language to be used in the classroom or schoolyard.

2. **Research the topic or the offensive language.** When caught off guard with hate language, use it as a teachable moment, for yourself and for your students. But always keep in

mind that we cannot teach what we do not know. If we do not know the history of hateful language used to demean different racial/ethnic groups, women, LGBTQ+ members, people of particular religious backgrounds, or people who are born in another country, then we need to learn. It is incumbent for teachers to educate themselves and study about topics, issues, and language that are divisive or hateful. Then share with students about the way hateful language has led to many people dying in our country and beyond.

3. **Increase your own racial literacy.** Demographers state that in the year 2042, our nation will be predominantly comprised of non-white people. Our country's racial, ethnic, and linguistic demography is changing rapidly. Thus, teachers need to increase their racial literacy to better understand, connect with, and teach today's learners. Race-based hate crimes remain the number-one type of hate crime in the United States. Hate is learned, and all adults must speak out about it. Approximately 80% of our teaching population is white, and over half of our student population is non-white. All teachers must work to increase their racial literacy. Ignorance and indifference fuel hate. Much of the hate speech in schools today is focused on racial hatred or discrimination. Increase your literacy to inform your students.

4. **Examine content in the curriculum.** Frequently, school content and curriculum can have language, examples, or images that implicitly or explicitly convey hateful messages. Teachers must be diligent in examining anything that could be controversial in textbooks, literature, or examples in videos shared in the classroom. Such content should be excluded from what students are being taught, but skilled teachers may choose to have educative discussions about why certain language is used in content and why it should be removed.

5. **Generate discussion in your class around hate language.** No matter the grade level or subject matter, teachers need to have conversations early and often about the zero tolerance for hate speech in their classrooms and across the school. Introduce concepts and lessons about the history of certain words and how they were used to dehumanize people. I recall a middle school teacher I worked with in Ohio who was masterful in teaching a lesson about the death of Matthew Shepard and how hate, ignorance, and violence toward members of the LGBTQ+ community were at the root of his tragic death. The discussion the lesson generated was powerful, insightful, and emotional. Students talked

about how they did not realize that phrases such as "that's so gay" contribute to the mistreatment of people, and learned not only that they need to stop using such language but also how they can speak up and be upstanders when they hear friends and peers using such language.

6. **Bring in guest speakers.** One of the more powerful approaches that teachers can take to help students learn about diversity is to hear firsthand from people from different groups who can talk about cultural practices, lived experiences, or historical events that are age appropriate and tied to particular subject matter. Ask colleagues or parents/caregivers about who might be ideal speakers to talk to your students.

For additional resources, see the following:

- *Start Where You Are, but Don't Stay There* by H. Rich Milner (2020)
- *Why Race and Culture Matter in Schools* by Tyrone C. Howard (2020)
- *Everyday Antiracism* by Mica Pollock (2008)
- *White Fragility* by Robin DiAngelo (2018)
- *Promoting Racial Literacy in Schools: Differences That Make a Difference* by Howard Stevenson (2014)
- *So You Want to Talk About Race* by Ijeoma Oluo (2018)
- *A Kids Book About Gender* by Dale Mueller (2023)
- *How to Be an Antiracist* by Ibram X. Kendi (2019)
- *Trans Kids: Being Gendered in the Twenty-First Century* by Tey Meadow (2018)
- *Feminism Is for Everybody* by bell hooks (2000)
- *Black Feminist Thought* by Patricia Hill Collins (1990)
- *Sister Outsider* by Audre Lorde (1984)
- *Queer Intentions* by Amelia Abraham (2019)

ADDRESSING THE N-WORD!

As I spend time in schools, one of the bigger issues that I hear students, teachers, and administrators talk about as a significant hate speech issue at schools is the use of the N-word. Unfortunately, I have heard a number of white teachers say that "it is not my place to tell Black kids not to use the N-word." Such a stance is a cop-out. Teachers have the moral grounding to tell students that any language, be it cultural or not, is not allowed. Talk about how that word is disrespectful to many people and hurtful to lots of others, and even though it may be used in spaces away from school, it is not allowed on school premises. My take has been straightforward and simple: Schools should immediately ban the word. Educate students about it. Tell students use of the N-word will be met with immediate restorative action. This approach would apply for students who are African American, Latinx, Asian American, white, Native American, mixed race, and from any other racial or ethnic background. And, yes, even white administrators and teachers need to step up and tell African American students not to use the word at school. How might a school enact and normalize such a policy? Following are some recommendations:

- Provide mandatory lessons based on the *New York Times*'s masterful and informative "The 1619 Project," helmed by Nikole Hannah-Jones (2019–present), which explores the history, horrors, and brutalities of slavery. All students need to understand the horrors of lynching and how countless African Americans died hearing this racist slur as they took their last breath.

- Clearly communicate the consequences of using the N-word; for example, the first occurrence necessitates notification of parents or caregivers. Second uses of the word trigger in-person meetings between school personnel, the students, and their parents or caregivers.

- Finally, third offenses result in suspension. While I typically am not an advocate of suspension, I think it would send a powerful message about what language is unacceptable. I wonder how many non-Black parents/caregivers even realize that their children use such an offensive word so often and so freely. Moreover, how would they respond if large numbers of their children were being suspended in ways that many African American and Latinx students are unfairly suspended for far lesser offenses such as willful defiance, tardiness, or talking back to teachers?

The N-word must go. The word has no place in our students' vocabulary, and even the most cursory research would reveal its long, ugly, and sordid history in our nation. Our students must know and understand that. School staff must know and understand that. Will there be resistance to schools taking a stance? Yes. However, I think schools can and should play a transformative role to create safe spaces for learning free of hate, bigotry, and harmful language. Let's be clear: The N-word is one of the most hateful, inhumane, racist, and useless words in the English vocabulary. Its history is rooted in degradation, enslavement, dehumanization, hate, anti-Black racism, and a belief in the inferiority of Blacks and African Americans. No student should use the N-word at school *ever*.

In some of my recent work with hundreds of Black students at local high schools in Los Angeles, I have heard them discuss the pain, anger, frustration, and sadness they endure when hearing other students of color using the N-word, not in a pejorative manner but as a term of endearment, in their presence. There is a large body of literature on the N-word and its usage when it comes to whether it ends with the letter *a* (meant to be endearing) or with *er* (meant to be derogatory; Kennedy, 2000). The students that I have worked with have made it abundantly clear that either usage is unacceptable. Moreover, most of the Black students that I have worked with have said that they have heard non-Black students use the word in the presence of school personnel, who fail to condemn the language or speak out about its inappropriateness. Even when it comes to textbooks and literature that contain the N-word, school personnel need to preemptively inform students that the word should be read out loud as "N-word." I also totally reject the contention that African American students have a "pass" on the use of the word because they have reclaimed and renamed the word. It is time for school personnel to increase their racial literacy and be much more active in eliminating the N-word.

SUPPORTING OUR MOST VULNERABLE STUDENTS

To ensure that schoolwide equity efforts are persistent and effective, the focus must always be on inclusion. Schools face ongoing challenges in helping to ensure that all children have access to a high-quality education. However, a closer look at today's schools reveals a disturbing demographic trend that shows little indication of slowing down: increasing numbers of vulnerable children. Although a number of children's circumstances can fall into the "vulnerable" category, those who are mired in chronic poverty, homelessness, or challenging home lives; facing untreated mental health issues; or part of the foster care system are among the most vulnerable in our schools and society today. An equity-focused approach to schools needs to consistently keep a focus on student groups who face more challenges than most. Cumulative disadvantage can lead to countless challenges that affect school experiences and outcomes.

To state the obvious, growing numbers of children face arduous circumstances before ever entering school. Although many courageous and dedicated teachers, staff, and leaders work tirelessly in these schools, the reality is painfully clear: Most schools are ill equipped and underprepared to understand, let alone address, the depth, breadth, complexity, and seriousness of the challenges that many students face daily—from food insecurities, homelessness, and parents with untreated mental health issues, to continuous caring for younger siblings and family members. Why can't we find ways to house, feed, care for, educate, and support all children? It is difficult, if not impossible, to inspire children when they are hungry, and children's ability to concentrate on learning is compromised when complex trauma has been a staple in their lives. Think about it: Would you be preoccupied with tonight's homework if you did not know where you would sleep tonight? School personnel cannot be blamed for low test scores (an unreliable indicator of a child's potential to begin with) when chronic violence, despair, and hopelessness are on full display every day for many young people. So, what is our response? How do we help those in direst need? To respond to the complex needs of vulnerable populations, everyone—educators, policymakers, and communities—can start with a three-pronged approach:

1. **Acknowledge the complexity of contemporary circumstances.** The first step to supporting children in vulnerable circumstances must be recognizing the complexity of these challenges. Issues tied to inequality, poverty, racism, homophobia, and sexism remain very much enmeshed in our nation's fabric, despite the apparent progress we have made. To that end, we need to realize that complicated problems are not solved with simplistic approaches, silver-bullet solutions, or mundane how-tos. We all must recognize the all-too-clear connections between race, class, gender, and poverty; between gender and exclusion; and between immigration and opportunity. This can be accomplished, in part, by keeping inclusion front and center in our efforts to enact equity.

   We must recognize the dearth of affordable housing in many cities as well as the grave implications for students struggling with housing insecurity (Aviles de Bradley, 2015). As a responsible society, we must also understand the relationship between mental health and substance abuse. The unacceptable numbers of children who are abused, neglected, or under the auspice of child welfare services often can be traced back to the deep pain, frustration, despair, suffering, marginalization, and desperation of their parents/caregivers. A close look at many children's circumstances reveals high levels of depression, anxiety, substance abuse, and mental health challenges for the adults who care for them. These are complex problems that are compounded by the complicity, indifference, ignorance, or carelessness of many adults. Compassion and understanding is vital.

2. **Build a robust, multidisciplinary, solutions-oriented approach.** An irony of today's circumstances is that our expertise and knowledge about how to address and solve difficult problems has never been higher. We often try to use simple approaches for complex problems and complex solutions for simple problems. As a society, our discoveries and innovations in science never fail to amaze. Driverless cars and trips to Mars are well within our reach. All of this begs the question: Why can't we find ways to house, feed, care for, educate, and support all children? We have not yet developed a consistent, evidence-based mechanism to work across disciplines to support our most precarious populations. The complexity of today's problems demands that we look beyond our siloes and work collaboratively with experts across disciplines and professions to solve this most urgent of problems. The challenges that our children face have critical connections not only to education but also to public policy, law, medicine, social welfare, and mental health. However, academics and advocates often fall painfully short in creating the partnerships that allow sustainable, cross-discipline collaborations to address multifaceted problems. Take, for example, a child who struggles academically, suffers from food and housing insecurity, has undiagnosed mental health and learning problems, and also has a parent or caregiver facing severe financial challenges. Yet, rarely does the teacher of that vulnerable child talk to the mental health advocate. The child's therapist rarely engages the social worker, and the social worker seldom shares ideas and insights with a pediatrician. The pediatrician, in turn, does not know the student has an individualized education plan (IEP), which requires regular monitoring. Our inability or unwillingness to talk, think, plan, research, and problem solve across fields only compounds the disconnect. We must popularize transdisciplinary approaches to our efforts to support vulnerable populations.

3. **Develop the moral conviction to support our most vulnerable youth.** Finally, everyone can and must play a role in sustaining the moral conviction to respond to our most vulnerable student populations. Elected officials must work in sync with social service agencies to ensure bureaucracy and lack of information do not impede families' access to desperately needed assistance. Community-based organizations must work with educational institutions to offer needed supports. Faith-based organizations can connect to philanthropic organizations to seek additional funding to help struggling families.

SUPPORTING STUDENTS
IN FOSTER CARE

One of the most vulnerable and underserved groups of youth in today's schools is youth who are in foster care. Foster youth are children under the age of 18 who have been removed from their parents and placed in the care of eligible relatives, nonrelatives, or institutions such as residential care or group homes, also referred to as Short-Term Residential Therapeutic Programs (STRTPs), for reasons related to maltreatment such as abuse or neglect (Bîrneanu, 2014). There are currently approximately over 400,000 youth in foster care in the United States, according to data from the U.S. Department of Health and Human Services (2021), and approximately 20,000 youth age out of the system each year. The foster care system is primarily tasked with protecting children who are at risk of abuse, but it is also responsible for ensuring safe placement and seeking permanency such as adoption, as well as facilitating the reunification process when possible. It is worth mentioning that despite family reunification or permanency being the stated goal for all children entering the system, as many as 74% stay in out-of-home care for multiple years (Massinga & Pecora, 2004). Youth in foster care in the United States, all of whom are connected by the shared experience of being removed from their families of origin, face significant challenges in schools compared to their nonfoster peers—a difference that is important to note in any discussion of equitable schools (U.S. Department of Health & Human Services, 2020). From the outset, separation from family, which for many foster youth ends up being permanent, is an experience steeped in pain and ongoing emotional scars and prolonged trauma, and these experiences can have an enduring impact on brain development and subsequently academic experiences and outcomes (McCormack & Issaakidis, 2018).

Research overwhelmingly demonstrates that foster youth are more susceptible to experiencing a host of health, behavioral, and educational problems compared to youth not in care. Foster youth register some of the most alarming educational statistics. These include being most likely to change schools frequently due to change in placements, being in special education classes due to a higher incidence of learning problems, chronic absenteeism, attending low-performing schools, and graduating high school at only a 50% rate (Allen & Vacca, 2010; Emerson & Lovitt, 2003). Additionally, in a recent study of over 350 foster youth (ages 15 and older), health and child welfare records were screened for those presently contending with health and mental illness and general high-risk status, including but not limited to drug abuse and risky sexual behavior (Beal et al., 2018). Of all the screened cases, an astounding 41.6% had a mental health diagnosis such as depression and behavioral challenges, while 41.3% were identified as having chronic health issues including obesity and loss of vision and hearing. In addition to health issues, nearly 40% were identified as drug users and participants in risky sexual activity (Beal et al., 2018). Furthermore, data provided by the American Academy of Pediatrics (Szilagyi et al., 2015) suggest that young adults who spent their adolescent years in foster care are far more likely to face high unemployment rates, experience homelessness, and suffer from post-traumatic stress disorders (Morton, 2012). According to Huff (2015), youth in foster care consistently demonstrate lower academic achievement because of increased rates of school transfer and psychological issues stemming from abusive and neglectful circumstances. Supporting youth in foster care is an issue that is rarely discussed in the equity framework and is one of the reasons I lift up this population in this chapter. Schools across the country have youth in care, and many school personnel do not know their status. Even in those cases where foster youth have been identified, they may not be receiving adequate supports.

Supporting youth in foster care is an issue that is rarely discussed in the equity framework and is one of the reasons I lift up this population in this chapter. Schools across the country have youth in care, and many school personnel do not know their status. Even in those cases where foster youth have been identified, they may not be receiving adequate supports.

EXAMINING ADVERSITY IN CHILDHOOD

For many children in foster care, the stress response of the brain becomes overused and therefore overdeveloped at the expense of other functions. In other words, sustained trauma and the overused stress response can provoke the emotional and cognitive learning problems many foster children experience throughout their lives (A. R. Garcia et al., 2012). Schools must make a concerted effort of identifying students in their respective schools who are in foster care, because in many instances they will require additional support. Additionally, children placed in out-of-home care face the types of events that expose them to higher levels of social, emotional, and behavioral risk and can provoke violence, disengagement, depression, aggression, and mental illness in adulthood (Bîrneanu, 2014).

According to R. T. Muñoz et al. (2019), these types of childhood trauma are so widespread that it has risen to the level of being a public health crisis, not just for youth in foster care but for youth in general. Added to this is the high incidence of adverse childhood experiences (ACEs) identified among youth in care. ACEs are traumatic events that can occur both in care within the biological family and during foster placement (Bîrneanu, 2014) and can be experienced at both the family and community level. Among the types of ACEs that educators should be mindful of, which are unfortunately common in many children's lives, are the following:

- Physical, sexual, verbal, or emotional abuse
- Physical or emotional neglect
- Substance dependence
- Parental incarceration
- Parental mental health issues
- Domestic violence
- Parental divorce or separation

In the late 1990s, Dr. Vincent Felitti at Kaiser Permanente in San Diego, California, and Dr. Robert Anda with the Centers for Disease Control and Prevention (CDC) examined the impact of ACEs on adult physical and mental well-being and the implications they have on adulthood (Felitti et al., 1998). The first ACEs study was conducted from 1995 to 1997 with two waves of data collection. Over 17,000 health maintenance organization (HMO) members from Southern California receiving physical exams completed confidential surveys regarding their childhood experiences and current health status and behaviors. The researchers discovered that the chronic nature of ACEs has a significant influence on adults and compromises overall health, stability, and functionality of adults. While ACEs have become widely known, the concept has been critiqued for relying on data predominantly from white, middle- to upper-middle-class participants and focusing on experiences within the home. Subsequently, the Philadelphia ACE Project was conducted in 2012–2013 to examine people living in urban communities to assess additional factors that might bring particular stresses not covered in the original ACEs study. The community-level indicators that the Philadelphia ACEs study examined included witnessing violence, living in foster care, bullying, experiencing racism or discrimination, and feeling unsafe in your neighborhood.

Hence, addressing the issues of adversity for youth today has significant ramifications for the next generation of adults. It is vital to understand the complexities of ACEs when it comes to youth in general, and youth in foster care in particular, for several reasons: (1) Adverse experiences can be, and usually are, long lasting; (2) students' "misbehavior" tied to adverse experiences usually has deeper causes that educators need to understand; and (3) more recent work on urban ACEs revealed that historically marginalized groups (people of color, LGBTQ+ individuals, women) face additional adverse experiences than what were covered in the first ACEs study (Matthews, 2019).

Much of the research on foster youth treats the community as monolithic. However, a growing amount of research is exploring the differential experiences and outcomes for foster youth based on race, gender, sexuality, or ability status (Williams-Butler, 2018). For example, Brianna Harvey (2023) has raised important questions about the experiences of Black youth in foster care. Yet, from the scant literature that does exist, we come to understand that Black foster youth experience marginalization in the carceral family system as well as in education (Dettlaff et al., 2020; Harvey & Whitman, 2020; Harvey et al., 2021; Stephens, 2020). Harvey's research highlights that Black children have been disproportionately removed from the care of their families for generations and continue to be displaced in foster care (P. C. Davis, 1998; Dettlaff et al., 2020; Roberts, 2009, 2011, 2022). She highlights that Black youth are approximately 14% of the overall child population (Kids Count Data Center, 2020) but 26% of allegations of child maltreatment from school personnel concerned Black children (Child Welfare Information Gateway, 2021). The disproportionate reporting of Black children also cumulates across childhood; 53% of Black children will be subject to a Child Protective Services (CPS) investigation before turning 18, compared to 37.5% of all children (Kim et al., 2017). Emily Putnam-Hornstein and her colleagues (2021) found that in the state of California, which has the nation's largest child welfare system, half of Black children, as well as half of Native American children, experienced a CPS investigation at some point during the first 18 years of their lives, compared to nearly a quarter of white children. One in eight Black children spent time in foster care—a rate three times as high as white children. Three percent of Black children experienced termination of parental rights, compared with 1% of white children.

It is important to note that school personnel are a critical cog when it comes to children in foster care. Nationally, school personnel are the second-largest group of calls and reports to CPS agencies, only behind law enforcement (Harvey et al., 2021). It is without question that educators see and hear many things that raise questions and concerns about child safety. However, one of the key considerations for educators is to recognize that there can be lifetime consequences for young people when they are placed in care, or even when an allegation is made. Unfortunately, in many cases CPS agencies are not always protective of the young people they are tasked with caring for (Roberts, 2022). While educators are mandated reporters, it is important to think about a shift from "mandated *reporters*" to "mandated *supporters*" (see Table 3.1).

TABLE 3.1 ● Mandated Reporters Versus Mandated Supporters

MANDATED REPORTER	MANDATED SUPPORTER
If there is anything that appears wrong, call Child Protective Services.	If something appears wrong, talk to the student and to colleagues.
If a student appears to be food deprived, call Child Protective Services.	If a student appears to be food deprived, identify food banks that can support their family.
If a student appears to be unhoused, call Child Protective Services.	If a student appears to be unhoused, call the homeless liaison in the school or district to identify support for their family.
If a student talks about observing domestic abuse in the home, call Child Protective Services.	If a student talks about observing domestic abuse in the home, talk to the school social worker and talk to the student's parent/caregiver about supports for abuse survivors.
If a student seems to be living in deep poverty, call Child Protective Services.	If a student seems to be living in deep poverty, identify community resources that can assist families.

Mandated supporters recognize the importance of providing families and children essential assistance for basic needs. The overwhelming number of families that have children in foster care (80%) are there not for abuse but for neglect. The term *neglect* is quite amorphous and usually signifies families living in poverty or deep poverty. Families should not be torn apart due to poverty. Children should not be taken away from parents/caregivers and siblings because of financial instability, yet tens of thousands are every year. Doing the work of equity means that educators must prioritize an asset-based approach to providing supports to families and children first and foremost as opposed to reporting families to CPS. Calling CPS should not always be the first line of defense when there appears to be something wrong with a student. There needs to be a move away from constant surveillance of families, many of whom are not engaging in neglectful or abusive behavior, toward addressing the conditions of those who are living in poverty.

Mandated reporters operate from a standpoint that it is their obligation to report any suspected neglect or abuse—not to ask any questions or investigate, but to call it into CPS and assume that the system will always lead to an outcome in the best interests of the child. Mandated supporters, in comparison, function through a strength-based, equity lens on being familiar with resources from tangible items (food, cleaning supplies, counseling, clothing, and furniture), to housing and jobs, to community- and school-based family supports, to interventions with an obligation to shore up families as opposed to reporting families to CPS. The transformation from mandated reporters to mandated supporters depends upon a robust transformation in training and ongoing coaching of educators, law enforcement personnel, medical and mental health service providers, child care providers, coaches, and other current mandated reporters. This is well aligned with the nation's 2-1-1 system and the national platform 1degree.org. It is important to note that 1degree.org is a national platform that provides individuals in need with access to social services, including housing, food, health care, education, legal help, employment, and financial support. The platform only requires the entering of a zip code to generate a list of various services and resources in the surrounding area.

In many states, dialing 2-1-1 provides individuals and families in need with a shortcut through what can be a bewildering maze of health and human service agency phone numbers. By simply dialing 2-1-1, those in need of assistance can be referred, and sometimes connected, to appropriate agencies and community organizations. According to 211.org, dialing 2-1-1 helps direct callers to services for, among others, older individuals, individuals with disabilities, those who do not speak English, those with a personal crisis, those with limited reading skills, and those who are new to their communities. The website also reports that 2-1-1 is available to approximately 309 million people, which is 94.6% of the total U.S. population. The 2-1-1 resource covers all 50 states, the District of Columbia, and Puerto Rico. To find out whether 2-1-1 services are offered in your area and to obtain more information, visit 211.org.

Sources such as 2-1-1 are critical because they are crucial to creating equitably and racially inclusive schools. Many Black families are often surveilled in ways that non-Black families are not. An equity-based focus would ask school personnel to make greater efforts to connect families to sources of support, assistance, and resources to provide for children. Such connections must be prioritized and not the criminalizing, excessive supervision, and scrutiny that has become commonplace for many families of color, including Black families. Acknowledging and repairing harm as a pillar of equity is paramount here.

A growing body of research has shown that social determinants of health, particularly those that lead to toxic stress, can stunt a young child's brain development, psychosocial development, and learning potential and thereby impact their lifelong health. We must work toward widespread awareness that the social determinants of health are integral to holistic development, and have culturally responsive services, interventions, and supports for children and families in need. The UCLA Center for the Transformation of Schools in a recently released report titled *Beyond the Schoolhouse* (Noguera et al., 2019) revealed that there are significant implications for environmental, economic, and social factors that severely and disproportionately impact Black families in Los Angeles County. We must first be deliberate in acknowledging such harm while continuing to further our awareness of the physical, social, emotional, and psychological state of Black and other families of color who have been profoundly impacted by structural racism, apparent in economic, housing, health, and social patterns, especially in our education systems. Engagement around the social determinants of health is an essential variable in supporting students and families. This type of comprehensive approach also lays the foundation for shared responsibility across departments and communities when families do engage with service systems.

HOW CAN SCHOOLS RESPOND?

Schools can offer an intensive set of mandated professional learning opportunities that would go beyond onetime training sessions and move toward sustained annual training, continuous coaching, accessing culturally responsive local resources, and engaging in confidential consultation. Moreover, working with colleges and universities that provide education and support of educators is essential to help school personnel recognize how to best support students and families without engaging CPS first and foremost. This is an important transformation that can reframe the way that we think about supporting children and families. It necessitates unlearning "when in doubt, report" as a default response and taking back a "protect yourself" culture of fear. The counternarrative is sensitizing individuals to recognize the important role they play in child safety and welfare.

Here are some steps that can be taken to support foster youth:

- Understand that the emotional challenges that come from being removed from home and separated from parents and siblings can be quite traumatic and affect students' behavior in a multitude of ways.

- Recognize that not all youth in foster care are with total strangers. Often relatives serve as caregivers. Get to know the home situation as best as you can.

- Not all youth in care are comfortable talking about their situation, so assess on a case-by-case basis. Bringing up the current situation for some students can be quite upsetting.

- Many foster youth have spent time in an ordinate number of schools, so academic shortcomings can be a result of missed school time or frequent moving from school to school.

- Understand that for many foster youth, school is their refuge and source of stability and familiarity. Do not be surprised if youth in care do quite well in school. Many of these young people possess uncanny resilience and intellect that is not always recognized.

- Provide as much predictability, familiarity, and consistency as possible. For many youth in care, their lives out of schools are full of uncertainty, so school can be a stabilizing and affirming place.

- If possible, try to engage a young person's social worker about the best ways that you can support the student. Do not ask why the student is in care but seek ways to better assist the student academically and emotionally.

SUPPORTING YOUTH EXPERIENCING HOMELESSNESS

In addition to foster youth, another vulnerable student population that warrants additional time, support, and resources is youth who are experiencing homelessness. According to the National Center for Homeless Education, there were approximately 1.3 million youth experiencing homelessness in the United States in the 2018–2019 academic year. The actual number is difficult to estimate, and some put the numbers considerably higher when we consider youth who are living doubled up, in shelters, and in cars (E. Edwards, 2019). Youth who are experiencing homelessness require additional supports and interventions, but we must be careful to not label them as "less than." Educators need to recheck biases and preconceived notions about what they think about students experiencing homelessness. They are among the most resourceful and resilient students served in schools. In short, many of us would struggle to survive in the reality they inhabit. Such realities need to be a part of every equity discussion that is had at schools across the nation. What needs to inform these discussions is an under-standing of the challenges and complexities of life for those experiencing homelessness. Most of the students experiencing homelessness and their parents and caregivers are not panhandlers. They are not drug users. Many of the adults are the working poor, who are striving daily to provide for themselves and their children (Aviles de Bradley, 2015).

All educators should be aware of the McKinney-Vento Homeless Assistance Act—the primary piece of federal legislation related to the education of youth experiencing homelessness. Among other things, this policy provides a common definition of homelessness and includes students finding temporary housing by doubling up with another family (E. Edwards, 2019). The policy also provides students and families experiencing homelessness with explicit rights to ensure the same access to education as their stably housed peers. Finally, the McKinney-Vento Act ensures educational rights and protections for unhoused children and youth. It is critical that all educators know the requirements of the McKinney-Vento Act legislation:

- Unhoused students who move have the right to remain in their schools of origin (i.e., the school the student attended when permanently housed or in which the student was last enrolled, which includes preschools) if that is in the student's best interest.

- If it is in the student's best interest to change schools, unhoused students must be immediately enrolled in a new school, even if they do not have the records normally required for enrollment.

- Transportation must be provided to or from a student's school of origin, at the request of a parent, a guardian, or, in the case of an unaccompanied youth, the local liaison.

- Unhoused students must have access to all programs and services for which they are eligible, including special education services, preschool, school nutrition programs, language assistance for English learners, career services, and technical education, gifted and talented programs, magnet schools, charter schools, summer learning, online learning, and before- and after-school care.

- Unaccompanied youths must be accorded specific protections, including immediate enrollment in school without proof of guardianship.

- Parents, caregivers, guardians, and unaccompanied youths have the right to dispute an eligibility, school selection, or enrollment decision.

The focus on unhoused students and families is a key equity area of focus, given the large numbers of families that are in this category. According to the National Center on Family Homelessness, here are some troubling statistics:

- Families experiencing homelessness comprise approximately 34% of the total U.S. unhoused population.
- 1 of every 4 unhoused women is homeless because of violence committed against her.
- 63% report that this abuse was perpetrated by an intimate partner.
- By age 12, 83% of homeless children have been exposed to at least one serious violent event.
- Almost 25% have witnessed acts of violence within their families.
- 15% have seen their father hit their mother.
- 11% have seen their mother abused by a male partner.
- Children who have witnessed violence are more likely than those who have not to exhibit frequent aggressive and antisocial behavior, increased fearfulness, and higher levels of depression and anxiety, and they have a greater acceptance of violence as a means of resolving conflict.
- People counted in the single adult homeless population (about 2.3–3.5 million annually) are also part of families:
  - Among all homeless women, 60% have children under age 18, but only 65% of them live with at least one of their children.
  - Among all homeless men, 41% have children under age 18, but only 7% live with at least one of their children.
- Inadequate housing and shelter options, evictions, discrimination, poverty, and other factors contribute to the crisis of homelessness caused by family violence. Furthermore, many women remain in an abusive relationship because of these barriers.
- Approximately 1.6 million children will experience homelessness over the course of a year. In any given day, researchers estimate that more than 200,000 children have no place to live.
- Furthermore, many women remain in an abusive relationship because of these barriers.
- Most single-parent families are female-headed (71%). Single-parent families are among the poorest in the nation and, as such, are extremely vulnerable to homelessness.

- Many family shelters do not accept men into their programs, causing families to separate when they become homeless.

- Over 92% of unhoused mothers have experienced severe physical and/or sexual abuse during their lifetime.

- Families experiencing homelessness usually have limited education:

  - 53% of homeless mothers do not have a high school diploma.

- 29% of adults in homeless families are working.

- 42% of children in homeless families are under the age of 6.

These sobering statistics should drive home that an equity framework must be inclusive and cognizant of the unique needs of students who are unhoused. At the same time, our focus on these children cannot be centered on pity and low expectations, but rather should emphasize the supports and services that can assist students as they deal with the complexities and challenges of experiencing homelessness. Education researcher Earl Edwards (2019) has done extensive research on youth experiencing homelessness and contends that there are at least six approaches or principles that educators can take to best support them:

- **Attend to students' basic needs.** Providing a resource room for clothing and hygiene products, as well as healthy food and snack options in classrooms, can be helpful.

- **Create a supportive environment.** Modeling honesty and vulnerability can help to foster relationships.

- **Provide effective instruction.** Refuse to lower expectations because of students' housing status. De-emphasize the importance of attendance in grading policies.

- **Use a multilevel approach to provide resources to students experiencing homelessness.** Consider creating a McKinney-Vento team that works collaboratively to support students and families.

- **Raise awareness of the McKinney-Vento Homeless Assistance Act.** Consider all-staff professional development to increase awareness of school personnel.

- **Use data to identify and respond to subpopulations of students experiencing homelessness.** Disaggregate data for students experiencing homelessness by race, gender, and zip code, and monitor trends over time.

An equity framework must be inclusive and cognizant of the unique needs of students who are unhoused. At the same time, our focus on these children cannot be centered on pity and low expectations, but rather should emphasize the supports and services that can assist students as they deal with the complexities and challenges of experiencing homelessness.

MENTAL HEALTH MATTERS

One of the biggest challenges that all educators face in this new moment is the salience of mental health. As I discussed in Chapter 2, there are a number of various mental health challenges that students faced before the pandemic, and those numbers have increased exponentially since the pandemic. The challenge before most of us is that there has been a reluctance on most of our parts to discuss mental health. The reason for our reluctance, and in many cases fear, is rooted in the unknown. As I have worked with many school districts across the country, I regularly ask teachers, leaders, and board members whether they feel comfortable discussing mental health. The overwhelming response is usually *no*. When I ask why they are uncomfortable discussing the topic, these are among the reasons I get:

- I'm afraid of being judged.
- I don't know what to say.
- It's a scary topic.
- I was never taught how to discuss mental health.
- I don't want to be labeled or to label someone else as crazy.
- I am not a therapist or psychologist.

The bottom line is that all educators need to develop skills, knowledge, and strategies to discuss mental health, because it is a necessity in today's schools. The bottom line is that mental health is an integral part of children's overall health and well-being. Mental health includes children's mental, psychological, emotional, and behavioral well-being. It affects how students think, feel, communicate, and act. It also plays a role in how young people handle stress, problem solving, and conflict; relate to others; and make prosocial choices. According to mental health experts, attention deficit hyperactivity disorder (ADHD), anxiety, behavior problems, and depression are the most diagnosed mental disorders in school-age youth. Estimates for the number of diagnoses among children aged 3–17 years, in 2016–2019, are provided by Rebecca H. Bitsko and colleagues (2022):

- ADHD: 9.8% (approximately 6.0 million)
- Anxiety: 9.4% (approximately 5.8 million)
- Behavior problems: 8.9% (approximately 5.5 million)
- Depression: 4.4% (approximately 2.7 million)

Hence, the reality is that there are literally millions of students in schools across the nation struggling with mental health challenges. Moreover, since these are only the cases that have been identified and diagnosed, one can only wonder about the millions of undiagnosed cases. Equity centers itself on justice and doing what is right for students. In this moment, the right and just thing to do with students is to destigmatize mental health. We must make it acceptable for our students to talk about how they are feeling, because it has a direct correlation to how they show up in schools. Many of us have been taught implicitly and explicitly not to talk about our emotions or feelings. We can no longer use such an approach in schools. The right thing to do now is to develop our own literacy about mental health. Failure to do so may very well make us complicit in harming students who are truly struggling with depression or anxiety. In this moment, silence is not the answer. All school personnel must become comfortable being uncomfortable to talk to students about how they are feeling. This fundamental question is more important than any academic task that we can ask students to perform. One of my favorite mantras is *Maslow before Bloom*. Abraham Maslow's (1943) hierarchy of needs is a psychological theory of motivation stating that five essential categories of human needs dictate an individual's behavior. Those needs are (1) physiological needs, (2) safety needs, (3) love and belonging needs, (4) self-esteem needs, and (5) self-actualization needs. Bloom's taxonomy refers to a classification system used to define and distinguish different levels of human cognition— that is, thinking, learning, and understanding, *namely knowledge, comprehension, application, analysis, synthesis,* and *evaluation*. In the context of mental health, we cannot expect our students to achieve at high levels if they are suffering from anxiety. We cannot expect students to do well on standardized tests if they are suffering from depression. If a student has undiagnosed ADHD, it is unrealistic to think that the student will be able to function with peers and engage in school-related activities.

Remember: Maslow before Bloom.

Failure to act and intervene when students appear to be struggling with mental health can have more serious consequences, where students engage in self-harming and even suicidal behavior. These matters should be taken seriously by all school personnel, because some of the data on youth suicidality are alarming. According to the CDC, in 2020, suicide was among the top nine leading causes of death for people ages 10–64. Suicide was the second-leading cause of death for people ages 10–14 and 25–34 (Czeisler et al., 2020). The teen suicide rate is highest among the following groups (Ivey-Stephenson et al., 2020):

- Males compared with females. Females attempt suicide more often than males; however, males are more likely to complete suicide.

- American Indian/Alaska Native adolescents compared with other racial and ethnic groups, by an extreme margin. White adolescents have a higher suicide rate compared with Asian/Pacific Islander, Hispanic, and Black adolescents, though the number of Black and Latinx youth who have died by suicide has increased dramatically over the last 10 years.

- Suicide attempts are higher among students who identify as gay, lesbian, transgender, or bisexual compared with students who identify as heterosexual.

Youth suicide according to many mental health experts is preventable in most cases. Experts say that adults who are in close and consistent contact with youth who are struggling mentally should be mindful of various signs. Though many educators may believe that they are not equipped to handle youth dealing with serious mental health challenges, the reality is that they often see students who are going through difficult times, and they have the capacity to act. Steps that educators can take include all of the following:

- Pay attention to drastic mood swings.

- Pay attention to students' comments in writings and drawings that may be disturbing.

- Pay attention to students' peer group and social interactions.

- Discuss social media with students, as this is a major culprit in students' well-being.

- Tell students, and demonstrate, that you care deeply about them and you are concerned and worry about their well-being. But don't stop there: Tell them how much you love them (if this is, indeed, authentic). Many students may believe no one cares about them.

- Increase the emotional access for students (especially for boys and young men).

- Be reasonable and teen-focused in your expectations for students' academic performance.
- If you see something that does not seem right, say something to an expert.

When working from an equity standpoint, one of the goals is to do our best to meet students where they are, and when it comes to mental health, some of our students are in dark and dangerous places. It is not your role to go to that dark and dangerous place with students; rather, contact an expert who can provide the necessary support that a student may need. It is also important for educators to be mindful of the various risk factors that are connected to youth and suicide:

- Psychiatric disorders such as major depressive, bipolar, substance use, and conduct disorders
- Psychiatric comorbidity, especially the combination of mood, disruptive, and substance abuse disorders
- Family history of depression or suicide
- Loss of a parent to death or divorce
- Physical and sexual abuse
- Lack of a support network
- Feelings of social isolation
- Bullying

To best support students,

- Check in with them often.
- Expect different types of behavior.
- Listen and learn from them without judgment!
- Reestablish routines and familiarity.
- Be aware of family stressors.
- Create community-based partnerships with expertise on mental health.

Mental health is one of our biggest challenges in the current education moment. The seriousness of mental health challenges and its connection to learning cannot be stressed enough. The impact of the pandemic, and the shutting down of schools, created deeper challenges for many students. It should be noted that many mental health experts stated that investigators found young people are significantly more likely to develop depression in the future due to the social isolation, the impact of loneliness, and the disconnection from teachers and peers that can last for up to 5–10 years after traumatic episodes such as the school closures (Kirzinger et al., 2020). It has become clear that social isolation and loneliness increased depression and anxiety for millions of students. The duration of loneliness was more strongly correlated with mental health symptoms than the intensity of loneliness. What is abundantly clear is the need to provide clinical services that offer preventative support and early intervention where possible and to be prepared for an increase in mental health problems.

Equity Now Chart

JUSTICE	REPAIR	BELONGING
• Doing right by all students, but placing an intentional and sustained focus on *our most vulnerable students*	• Working systematically with outside agencies to address barriers that contribute to deep-seated poverty for children and families	• Creating policies and practices that are asset based and are focused on inclusion for students living in poverty
• Moving to a mandated supporter approach to support students in foster care or those who might have challenges • Recognizing the harm and injury done to families by way of Child Protective Services	• Providing teachers with names of community-based organizations and nonprofit entities within zip codes of the school to refer supports for families and children in need of basic services	• Destigmatizing youth in foster care • Creating curriculum that talks about diversity of family arrangements (foster families are important) • Remembering *Maslow before Bloom* and creating welcoming and inviting learning spaces
• Providing wraparound services in schools to support students who are unhoused or experiencing food insecurities	• Providing before- and after-school programs complete with food and academic support for families who need extended care	• Using careful language in curriculum that does not always talk about "home" and instead focuses on time with families or time away from school

Questions to Consider

1. How would I describe the culture of my school or district?

2. How does my school or district address (or not) matters tied to hate speech?

3. What professional learning does my district offer for vulnerable youth?

4. Are there supports in my school for youth who are in foster care?

5. Does my school or district have a homeless liaison? Do I know what resources are available at my school?

6. What supports does my school have in place for students who may be suffering from anxiety or stress?

7. Do I know the signs or symptoms of students who may be experiencing mild, moderate, or severe mental health challenges?

Recommendations for Reading and Resources

1. Roberts, D. E. (2022). *Torn apart: How the child welfare system destroys Black families—and how abolition can build a safer world.* Basic Books.

2. Aviles de Bradley, A. M. (2015). *From charity to equity: Race, homelessness and urban schools.* Teachers College Press.

3. McGhee, H. (2021). *The sum of us: What racism costs everyone and how we can prosper together.* One World.

4. Elliott, A. (2022). *Invisible child: Poverty, survival, and hope in an American city.* Random House.

5. Craig, S. (2018). *Trauma-sensitive schools for the adolescent years: Promoting resiliency and healing, grades 6–12.* Teachers College Press.

6. Bubrick, K., Goodman, J., & Whitlock, J. (2015). *Non-suicidal self-injury in schools: Developing and implementing school protocol.* Cornell Research Program on Self-Injury and Recovery. https://www.selfinjury.bctr.cornell.edu/perch/resources/non-suicidal-self-injury-in-schools-1.pdf

7. National Child Traumatic Stress Network. (2018). *Impact of complex trauma.* https://www.nctsn.org/sites/default/files/resources//impact_of_complex_trauma.pdf

CHAPTER 4

Leadership and Equity

The Foundation of Equity-Centered Schools

The role of leadership is vital in creating equitable schools. There has been an extensive body of literature that documents the importance of school leadership (S. M. Johnson, 2019; Khalifa, 2018). It is difficult to create equitable schools without strong, culturally responsive, and equity-focused leadership. In this chapter, I will discuss the important role that leadership plays in creating equity-centered schools. Schools that are committed to attaining justice for students need to have bold and unapologetic leadership centered on helping all students feel that they belong to the school community. In many ways, it is almost impossible to create the types of schools that serve all students without consistent, empathic leadership. In this chapter, I will discuss leadership broadly. While many iterations of leadership are centered on superintendents, principals, and other administrative positions, leadership can and should manifest across multiple positions. In this chapter, leadership will include teacher leaders, school staff leaders, and other individuals in the education ecosystem who play a role in building a culture that helps students thrive, helps teachers excel, and helps parents and caregivers feel like authentic partners. To help ground the focus on why leadership matters, consider that a national study (S. M. Johnson et al., 2012) that surveyed over 15,000 teachers who responded to questions about their schools' work environment found that the three most important factors involved in their satisfaction and efficacy were (1) having effective leadership by the principal, (2) having capable and collaborative colleagues, and (3) working in a school culture that is purposeful, orderly, and supportive. Research has consistently and repeatedly shown that effective school leadership is the most important factor in school quality and overall environment. Moreover, leaders who are responsive and inclusive create the most optimal conditions for teachers to thrive (S. M. Johnson, 2019).

Leaders are critical in establishing how educational policies and practices are enacted, how students are prioritized, how school personnel engage with families, and how staff feel supported to reach the educational objectives of the school or district. But to be clear, the work of leaders is not easy, and not for the faint of heart. Leaders make countless decisions throughout the course of a given day to ensure that the schools operate smoothly. While some of these decisions can be made quickly, leaders must engage in deep-seated reflection about the role that they play in creating equitable schools. In his work on culturally responsive leadership, Muhammad Khalifa (2018) states that leadership must be built on the connection between culture, community, and leading and that culturally responsive school leadership (CRSL) "engages students, parents, teachers, and neighborhood communities in ways that positively impact organizational and leadership practice, teacher practice, and student learning" (p. 13). He anchors his framework of CRSL on four core principles:

- Critically Self-Reflects on Leadership Behaviors
- Develops Culturally Responsive Teachers
- Promotes Culturally Responsive/Inclusive Environment
- Engages Students, Parents, and Indigenous Contexts

The work of leaders is demanding and never ending in the traditional sense, but for leaders who are committed to equity and excellence, the work can be even more challenging. The primary reason for these challenges is that leaders are contending with students and families who are facing deep-seated structural challenges, namely generational poverty and all its associated challenges, racial inequity and all its corollaries, and the quest of helping students play a seemingly never-ending game of academic catch-up. A second challenge that equity-focused leaders contend with is the resistance and apathy that comes from adults on their staffs. Though many would never want to admit this publicly, most administrators will tell you that their biggest challenges in schools are not always the students; sometimes it is the adults. Not all the adults on staff are resistant, but those who are I will refer to as the vocal minority. Getting staff to buy into the idea that schools can be better, and students can have better outcomes, is one of the biggest obstacles for leaders. Frankly, many teachers resort to blame tactics by saying that parents/caregivers are not doing their jobs or do not care, which makes leaders' jobs even more challenging. The problem with such judgments is that many teachers fail to self-reflect before pointing the finger elsewhere. The job of equity-focused leaders can become quite daunting when adults who have chosen to be educators in particular schools or districts become hypercritical about others but lack honest self-reflection. Leaders must find ways to hear out the concerns of resistant staff and colleagues but then get them to remember their *why*, focus on what they can control, and buy into the idea that educators can and do make a difference every day.

I recall working with a principal in Massachusetts. He informed me that he longed to be a principal and worked his way up to ultimately being asked to take over a school that had some of the lowest scores not only in the district but across the entire state. He lamented that this is often the case for aspiring principals of color, getting really challenging schools as their first principalship. Mr. Jones, the principal, described his school as predominantly Latinx and Black, high poverty, and "even higher teacher apathy." He talked about how as a product of the community where his school was located, he felt great pride and deep worry about how to best support his students, who he felt were being failed by the school. Yet, he said the single biggest obstacle he faced in his first year was the fact that "so many teachers had checked out." Mr. Jones described a lengthy process of having "come-to-Jesus meetings" with some of his staff where he asked them about their *why*, their purpose, and what they were willing to do in order to help make the school better. Mr. Jones said that it took him approximately four years to get the right people in place to build the type of culture that was needed for his school to succeed. He said it meant having hard conversations with certain teachers that his school may not be the best fit for them, developing other teachers with additional instructional support, developing and upholding policies and procedures around how the school would operate, and then finally building a "students-first culture" that he said was sorely lacking. Now in his 10th year as a principal, Mr. Jones shared that his school has among the highest scores in the state and the district, adding that his team deserves the lion's share of the credit because they are deeply committed to their students, they support each other, and they "see the big picture" in ways that his first staff did not. He said that he had to essentially replace close to half his staff who "would not buy into what I thought the school could become." I share my story of Mr. Jones because it is important to highlight the importance of getting the right adults in the building, and this is arguably the most challenging task that school leaders face.

The work of equity-focused leaders can also be limited by lack of resources when it comes to some of the neediest students. Many leaders struggle with having to make tough decisions that more affluent schools rarely have to contemplate, such as whether to hire an additional math teacher or put the money in an after-school program. Some leaders struggle when what should be necessities at every school become either–or propositions for them. Do I pay for an extra counselor, or do I allocate money for my students' senior activities and/or field trips for the end of the year? The work of equity-focused leaders is also predicated on knowing that many of the decisions that will be made will not make everyone happy. Every decision that a leader makes will have its fair share of supporters and distractors. Among the questions that leaders must contemplate are the following:

- Have I been as transparent as I can be with my decision-making process? (Sometimes confidentiality issues put limits on what can and cannot be shared.)

- Have I tried to hear multiple viewpoints on this issue?

- What data inform my decision making?

- Is my decision being made based on what's in the best interests of students?

- Have I effectively conveyed my decision-making process to stakeholders?

- Who will be directly (and indirectly) affected by my decision?

- Have parents/caregivers been informed about the rationale behind my decision making?

- Am I prepared for the fallout (dislike/anger) that will come from my decision making?

- Does my decision making create greater belonging?

- Is this the just and right thing to do?

- Does my decision making seek to repair past harm and injuries?

Being mindful of how teachers are understanding the leaders' goals, aims, and direction as they pertain to equity is essential in schools reaching them. In essence, clarity is key in school transformation (Fullan & Quinn, 2016).

The work of leaders is a never-ending set of decisions, actions, challenges, conversations, and moves to build a healthy environment for students to learn and for adults to work in. In today's schools, building leaders typically have strengths in one of five categories: (1) the instructional leader, (2) the building manager, (3) the visionary or inspirer of people, (4) the data miner, and (5) the fiscal expert. To be clear, exemplary leaders excel in all these areas, and it would be great for more leaders to have all these broad strengths—and many leaders do—but many leaders would say they are really great at one, or maybe two or three, but mastering all five is a challenging feat that is often aspirational. To further clarify, however, each of these categories and leader types can have a commitment to equity with a focus on justice, repair, and belonging. It is important to note their strengths in different areas.

The **instructional leader** is someone with an equity lens who was really strong as a teacher in the areas of planning, instruction, and implementing lessons. This leader has a strong knack for connecting content to standards and has a clear instructional focus. This leader typically can walk into a classroom and look for the goal of a particular lesson, evaluate instructional clarity, and assess to what degree (if any) students are engaged and making meaning of information. The instructional leader is not necessarily an expert in every content area but knows the power and importance of good instruction and is able to support teachers thinking about the usefulness of dynamic ways of getting students involved, such as creating student-centered discussions by way of think-pair-share, student-workgroups, or turn-and-talk strategies. The instructional leader is usually willing to learn beside the teachers (e.g., being an active participant in professional learning workshops). The instructional leader sees equity as justice being rooted in every student having a teacher in front of them who is sound instructionally—anything less is an injustice. For many instructional leaders, their focus is often about modeling but also about having a clear understanding of the kind of learning in which teachers are engaged, including its intended outcomes, measures of teacher growth, and student outcomes. The way that we become equity focused is to ensure that, every day, every student has access to high-quality, engaging instruction to help stimulate ideas, imagination, and possibilities to learn. The instructional leader often will be present in classrooms regularly, observing lessons, offering teachers formative feedback, identifying resources for teachers, and being incessantly committed to improving teacher pedagogy.

The **building manager** is one who has an equity focus and is highly efficient in overseeing and managing systems, structures, and policies to help the building operate smoothly and effectively. In many ways, schools are mini communities tasked with dealing with hundreds—and, in the case of secondary schools, thousands—of young people every day. There are countless tasks to perform daily for schools to be successful, including but not limited to the morning drop-off and managing buses; greeting and speaking to parents/caregivers dropping off students, including those who are walking; and making sure the system of just getting students into the building safely goes well. Then there is the matter of seeing that all staff have arrived and are working for the day. The building manager has a plan for classes that need substitute teachers and classes that need to be combined if there are no substitute teachers available. The building manager also must make sure that all students are in class, or otherwise where they are supposed to be, while talking to parents/caregivers and with staff to gauge any issues for the day. With such a myriad of details to stay on top of, it should come as no surprise that the building manager often can be exhausted before 9 a.m. The equity focus for the building manager is on creating systems in schools to support students who often do not have appropriate systems of support outside of school. Are students getting breakfast? Do students have everything needed to have an optimal day? How are school staff feeling this morning? There can also be focus on who is not in school and making phone calls and visits to homes of chronically absent students, thinking about why certain students are persistently absent, and thinking about stories shared by students and parents/caregivers during the drop-off in the morning. The building manager also ensures that passing periods are safe and lunch goes smoothly, engages parents/caregivers who show up unannounced, ensures that bathrooms are clean and operable, and deals with all the technical aspects of keeping the organization flowing. The building manager is great at problem solving; fixing structural challenges; dealing with last-minute emergencies, such as nonworking bathrooms, any safety hazards, or student safety issues; and often delegating with an effective support team. Building managers pride themselves on the idea that the organization called school is safe, functioning, and a viable place for learning and working.

The **visionary/inspirer** (VI) is often a person who has a strong conviction, commitment to equity, and sense of purpose about the work of education and educators. The VI often has a story rooted in their own personal challenges and life stories that typically culminates with how education literally transformed their life. Thus, they see the work of leading schools as transformational and are at odds with those who do not see the life-and-death implications of not getting education right. The VI often has excellent people skills, has the knack or ability to connect with all personality types, and is usually well liked by most of the teachers, staff, and parents/caregivers. The VI challenges educators to see the best in students and families and can often be demanding in insisting that everyone give their all to make the school the best it can be. The VI frequently has powerful anecdotes or stories that can truly inspire those that they work with daily. The VI also frequently asks educators to remember their *why* and does all that can be done to help make excellence possible. The VI often has a good working relationship with parents/caregivers, staff, and the larger community. This person is often quite charismatic and knows how to get people to buy into the vision of how the school can be better and the role that educators can play in creating equitable schools. In some instances, the VI has grown up in the community (or one similar) where they lead and can relate firsthand to some of the challenges and strengths of the community. The VI is often seen as the face of the school, sets the tone of the building, and is quite present talking to students daily, knows them personally, remembers names, asks questions about what they are learning, and is often a known entity in the community as well.

The **data minder** (DM) is an individual whose equity focus is closely tied to using data to inform decision making. For this individual, justice is centered on making data-driven decisions daily. One of the better approaches to programs, curriculum, teaching assignments, and particular interventions is steeped on what the evidence says is best for students. The DM rarely operates on hunches, gut feelings, assumptions, or hearsay. The DM builds on various forms of data, be it conversations with stakeholders, stories from students, test score data, observational data, district data, or trends over time. The DM is also focused on subgroups who consistently are behind, and will often analyze data on students with disabilities, students in special education, English learners, and Black students—groups that are often not served well in schools. I recall working with a superintendent in Illinois in 2022, and he explained to me that when he initially assumed his position he would get monthly data reports on schools within the district. He lamented that the data reports provided little specificity or disaggregated data. He informed me that his teachers did not know which problems, concepts, or skills students struggled to comprehend; had no idea which students were showing high levels of proficiency; and weren't sure which subgroups needed more immediate intervention. The superintendent then shared with me how he required the district to provide data to all schools that would be disaggregated by grade, subject areas, skill and concept, and subgroups, and required data managers to provide ongoing professional learning to all sites to help them understand the data.

Such steps can go a long way to help teachers not only understand data but then make instructional adjustments that are informed by such data.

In many ways, the DM tries to remove emotion or feeling out of most of the decision-making processing. To that end, they inform their staff or team about how they try their best to engage in "objective" decision making that is fueled by data. To be fair, many DMs understand that there are a host of variables that can influence what data look like. But by and large, the DM is consistent with showing the staff what data say about practically everything about the school. Those leaders who are DMs want to empower their teachers and staff and will take various steps to help individuals understand, interpret, and analyze data so that their classroom practice can improve. For example, if there is a teacher whose data show that their students have high proficiency in fractions but there are a handful of students in another class who struggle with fractions, there is an effort to match the high-performing teacher to the struggling students. If the data suggest that students are not performing with a particular teacher, then there might be a discussion about moving a teacher to a new grade level but one that is a better match with the strengths of that teacher. In the current information age that we live in, the DM believes that the job of leaders is to let data lead the way.

The **fiscal expert** is a leader who determines their effectiveness based on how well they can financially manage a school or organization. This is more frequently the case in schools where leaders may have greater autonomy such as pilot, private, or certain charter schools. Yet, this leader sees organizational efficiency being closely linked to fiscal well-being and germane to equity. Thus, the leader is clear from the outset about the annual budget. The leader may establish an emergency fund for unforeseen expenses and, when needed, may constantly advocate for additional resources from district leadership. The fiscal manager often works closely with the parent–teacher organization or other entities that focus on fundraising. This leader recognizes that resources matter for teachers to be at their best and for students to learn. Hence, the fiscal expert may also seek grants, scholarships, or other funding opportunities that exist beyond the district's parameters. The fiscal expert is also quick to tell staff that they may not be able to do certain things like field trips or extracurricular programs or acquire what might be essential resources because they do not have the funding. In many ways, the fiscal expert may challenge their staff to do more with less, while arguing that it is not always things, programs, or materials that are most vital to student success— highly committed people make the difference in classrooms.

In a lot of instances, they see recognizing and repairing harm for students who have historically been neglected as ensuring that they have the best resources, materials, curriculum, equipment, and amenities possible. Or in many cases, when requests are made to this particular leader, they want to know how a given purchase directly connects to benefitting students. The equity lens for fiscal experts is that resource efficiency ensures that core needs are met for students and that each dollar is spent wisely with students as the priority and with a particular focus on those in greatest need. If there is not a clear rationale for how a given purchase improves students' experiences or learning, this leader may see it as a nonessential purchase.

While these are prototypes, by no means are they meant to be exhaustive. These classifications are derived from my work in hundreds of schools over the past two decades and having interacted with hundreds of principals. Many school leaders embody some or all of these aforementioned characteristics. However, most leaders are strong in one or two of these areas and may need to improve in another area. The goal of laying out these characteristics is to spotlight the complexity and difficulty of being a school leader. The various tasks, duties, and responsibilities are enormous. What I have learned in my work with hundreds of principals over the last two decades is that when it comes to leadership, nothing is easy, and there are no magic bullets or special formulas or "how to" manuals about the accomplishments of high-performing schools. Hands down, it is one of the most difficult jobs on the planet. Find a school that is high achieving and showing steady growth and improvement for even our most vulnerable students, and there is a high likelihood that you will find a strong, dedicated leader surrounded by an incredibly hardworking and talented staff. Their accomplishments represent hard work by smart, dedicated, compassionate, and persistent people. Hard work and dedication are essential, yet insufficient.

> *What I have learned in my work with hundreds of principals over the last two decades is that when it comes to leadership, nothing is easy, and there are no magic bullets or special formulas or "how to" manuals about the accomplishments of high-performing schools. Hands down, it is one of the most difficult jobs on the planet.*

CULTURALLY RESPONSIVE SCHOOL LEADERSHIP

As mentioned at the beginning of this chapter, the culturally responsive school leadership framework seeks to recognize the salience of past harm to particular groups. When considering the persistence of racism, sexism, classism, and ableism, leaders must realize that history, culture, and context matter. Recognizing past harms has been a key pillar of the equity framework that I have used for this book. Khalifa (2018) states that for culturally responsive school leaders

> it is absolutely necessary to understand contexts and histories of the students and their communities. Oppressive structures and practices will remain in place unless (a) the status quo is challenged and (b) educators and leaders know how to properly push against oppression. (p. 7)

Leading against the status quo is an essential feature of equity-focused leaders. Leading against the status quo means having a mindset and commitment to leadership and practice that see all students as scholars, thinkers, and doers with unlimited potential and promise. It is also an asset-based approach that rests on identifying the strengths in every student, family, and community. It is a matter not of whether those strengths exist but of identifying what and where they are and building learning opportunities in line with them. That mindset recognizes that despite histories tied to deindustrialization, Jim Crow laws, racial housing covenants, health disparities, economic disinvestment, environmental hazards, and lack of social supports, families still fight for their children to have an opportunity, and education is the passport to a brighter future. Recognizing the history of oppressive structures is an acknowledgement of the past harms many families are still reeling from in seen and unseen ways. For those leaders who work in high-needs schools in urban and rural communities, leading against the status quo and being equity focused also means working against a history of disadvantage that young people and their families have faced for reasons not of their own doing. The various systems of oppression that affect people of color, people living in poverty, people who are gender or sexual minorities, and people with disabilities is a challenging task. Thus, the approach for leaders is to recognize that in a multitude of ways the odds are stacked against you, and systems and structures often do not want to see certain students succeed. One of the core pillars of the equity framework I have developed for this book is acknowledging and recognizing past harm and focusing on repair. Leaders possess tremendous influence to shape schools. However, equity-focused leaders realize that schools are in communities, and those communities have a long and complex history that has a profound influence on its members. Thus, leaders who have a justice focus realize that the current state of affairs for a school's performance (if it is not ideal) is not solely based on student effort and ability, but that issues tied to poverty, gentrification, environmental disparities, displacement, intergenerational trauma, lack of affordable housing, and decent-paying jobs are just as much a part of how students perform as is curriculum and instruction. Hence, leaders should walk into such opportunities with their eyes wide open, realizing the gravity and complexity of their tasks, but with a clear sense of conviction and commitment that students can and will succeed under their leadership. To be clear, pity is not needed here; feeling sorry for students does not improve their outcomes, better schools are what is needed, and it starts with strong leadership. Moreover, such leaders are clear in their focus to identify and develop teachers who share a similar understanding of working in understaffed and underresourced schools but are not intimidated by the challenge before them (Khalifa, 2018).

To be clear, pity is not needed here; feeling sorry for students does not improve their outcomes, better schools are what is needed, and it starts with strong leadership.

Questions that leaders should reflect on include the following:

- What do I think and feel about the community I serve?
- What do I think and feel about the children and families I serve?
- How do I understand structural and historical inequities?
- What type of leader do I aspire to be?
- How have I enjoyed privilege over other groups, especially those that I serve in my school?
- Are communications with my parents/caregivers in their native language? Do I affirm their cultural identities in such communication?
- How am I including parent/caregiver voice in governance and decision making?
- Am I hiring staff who are consistent with community demographics and willing to be self-reflective?

Sonia Nieto (2018) in her account of leaders who lead against the grain lifts up the example from a leader who inspired her, Antonia Pantoja, and she offers the following five characteristics of effective leaders:

1. Have a deep belief in people, particularly those who have been left behind, marginalized, and oppressed by society.
2. Believe that everyone learns best in communities: For this reason, creating spaces for leaders to collaborate is essential.
3. Mentor and learn from young people. They are our primary clientele, and there is a lot we can learn from them.
4. Share and do not hoard leadership: Part of our job is to look for leadership characteristics in others.

Here are a few simple ideas that help leaders improve relationships and contribute to a positive school culture.

- **Get to know your teachers as people.** Knowing teachers as people, with full lives with families and concerns, is critical to building a positive school culture. It tells teachers that you care about them beyond their professional roles. Caring about them can help improve cooperation and give them a more positive outlook on their jobs and where they work.

- **Be observant of staff.** Notice the teachers and staff who are the most and least engaged and start conversations with them. Recognize and support the efforts of the most engaged and seek ways to motivate the least engaged. Offer to participate in programs or take staff to lunch for get-to-know-you discussions.

- **Respect teacher time.** Avoid setting up long, overly bureaucratic, and repetitive meetings, which put a strain on a teacher's day and time. One of the most important gifts that leaders can give to teachers is the gift of time. Try to handle as many matters as possible via email or other means that do not always require big chunks of time from teachers.

- **Celebrate success.** Recognize the efforts of teachers and how those efforts translate into success. Publicly acknowledge what is going right at the school (and there is always something!). Encourage teachers and students to motivate them to learn and grow. Find the small tasks that teachers do, the extra time they devote, their volunteering efforts, and their willingness to always step up when there is a need.

- **Develop thick skin.** To be an equity-focused leader requires one to have the ability to not be focused on popularity or being well liked by everyone, but to be respected. Having thick skin means being able to stand in the face of constant criticism, having your decisions continuously scrutinized, and having people question your competency. Having thick skin also means not being deterred by people's opinions of you and your performance but realizing that not everyone has access to information that informs your decision making. Equity-focused leadership is not for the faint of heart.

Expect, but do not be deterred by, resistance when staff do not buy into the aims, goals, and direction in which you are going. Stay the course by doubling down on the following:

1. Focus on respect rather than popularity. Many school leaders desire to be liked by their staff, and, of course, this can have its benefits. But in my conversations with hundreds of school leaders, a consistent theme is being respected. To that end, leaders must aim for being consistent, true to their word, and anchored in core values, with a firm, authentic, and unwavering commitment to children. More times than not, these characteristics will earn respect. Being liked or being popular does not always lead to effective leadership. Being respected does.

2. Listen to input from your staff. One of the most useful ways to earn the respect of staff is to truly listen to their thoughts, ideas, and feedback about how to make schools better. This does not mean that you will always agree with everything your staff recommends, but having an open-door approach where staff can offer constructive criticism (publicly and privately) can go a long way. Implementing certain ideas can communicate to staff that their input is being taken to heart. Listening to staff can take place in staff meetings, hallway conversations, emails, one-on-one conversations, or other modes of communication. Finally, consistently asking teachers and staff for their input can be transformative.

3. Provide regular, constructive feedback. The overwhelming majority of teachers take their work seriously. They see the task of helping students as an important one. However, many are often looking for ways to get better, especially novice teachers. Whenever possible, spend time offering formative feedback to teachers and provide suggestions on how they can improve their practice, how they might connect to students and families, and ways they can improve overall. Approach matters here.

4. Delegate, delegate, delegate! One of the most essential features of effective leaders is to recognize that they cannot do everything. Many leaders place undue pressure on themselves because they take on the responsibility of all things, at all times. Attempting to be the fixer

for everything is a recipe for fast burnout. Effective leaders learn the importance of and practice delegation. Surrounding yourself with competent allies who share your vision for the school is essential. Effective leaders also understand the importance of training and mentoring aspiring leaders so that they can take on various issues at the school. No leader can do it all. But effective leaders develop trust in those around them to carry out their tasks in order for the school to reach its optimal levels.

EFFECTIVE LEADERS EMPOWER TEACHERS AND CULTIVATE LEADERSHIP SKILLS. The most effective leaders seek to identify others on their staff who possess the disposition, work ethic, skills, and desire to be leaders. Many leaders recognize that when they were classroom teachers, someone saw something in them that led to THEIR leadership journey. As a result, many effective leaders do the same for the next generation of leaders. Effective leaders often empower their teachers with tasks, special projects, or responsibilities that are helping to bolster their leadership skills. Often teachers may not recognize what is being done, but leaders are essentially saying "I believe in you." Moreover, leaders who are equity centered recognize that they are only as strong as the people around them. Thus, mentoring and empowering up-and-coming leaders serves multiple purposes; it builds skills in up-and-coming leaders and supports the school to become better. Moreover, equity-minded leaders may even seek out leadership classes, seminars, and professional development opportunities that will aid their teachers in varying capacities.

BUILDING A CULTURE MATTERS. Effective leaders recognize that in order for schools to be their best, it is vital to have a structure predicated on core values, norms, and practices that are rooted in a deep belief tied to student success. In other words, we are talking about the importance of culture. Every school has a culture, but that does not mean it is a culture that is conducive to school success. Some schools have a toxic culture, which is centered on blaming students and families, lack of trust and collaboration amongst staff, no vision from leadership, and a place where no one can grow and thrive (Safir, 2017). Conversely, when done right, a more positive culture is centered on core ideals that inform how the school operates and is not shaped by one person but grounded in systems, structures, behaviors, and understandings that allow people—adults *and* students—to be their best. Leaders should be intentional in how they seek to build a culture at their school but must be patient and deliberate and recognize that building a positive school culture does not happen overnight and may take years to establish. Moreover, leaders must recognize that often there are certain individuals who are major obstacles to building a healthy, positive culture. It doesn't necessarily mean that such individuals cannot be brought on board. In some cases, when leaders take the time to listen, understand the source of the resistance, work to meet the person's needs (that is, assuming that such needs are not inconsistent with the core values of the culture), and foster a sense of belonging, that person can not only change but also become a valuable member of the team. However, the hard work of leaders is to recognize that some adults are quite toxic and persistently negative. In such cases, leaders must have the courage to engage in uncomfortable conversations, including asking the individual if this is the best place for them while underscoring that they are in the way of building an equity-centered culture and helping students thrive. The work of a leader is to take steps to help such individuals realize that this school is not the right fit for them.

---

when done right, a more positive culture is centered on core ideals that inform how the school operates and is not shaped by one person but grounded in systems, structures, behaviors, and understandings that allow people—adults and students—to be their best

---

DON'T AVOID THE HARD CONVERSATIONS. The task of the school leader is to make sure that pressing issues that occur at the school are not avoided but addressed directly. To be equity minded, sometimes the issue can be a nagging parent/caregiver who has been giving staff a hard time, or in some cases it is a teacher who engages in bullying behavior with colleagues. No matter how awkward or uncomfortable the situation is, effective leaders tackle it head on. The approach typically involves gathering information, going to the source, and seeking clarity; then conveying the problem with certain types of behavior; and subsequently identifying a solution. Another area where courageous conversations are warranted is when matters of racism, misogyny, homophobia, or transphobia arise. In today's school climate, students and adults can engage in problematic behavior and use language that harms members of minoritized communities. Once leaders hear about such situations, swift, informed decision making is vital. Refusal to address various topics can convey a lack of concern or care for those who are injured. Equity now leadership requires what H. Rich Milner (2023) calls "frontline leadership" where leaders must commit themselves to building anti-racist leadership capacity in today's turbulent political environment.

WHY EMPATHY AND LISTENING MATTER FOR LEADERS

One of the most essential characteristics that school leaders can adopt is trying to put themselves in the shoes and situations of others. In short, empathy matters when it comes to equity-minded leadership. Trying to understand what teachers may be going through; recognizing parents/givers are doing the best that they can; attempting to think about what it means to be a teenager today—all these approaches can endear leaders to those whom they are working alongside. Empathetic leadership is born from an authentic understanding of other people's needs and is an essential component of equity-based school leadership (Sinek, 2009).

Empathetic leadership can be one of the most essential tools in a leader's tool kit because it is centered on trying to understand their team members' thoughts, feelings, and emotions. One of the essential elements of equity in this work is about justice and fairness. People we work with want to be seen, heard, and valued. At the outside, I talked about how justice is doing the right thing. Empathetic leaders usually have excellent communication and active listening skills, and they inspire co-workers to improve their own communication skills. They want to do right by them. Empathy drives a leader to try to understand people's behaviors and individualize strategies for increasing work efficiency and productivity. It is a key element of servant leadership, a leadership style in which the focus is on the team's growth and well-being to put their needs first. The theory is that instead of employees serving the leader, the leader serves the employees. Such an approach can make people feel more understood and less alone as they encounter challenges in life since empathy is the ability to experience, feel, or imagine what another person is going through (Sinek, 2009).

Empathetic leadership is a mindset that should inform decision making and help establish a schoolwide culture of purpose and respect. Empathic leadership is anchored on school leaders being mindful of (and never forgetting) their time as teachers and what they needed or wanted from their leaders. Such an approach conveys to staff that "I am with you" or "I want to see you succeed." Though the realities of teaching are always in a state of flux, empathetic leaders make themselves available as much as possible. Empathetic leaders schedule listening tours with their staff to hear their concerns, frustrations, or ideas. Shane Safir (2017) talks about the importance of what she calls *listening leaders*. She states that "listening leadership extends well beyond the act of listening; it is also an orientation towards collegiality, shared leadership, professional growth, and equity. It's a mindset and a way of being" (Safir, 2017, p. xvii). Listening leaders are also comfortable making classroom visits—not in an evaluative manner, but in a manner to see how they might best support their teachers; they listen to and learn from students and frequently leave a note with positive praise or constructive feedback. Furthermore, many empathetic leaders see signs of leadership in their teachers and other staff members and offer them professional leadership opportunities that may assist them with other career goals. The importance of empathetic and listening leaders can have multiple benefits. Listening leaders can equip individuals with the strategies and skills for a variety of issues that they confront in school:

- Managing difficult conversations
- Understanding how to get the best out of individuals with challenging behaviors
- Understanding yourself better and knowing how to draw upon your strengths to get the best out of others
- Facilitating better teamwork and minimizing team conflict
- Developing your relationship management skills by helping you understand how to identify and respond to different personality types

An additional benefit of an empathetic and listening approach is that it lends itself to creating working and learning environments. Equity-focused leaders work to create spaces where teachers, staff, and others in the school are willing to engage in courageous and difficult conversations. While never easy, often the job of leaders is to make sure that adults and students can engage in discussions that are uncomfortable but are necessary when it comes to equity. Some might argue the most important condition for enacting such conversations is safety. I seek to go further and say we need more than safe spaces. We need *brave* spaces. A safe space is ideally one that does not incite judgment based on identity or experience—where the expression of both can exist and be affirmed without fear of repercussion. While learning may occur in these spaces, the ultimate goal is to provide support. A *brave space* encourages dialogue, often difficult dialogue. Such approaches recognize differences that we all possess, and we commit to holding ourselves accountable, and holding each person accountable, to doing the work of sharing experiences and coming to new understandings—a feat that is often hard and, typically, uncomfortable. Brave spaces often require vulnerability, honesty, and courage to say things that may elicit emotions, intense disagreement, and at times anger. Frequently, in schools, there are many adults who have given up on students (or never believed in them) and do significant harm to students. Frequently, in these situations, adults in the building know who these individuals are yet never say a word to them. Brave spaces ask us to enter discussions either individually or collectively about how we lovingly challenge our colleagues to do better by students. Leaders cannot be passive or indifferent in such conversations. Frequently, leaders must initiate and lead such discussions to create equity-centered schools. Avoidance of hard conversations makes leaders complicit in the obstruction of making equity a reality in schools. Brené Brown (2018) says that

> too many people are opting out of vital conversations about diversity and inclusivity because they fear looking wrong, saying something wrong, or being wrong. Choosing our comfort over hard conversations is the epitome of privilege, and it corrodes trust and moves us away from meaningful and lasting change (p. 18).

Hence, equity-minded leaders work to make sure people can be themselves and feel a sense of belonging, purpose, vision, and conviction. These leaders are often egoless and create a culture that allows individuals to be creative, autonomous, and focus-driven on improving students' experiences and outcomes. It is essential for leadership to remember that equity-based approaches should be mindful of the fact that inequity is historical and systemic, operating at structural, institutional, and individual/interpersonal levels that often overlap. Since a core pillar of equity in this work has been recognizing and repairing past harms, leadership must always be mindful of the historical contexts of various groups. Moreover, teaching is political, and so is leadership. There are no easy fixes, but there can be a consistent focus and unapologetic commitment to have schools become places that seek to undo and dismantle inequitable practices, policies, and procedures. Moreover, leaders must consistently remind their staff that while educators are not responsible for structural inequities or the current state of affairs that disadvantage students, they can play a role in undoing some of the harm. Finally, leaders can and should continuously ask their staffs, "What is your *why?*" Why have they chosen to do the work of being educators? This anchoring question is vital because for many educators their reasoning for pursuing teaching is rooted in a commitment to justice, equality, and providing an opportunity to students who have been historically marginalized. However, oftentimes when trapped in a system that was intentionally designed to marginalize some students at the expense of others, educators become detached from the pure ideals that brought them into the profession in the first place. Leaders must remind teachers that if their *why* is to "save kids" or "love students," that is not sufficient. Such monikers reek of a missionary approach to teaching, which is often situated in white saviorism where adults see it as their role to liberate students from harsh and difficult circumstances in their homes and communities. Such approaches do more harm than good because most of those beliefs are anchored in racist, classist, and deficit beliefs that see children, their families, or their communities as the problem (Valencia, 1997). Deficit-based views of children, families, and communities often are devoid of any structural context that explains how and why unequal circumstances exist in the first place. Leaders must constantly ask their staff to remember their *why*.

I seek to go further and say we need more than safe spaces. We need brave *spaces.*

Leaders must remind teachers that if their why *is to "save kids" or "love students," that is not sufficient. Such monikers reek of a missionary approach to teaching, which is often situated in white saviorism where adults see it as their role to liberate students from harsh and difficult circumstances in their homes and communities.*

Equity Now Chart

JUSTICE	REPAIR	BELONGING
• Doing right by all members of the school community • Being an active listener to all stakeholders	• Bringing in resources to schools and communities that have been historically underserved	• Including teachers, staff, and parents/caregivers as part of regular decision making • Reaching out to local businesses to establish partnerships with schools

(Continued)

(Continued)

JUSTICE	REPAIR	BELONGING
• Developing the courage to have "hard conversations" with adults who are not acting in the best interest of students • Having the willingness to have bold yet loving discussions with parents/caregivers about how they can best support their children's education	• Being willing to acknowledge your own shortcomings as a leader • Saying "I am sorry" when you have hurt others • Acknowledging your own mistakes.	• Having parents/ caregivers on budget and hiring committees • Garnering student input/feedback on how to best improve aspects of the school community
• Consistently reminding adults to remember what their *why* is • Consistently telling staff, students, and families what your commitment as a leader is to students' learning	• Having new leaders ask for input from staff on how they can best meet their needs • Listening to stakeholders who have felt excluded from decision making about what can make schools ideal for working and learning	• Holding regular staff appreciation days • Hosting community-building activities for staff at off-site locations • Having community forums and festivals for school staff, parents/ caregivers, and students to enjoy social activities

Questions for Leaders to Consider

1. How often do I have "listen and learn" sessions with my staff?

2. How often do I have "listen and learn" sessions with my students?

3. How often do I have "listen and learn" sessions with my parents/caregivers?

4. How much do I empower my team to take ownership of their tasks?

5. How much, if at all, do I delegate important tasks to my team?

6. How often do I affirm or offer supportive words to my team?

7. How do I empower my team to be better?

Recommendations for Reading and Resources

1. Milner, H. R. (2023). *Play the race card*. Corwin.

2. Blankstein, A. M., & Noguera, P. (2015). *Excellence through equity: Five principles of courageous leadership to guide achievement for every student*. ASCD.

3. Radd, S., Generett, G. G., Gooden, M. A., & Theoharis, G. (2021). *Five practices for equity-focused school leadership*. ASCD.

4. Khalifa, M. (2018). *Culturally responsive school leadership*. Harvard Education Press.

5. Safir, S. (2017). *The listening leader: Creating the conditions for equitable school conditions*. Jossey-Bass.

6. Kafele, B. K. (2021). *The equity and social justice education 50: Critical questions for improving opportunities and outcomes for Black students*. ASCD.

7. Brown, B. (2018). *Dare to lead: Brave work. Tough conversations. Whole hearts*. Random House.

CHAPTER 5

Equity in the Classroom

I have discussed what equity looks like at the district and school levels. Success at each of those levels requires organizational commitment to making equity a reality. School- and systemwide change truly takes a village, meaning systems, structures, policies, and procedures are in alignment with the goal of a synthesized effort to make schools work, especially for our most vulnerable students. Such an effort necessitates the design and implementation of macro-level interventions steeped in justice, recognition and repair of past harms, and belonging—admittedly formidable and complex challenges. One of the reasons why students need equity now is that far too many students sit in classrooms every day in our country, overlooked and underserved, and are seen as disposable to the adults who have chosen to teach them and the systems that are paid to serve them, and we accept it. Something different needs to happen because our students deserve better.

In this chapter, I address a more individual or micro-level approach to equity (i.e., what it looks like in classrooms) and the critical role of teachers in equity-focused change. However, before jumping into this topic, I believe it is only fair to acknowledge the current state of affairs for many teachers, conditions that only make enacting equity work even more challenging. Many teachers are frustrated and even downright angry with the working conditions in schools and the demands being placed on them. Such demands have only increased at a time when many are still reeling from the aftereffects of the COVID-19 pandemic. A national survey discovered that two-thirds of teachers said that they were frustrated and burned out with their jobs, and 55% said that they believed they would be willing to leave the profession sooner than anticipated

(Walker, 2020). A similar, and more recent, report by the California Teachers Association (CTA) and the UCLA Center for the Transformation of Schools (CTS) discovered high rates of dissatisfaction, frustration, and burnout from a majority of teachers in schools across the state of California that are probably similar in other parts of the country (Mathews, 2022). In the survey of more than 4,600 current teachers in California, the findings revealed that while teachers enter the profession to help students and make a difference, many teachers today are feeling acute levels of trauma, stress, and job dissatisfaction—all of which have led them to seriously consider exiting the profession. The report also found that teacher retention will be a challenge in the near term in many schools in the nation's most populous state. Four in ten current teachers have explored leaving the classroom either to continue in other capacities within education or to switch professions entirely. One in five current teachers say they will likely leave the profession in the next three years. Current teachers aged 55 and older are the most inclined to leave teaching within three years, and more than one-third of younger teachers have a similar outlook. There are also many equity concerns related to teacher diversity, the report revealed. Many current teachers of color, especially Black teachers, say they have experienced discrimination and do not feel comfortable expressing themselves in today's school climate. LGBTQ+ teachers have also experienced discrimination at high rates. Aspiring and former teachers of color share that feeling comfortable and being a part of their school community are directly tied to whether their students and their families, peers, and leadership have similar racial/ethnic backgrounds to their own. Any conversations that are concerned with equity need to place a high priority on teacher supports and well-being. It is critical in this moment to recognize and support the complex challenges that teachers are facing, because burnout is real, and many are considering leaving the profession. Particularly in such an environment, carrot-and-stick approaches to school reform and toxic positivity are not appropriate levers for change.

There are a variety of changes that current and former teachers believe would address burnout and improve teacher retention according to the CTA/CTS study (Mathews, 2022). Current and former teachers' top priority for state and local officials is better pay. Second-tier priorities are all things that could reduce the stress that current teachers are feeling in their jobs, including smaller class sizes, stronger discipline policies for students who behave disruptively, better staffing, a more manageable workload, and more support services for students like access to nurses, counselors, and behavioral specialists. So, to be clear, districts and states must do more to create better working conditions for teachers. This is undoubtedly an equity issue that requires action in order to support an essential cog in the equity wheel, teachers. Yet, even as the fight for better conditions is in full swing, students are still arriving with a diverse set of needs. Teachers need to be provided the supports to best support students.

MOVING BEYOND SELF-CARE

One of the more common responses offered to teachers in today's high-stress, high-demand ecosystem of teaching is to engage in more "self-care." The idea is that teachers need to take responsibility for taking on less stress; doing more to prioritize their health, such as more exercising; and doing more pleasurable activities to take their minds away from the intensity of the day-to-day work of teaching. While such mantras have been widely adopted slogans in schools and appear to be well intended on the surface, they are deeply problematic, and schools should consider moving away from the frequent reminders to take care of ourselves. While self-care in and of itself is certainly not a bad thing, the way it is framed in schools and districts is typically not helpful. The reason such statements are unhelpful, and in some cases even harmful, is that, like the parallel demand for students to "get more grit," the self-care trope asks teachers to do more work. It asks teachers to engage in labor to reduce their stressors, without paying attention to the sources that create the stressors in the first place—the bureaucracies and demands of schools. The continuous plea for teachers to do a better job of taking care of themselves does not ask the question, Why are teachers in need of so much self-care to begin with? Why has the demand of teaching become so intense in the last decade but supports (and pay) have not accompanied this demand? Suggesting that teachers do more self-care removes any institutional culpability that generates high stressors. When considering the complex needs of learners, students with behavioral challenges, unmanageable class sizes, little to no support from leadership, an influx of new district mandates, curricular directives, testing and accountability worries, and, more recently, attempts to suppress academic freedom in the form of book bans and education "gag orders"—policies that forbid conversations about race, gender identity, sexual orientation, and so on—it stands to reason that the challenges are more than enough to make even the least-stressed individuals highly stressed. Education advocates need to move away from telling teachers to practice more self-care and move toward reducing the very factors that have sparked the need for so much self-care. This is where school and district leaders need to mobilize and think more creatively about how to best support teachers. What should the steps in this process be?

1. Ask teachers what they need to be supported.
2. Listen carefully to such articulations of need.
3. Take action steps to implement the types of change that teachers need, want, and deserve, as they are the catalyst for maximizing student learning.

Why has the demand of teaching become so intense in the last decade but supports (and pay) have not accompanied this demand? Suggesting that teachers do more self-care removes any institutional culpability that generates high stressors.

While schools continue to place demands on teachers, the ability of many teachers to do incredibly supportive work for students cannot be stressed enough. In the following sections, I will discuss steps that teachers can take in their classrooms to support students, with an equity-focused approach to some of the more vulnerable student populations.

TEACHERS MAKING A DIFFERENCE THROUGH EQUITY

In doing equity work, it is important for teachers to understand what is working in schools and how teachers are making a difference in challenging times. In his work on star teachers of children living in poverty, Martin Haberman et al. (2018) stated that there are essential approaches that these teachers take in being effective with their students. Haberman (2018) also identified behaviors that star teachers do not do, which are essential to being effective, and in their study of effective teachers, Haberman et al. found that star teachers did not (1) focus on discipline, (2) mete out punishment, (3) give tests and grades, (4) give homework in the traditional sense, and (5) parent bash. Haberman and his team observed teachers who were more focused on students' effort, rather than their ability, and they looked for ways to engage them in interesting content so behavior would not be a problem and there would be no need to obsess over compliance. An important theme of Haberman's work on star teachers is that these teachers did not engage in reward-performance types of dynamics in their classroom and operated from the standpoint that students are naturally inquisitive. This fueled their desire to create a curriculum that builds on student curiosity, encourages question asking, and seeks to identify relevant content in the classroom that piques students' excitement. Moreover, the teachers that

Haberman studied found that they viewed parents as partners and frequently asked them about their students' interests, likes and dislikes, strengths, and areas of growth. Finally, another important theme was teachers' awareness that students have interests in a wide array of aspects of human experience including computers, games, sports, movies, TV, dancing, singing, acting, social media, chess, and a host of other activities. It is essential that teachers tap into the interests or proclivities that students have and allow those strengths to be a conduit of what students learn in the school curriculum.

RELEVANCE MATTERS: CULTURALLY RESPONSIVE TEACHING IN THE CLASSROOM

As schools become more culturally and linguistically diverse, it is vital for teachers to recognize the importance of diversifying approaches to teaching that meet the needs of today's learners (Banks, 2004, 2006, 2019; Gay, 2020; Milner, 2020). Like most humans, students have a healthy and natural curiosity and, given the right conditions, can get excited when developing new insights and learning new information. This is especially likely to happen if the content or information sparks curiosity, excites students' imagination, and piques their creativity. For most students, there is nothing more enticing than when new information has a connection to their world, their own interests, and their own lived experiences (T. C. Howard, 2003). In short, relevance matters. Relevance matters because it allows students to feel as if what they know, see, feel, and hear is important and can help them learn more information (T. C. Howard, 2020). Arguably, there is no more powerful stimulus to learning than when that learning is connected to students' worlds; there is no disconnect between "what I know" and "what I am expected to learn." When information is not reflective or connected to who students are, there is a tendency to disengage, disconnect, become frustrated, and turn off possibilities for learning. In this respect, our students are no different from ourselves as adults. Think of the times you've attended a lecture or watched a video that had no relevance or conceivable connection to your own lived experience: How long did it take you to mentally check out? When students can engage in relevant and stimulating content, the possibility for their learning is endless. Effort can improve, participation may increase, and, most importantly, learning can grow. The concept of culturally relevant and culturally responsive teaching was introduced by education scholars Gloria Ladson-Billings (1994) and Geneva Gay (2000). They both state that culturally responsive teaching is an approach to teaching that incorporates attributes, characteristics, or knowledge from students' cultural background into the instructional strategies and course content to improve educational outcomes. One of the primary ideas behind culturally responsive pedagogy is to create learning environments that allow students to utilize cultural elements, cultural capital, and other recognizable knowledge that they are familiar with to learn new content and information to enhance their schooling experience and academic success. According to T. C. Howard and Terry (2011),

> Culturally responsive pedagogy embodies a set of professional, political, cultural, ethical, and ideological disposition that supersedes mundane teaching acts, but is centered in fundamental beliefs about teaching, learning, students, their families, their communities, and an unyielding commitment to see student success become less rhetorical and more of a reality. Culturally responsive pedagogy is situated in a framework that recognizes the rich and varied cultural wealth, knowledge, and skills that diverse students bring to schools, and seeks to develop dynamic teaching practices, multicultural content, multiple means of assessment, and a philosophical view of teaching that is dedicated to nurturing students' academic, social, emotional, cultural, psychological, and physiological well-being. (p. 346)

Culturally responsive teaching matters because students' experiences matter. One of the key attributes of culturally responsive teaching is to affirm our students—to create learning environments that help them feel included, valued, and safe. To be clear, culturally responsive teaching is not only about content, but it starts with some of the following:

- **A fundamental belief in the ability of all students to learn.** High expectations are essential for every student, regardless of background. Teachers must have a set of positive attitudes and dispositions toward every student.

- **A wide range of curricular content** that is reflective of students' race, ethnicity, gender, gender identity expression, abilities, religion, language, home, and family configuration, among others. All matter. Therefore, literature, examples, and concepts that reflect and affirm students' identities should be present regularly.

- **Instruction should be dynamic.** Responsiveness recognizes that students learn in a multitude of ways. Therefore, teaching strategies should be dynamic and diverse, meaning students have whole-group instruction, pair-share, and small-group activities that require students to talk with each other, learn from one another, share, discuss, disagree, and think individually and collectively. Also, students should be allowed multiple ways to participate, share their understandings, and demonstrate mastery of content.

- **Bring community into the school.** Parents, caregivers, and grandparents, as well as various members of students' communities, should be asked to come to classrooms to share stories, offer supports, and provide cultural bridges between the larger community and the classroom.

- **Activate students' prior knowledge.** This might include asking students what they know about a particular concept and connecting that to the lesson you're introducing. For example, before you begin a story about a character adjusting to life in the United States, you might ask students to think about when they have encountered a new environment.

- **Make learning contextual.** When discussing a text or primary source that is from or about another time, place, or culture, encourage students to connect it to their lives or the current moment. Try asking questions such as these: "How is immigration different today than 100 years ago?" or "How would people who protested for voting rights in the 1950s feel about voter suppression today?"

- **Focus on political and contemporary issues.** Today's students are keenly aware of the social, political, and economic milieu in which they live and learn. Avoidance of important topics that are current in today's news cycle not only is a missed opportunity but can disenfranchise students whose lives are directly impacted by such topics. Relevance in teaching means addressing today's complex issues in a manner that gets students thinking, learning, analyzing, and discussing today's topics from multiple perspectives. To be clear, it is teachers' job not to tell students what to think, but to provide them with the knowledge, critical thinking skills, resources, and dispositions to make informed decisions. Sociopolitical awareness is vital to today's learning context.

In addition to developing a framework for safety—for teachers to teach and for students to learn—and an emphasis on cultural relevance, I would argue that there are five key steps that are essential to deepening equity-based approaches to teaching.

1. MINDSET

The first and arguably most important step that educators across all grade levels and subject matters must first examine is their beliefs about the students they teach, the families that support them, and the communities in which they live. In short, what is the mindset that you have about the very group of people you are responsible for? Important reflection is vital when thinking about mindset because everything that educators do from relational interactions, to expectations, to how discipline is handled flows from their mindsets about students (T. C. Howard, 2003). But, in particular, what is the mindset that educators have about students who come from diverse backgrounds racially, ethnically, linguistically, and socioeconomically? Questions about mindset are raised because all too often certain students face an uphill battle because teachers harbor deficit mindsets about students, wherein there is a fixation on some of the following deficit beliefs:

- Students do not have support at home.
- Students do not have the academic foundation to be successful learners.
- Students are not motivated to learn.
- Students have parents/caregivers who are not involved in their education.
- Students whose first language is not English do not have the skills to be successful academically.
- Students do not have the grit to effectively problem solve.
- Students lack the focus and concentration to be successful.

What is clear in each of these statements is that they are anchored in what students "do not have," what they "cannot do," or what they "are lacking." Such approaches start students off on the wrong foot because teachers fail to see any of the students' strengths, or what they *can* do. The persistence of negative thoughts and ideas about students and their families is dangerous and can cause significant injury because students pick up on the attitudes, lack of belief, apathy, and often outright lack of care that adults have toward them, and as a result they can begin to disengage and put forth limited or no effort (Shalaby, 2017). To disrupt the prevalence of deficit-based viewpoints and ideas, teachers who harbor such beliefs need to have a significant shift in mindset, one that is asset based, steeped in possibilities for students, and anchored in how and where students can grow. One of the more popular phrases that has been used in education circles is the importance of students needing to have a "*growth* mindset" as opposed to a "*fixed* mindset." Education scholar Carol Dweck (2006), in her book *Mindset*, describes people who believe that their success depends on time, persistence, and effort. People with a growth mindset feel their skills and intelligence can be improved with effort and persistence. They embrace challenges, persist through obstacles, learn from criticism, and seek out inspiration in others' success. Fixed mindset, in contrast, describes people who see their qualities as fixed traits that cannot change. The irony for educators is that many challenge, push, or strongly encourage students to develop a growth mindset while many of these adults maintain a very strong fixed mindset about their students. Mindset matters for adults, just as it matters for students. To that end, educators must hold themselves accountable in the same manner that they expect of their students, by working to replace such fixed beliefs about their students' capacity and intelligence with a growth mindset by envisioning students' potential, areas of growth and academic progress, the effort being put forth, and the sheer determination that even some of their most vulnerable students exhibit on a daily basis. If equity-minded practitioners want to acknowledge and repair harm done to students over years from being in classrooms, mindset shifts are an absolute must.

2. EXPECTATIONS

Once teachers have engaged in deep reflection about their perceptions, beliefs, and attitudes about students, their families, and their communities, they can begin to adjust their expectations. Expectations, beliefs, and mindsets are all in sync when it comes to equity in the classroom. Gersheson et al. (2016) explains that teachers' expectations might be able to influence student outcomes in at least three primary ways that have important equity considerations. First, the perception that teachers have low expectations may exacerbate the harmful effects of stereotype threat, whereby low expectations have the potential to cause emotional responses that directly harm or impede performance or cause students to disidentify with educational environments (Steele, 1997). Second, stigmatized students (who are often students of color, low income, or multilingual learners) may modify their own expectations, and in turn their behavior, to conform to teachers' negative biases (Ferguson, 2003). In each of the first two cases, teachers' negative beliefs about students could create a mental map for students that becomes a self-fulfilling prophecy (i.e., if the teacher thinks I cannot learn, then it must be true: I cannot learn) and can become internalized by students (Burgess & Greaves, 2013; Loury, 2009). Finally, teachers who stigmatize certain types of students may modify how they teach, evaluate, and advise them, again leading to poor educational outcomes for stigmatized students (Ferguson, 2003). Each of these scenarios potentially perpetuates equity gaps in educational experiences and attainment.

An additional barrier to establishing realistic and high expectations for stigmatized students is that many of the unique skills and strengths of these students simply do not manifest in most classroom settings. Examples include different ways of learning, creative processing mechanisms, multilingualism, or leadership skills. If we truly want to tap into our students' potential, we will want to have a myriad of ways to take inventory of these "hidden" strengths both inside and outside of the classroom. Moreover, there is a litany of data (Dee, 2005, 2007; Holt & Gershenson, 2015; Shalaby, 2017) that highlights the way teachers tend to have lowered expectations of students based on their essential identities, including race, ethnicity, socioeconomic status, and gender. Hence, it is important for all educators to take stock of the ways that they see students as learners, and recognize how larger societal images and stereotypes may shape their attitudes and perspectives. The research on implicit bias (Watson, 2019) and how it shapes human behavior continues to grow and evolve. According to the Kirwan Institute for the Study of Race and Ethnicity (2013), implicit bias refers to

> the attitudes or stereotypes that affect our understanding, actions, and decisions in an unconscious manner. These biases, which encompass both favorable and unfavorable assessments, are activated involuntarily and without an individual's awareness or intentional control. Residing deep in the subconscious, these biases are different from known biases that individuals may choose to conceal for the purposes of social and/or political correctness. Rather, implicit biases are not accessible through introspection.

The concept of implicit bias first gained traction and attention in the late 1970s as researchers tried to make sense of why individuals who claimed they did not hold prejudiced beliefs or attitudes about certain marginalized groups (namely people of color, women, members of the LGBTQ+ community, etc.) seemed to discriminate against them in overt and covert ways, despite their espoused beliefs (Kahn, 2017). These early studies, as well as recent findings, suggest that whereas explicit intent or bias may be less likely to be admitted or confronted—because it is less socially acceptable and occurs less regularly—unconscious intent or implicit bias is widespread and observable with the help of such tools as the online Implicit Association Test, or IAT (Banaji & Greenwald, 2013).

Bias has real-life consequences for students and can serve as the reason why opportunities are afforded to some students and vehemently denied to others. Not only does bias play a role in areas such as students who are praised and affirmed in the classroom. Bias can also shape who gets teacher recommendations for gifted and talented programs, leadership opportunities, extracurricular opportunities, and other pathways that possess high capital in schools. Conversely, there are data that show how bias can influence students who are more likely to face persistent reprimand, punishment, and school discipline. A number of studies have highlighted the way Black students in particular are overpunished and severely disciplined in schools (Morris, 2016; Wood et al., 2016). With such serious consequences, the need for educators to work toward reducing or eliminating bias is an urgent priority. It should be noted, though, that many schools have moved to one- to two-hour "bias trainings" to help teachers eliminate bias. Data on such efforts show that they have little to no effect on teachers' practices. To truly address bias in an effective way requires teachers to engage in ongoing reflection, reading, and meta-analysis of their thoughts and actions with students.

For teachers who are looking to identify and subsequently address their biases, know that there are no easy answers, because as humans we all have various types of bias, but there are steps that can be taken to address bias in classroom instruction and overall practices:

1. **Raise awareness of our own biases.** All human beings have some type of bias. Being biased does not make you a bad person; it makes you human. Try to focus on your thoughts and actions about particular people and situations and ask, "Why do I think that?" "Where did those thoughts come from?" And "Are they accurate?"

2. **Consider our interactions with others.** Think about language with certain individuals—how you engage, what you say, and how you say it—and think about whether it changes across groups. If it does, why? Frequently our interactions reveal our bias about what we believe about certain people, who we avoid, who we like being around, and our comfort levels with people who are different from us.

3. **Practice empathy, mindfulness, and communication.** Thinking about others' experiences and being mindful about our interactions can go a long way in eliminating bias.

Not all students will have the same cultural assumptions as their teachers, and it should be the teacher's responsibility to bridge the gap. Listening to others' realities about how they have been othered can garner empathy, which is known to reduce bias.

4. **Slow down.** Often our biases become our default when we have limited time, limited information, or competing demands on our time and attention. Slowing down during the process of decision making and gathering adequate information, and while processing thoughts, language, and actions, can help us to make decisions that are informed by accurate, not biased, information.

5. **Hold all students to a high standard.** This does not mean holding all students to the same standard because individuality matters. However, assuming the best of intentions of all students can help to eliminate bias and provide students the benefit of the doubt that they deserve. In addition, holding all students to a high standard aligns with high expectations and seeing the best in our students.

3. RELATIONSHIPS

Relationships are arguably the most important feature in building equity-based classrooms that facilitate engagement, belonging, justice, and learning (J. R. Howard et al., 2019; Milner et al, 2019). The emphasis on student–teacher relationships in teaching and learning is important given the growing body of research that has demonstrated the importance of relationships, connections, and social–emotional well-being to student learning (Sparks, 2016). For many students, learning occurs within a social context of caring, emotional supports that center students' humanity first and foremost. In absence of such supports, learning is unlikely for these students. In short, relationships matter where teaching and learning is concerned.

We have known about the importance of relationships for many years. The influential child psychiatrist James Comer (1995) stated decades ago "no significant learning can occur without a significant relationship." The focus on relationships in education has been critical for some time but has become more central given all that students have encountered since the COVID-19 pandemic. And even prior to the pandemic, the damaging effects of structural inequities such as poverty, displacement, racial discrimination, homophobia, transphobia, and homelessness underscored the need to connect with students on deeper levels (Berson & Baggerly, 2012). Such damaging influences contributed to the escalating rates of depression, anxiety, stress, and grief alluded to earlier in this book. In addition to mental health supports, there has been widespread recognition of the importance of social–emotional learning and its connection to academic learning. One of the casualties of *No Child Left Behind* was the compartmentalization of "student achievement" with little to no attention to the affective domain. The connection between the affective and cognitive domains matters and is known to improve student experiences and outcomes. In short, relationships and connectedness matter in meaningful ways that perhaps are not understood by many educators and can be used to disrupt the potential for healthy teacher–student relationships (J. R. Howard et al., 2019).

Positive teacher–student relationships contribute to school adjustment and academic and social performance in countless ways. A large body of research has uncovered the value of positive teacher–student relationships. Teachers have reported a number of positive outcomes including low conflict, a high degree of closeness and support, and increased student agency, all of which contribute to students' adjustment to school, social skills and development, academic performance, and resiliency in academic performance (Battistich et al., 2004; Curby, Rimm-Kaufman, & Ponitz, 2009; Ewing & Taylor, 2009; Rudasill et al., 2010).

Teachers who experience close relationships with students also reported that their students were less likely to be chronically absent, were more self-driven, and were more cooperative and more engaged in learning (Decker et al., 2007; Klem & Connell, 2004). Teachers who value teacher–student relationships tend to use more learner-centered practices (i.e., practices that show sensitivity to individual differences among students), include students in the decision making, provide more voice and choice in daily activities, and acknowledge students' developmental needs—all of which can go a long way toward building trust, rapport, and a desire to want to learn from educators.

While most educators would now agree that relationships can be vital to learning, the bigger challenge is how to *do* it. Relationships can also be instrumental in creating a sense of belonging for students. Many educators have a natural ability to connect with students that can appear effortless. However, others may struggle with a knowing–doing gap that can surface in the form of questions like these:

- *How can I connect with students who are more reclusive?*
- *What if I am more reclusive?*
- *How can I build relationships when I only have 55 minutes a period, and I have so much material to cover with so many students?*

These are all legitimate questions. Moreover, I would contend that relationship building, while easy for some, takes time, requires patience, and does not always happen quickly. Like any human relationship, connecting with students requires time, reciprocity, and a level of respect that is felt and honored by students. Furthermore, relationship building does not come at the expense of learning; rather, it is a conduit to learning, and building skills and content knowledge is never compromised in the promise. Finally, I should note that I advocate for relationships, not friendships. There is a monumental difference between the two (see Table 5.1). It is important to note that as adult professionals, it is never okay to seek to build friendships with our students, and we need to be very clear about where and why that line is drawn. One of the mistakes many new teachers make is seeking student friendships over relationships.

Another area to consider when relationship building is forming connections across differences. As noted in Chapter 1, most teachers are middle-class, white, monolingual, and women, while the growing makeup of students in schools is not from these same groups. To that end, cultural context matters. When being committed to being equity minded, teachers must realize that healthy teacher–student relationships can be formed across differences, but they are not always easy to build and maintain, and they can take time. One of the first things to consider when building relationships across differences is trust. For many students from marginalized backgrounds, people from different groups (racial, gender, sexual orientation, social class) have been seen or viewed as people to be leery about, or to be careful with, because of how certain groups have been mistreated by them in the education system. So, it may be difficult for some Black or Latinx students to initially feel comfortable with white teachers. Or some girls may have a hard time opening up to men who are teachers. Teachers must not personalize the reticence that some students might have initially toward them. Moreover, teachers need to acknowledge the harm that students have received from adults (e.g., adults making homophobic or transphobic comments) and understand the root of the mistrust. Second, realize that language and humor have a cultural context. For many communities, tone, volume, and pace of speaking have meaning and cultural connotations. So, it is imperative for teachers to observe student speech patterns and inflection points and to realize that certain jokes, comments, and nicknames that are made within a group are not fair game or for usage among individuals who are not part of the group. Third, teachers must exhibit cultural humility, meaning they need to demonstrate the ability to know that their cultural frames of reference are not everyone else's and that having an "other" orientation in relation to aspects of cultural identity is important (Nasir, 2011). Finally, cultural humility is rooted in the understanding that we will never fully understand the experiences of every cultural group that is different from our own. However, if we acknowledge our lack of understanding, then we can be more open to learning about those realities.

When being committed to being equity minded, teachers must realize that healthy teacher-student relationships can be formed across differences, but they are not always easy to build and maintain, and they can take time.

TABLE 5.1 ● Friendships vs. Relationships

FRIENDSHIPS	RELATIONSHIPS
Seen as peer	Seen as authority figure
Seeks to be liked	Seeks to be respected and trusted
Shares lots of personal information that goes beyond professional boundaries	Shares limited, age-appropriate personal information within professional boundaries
Blurred or no line between teacher and student	Clear line between teacher and student
Goal is social	Goal is learning

Once there is a clear commitment to build relationships and not friendships, there is no set recipe on how this can be done. In the book *No More Teaching Without Positive Relationships*, J. R. Howard et al. (2019) lay out a number of approaches that educators can take. The following are a few strategies that educators may consider in their efforts to build relationships with students.

STRATEGIES TO BUILD RELATIONSHIPS

- **Journaling:** 10–15 minutes of creative writing or free writing for students to write about their thoughts, feelings, and emotions about anything they choose as a way for teachers to get to learn about students' likes, dislikes, interests, hobbies, hopes, family, friends, wishes, and ambitions (task is ungraded).

- **Finding common ground:** Finding out what common interests you share with your students (e.g., music, art, movies, TV shows, sports, hobbies).

- **Sharing yourself:** Disclosing the school-appropriate things that are happening in your life (e.g., new pets, moving, family, children, or vacation).

- **One-on-one check-ins:** Providing students with individualized one-on-one time.

- **Noticing the quiet ones:** Taking out the time to talk to students who will not regularly communicate with peers or teachers. Sometimes, these students have serious challenges that result in their disengagement or silence.

- **Duty time:** Spending time getting to know students in a less formal setting during breakfast or lunch.

- **Out-of-school support:** Attending students' significant life events outside of school (e.g., sporting events, birthday parties, quinceañeras, cheer competitions).

- **Weekend check-ins:** Giving students time on Mondays to discuss their weekends, and time on Fridays to share weekend plans.

In short, relationships convey an important element of care that is essential to learning. Irvine and Fraser (1998) described educators who care as "warm demanders." Borrowing from Judith Kleinfeld's (1975) work, they stated that warm demander teachers know their students as individuals, always demonstrate unconditional positive regard, and are adamant about always setting high standards and expectations for students.

FROM RELATIONSHIPS TO LEARNING

As a foundational approach to learning is established—one that is based on mutual respect, getting to know students, engendering trust, and agreeing upon a clear sense of collective goals—an equity now–based approach is unapologetic in its focus on creating these conditions in the interest of enhancing student learning. Relationship building is empty if no learning emerges from it. To that end, one of the most harmful things done to students in classrooms today is apathetic instruction, or instruction that is void of creativity; teacher-centered approaches are antithetical to what equity in the classroom should look like.

To that end, teachers should always engage in meta-analysis of thinking about processes, approaches, interactions, and instructions that they use with students. Learning is often socially constructed for many students, and culture and multiple means of engagement and representation make up a big part of the process. We know that no two students are alike, so teachers have the complicated task of avoiding cookie-cutter approaches and should regularly engage in reflective processes about the quality of their exchanges and the cultural congruity with their students. Among the questions that teachers can consider are the following:

What is a student's home language?

- Do I have multilingual learners whose first language is not English?
- If so, how am I supporting them?
- Do I have African American, Native American, or Asian American/Asian Pacific Islander students whose first language is English and for whom standard English is not native?
- How can I both honor and affirm these home languages while also explicitly teaching academic language in the interest of promoting access to rigorous content?

What does engagement look like?

- How does my tone of voice affect how students receive information?
- What does silence from students mean?
- Do I recognize that students can be engaged without speaking?
- Do I realize that I can have lots of talking and movement in my classroom, and that can mean powerful learning is taking place?

Are my students contextualized learners?

- Do my students do better when information is authentic and connected to real-world situations and activities?
- Do my students prefer hands-on activities and information?
- Am I providing concrete activities and applications for them to apply new knowledge and skills?

4. ENGAGEMENT

Student engagement is often described as meaningful student involvement in the learning process, with a heightened level of attention and focus on the given task or tasks. Education scholar Maisha Winn (2018) says that "engagement is the opportunity to practice justice and freedom while cultivating participatory democracy" (p. 21). Student engagement typically occurs when teachers take time to investigate who their students are and what their students like, and subsequently find ways to incorporate students' interests and identities into meaningful academic tasks. Promoting engagement requires a commitment to uprooting deficit beliefs about marginalized students to ensure that classroom materials, culture, and environment are culturally responsive, inclusive, and affirming of students' lives, histories, and backgrounds. Student engagement is a function of both the individual and the context and can vary in intensity and duration depending on circumstances (Fredricks et al., 2004). For example, a student may be engaged one semester but not so much the next; another student might enjoy one of their classes but be bored in others. Student engagement often correlates with student motivation and interest, which is one reason that engagement has been increasingly viewed as one of the keys to addressing problems such as low achievement, boredom, alienation, absenteeism, and high dropout rates. A growing body of research points to such engagement as particularly linked to favorable learning outcomes for minoritized student groups who have been placed at risk for academic failure (Borman & Overman, 2004). I recall teaching a group of high school students one year as part of my summer course at UCLA, and for the most part, most of the students were engaged and participating. However, one of the students, let's call her Candyce, frequently sat quietly without much participation. First it is important to know that just because students do not talk in class does not mean that they are not engaged. For many students, engagement can be their mental processing of class content. But for Candyce, even when I asked her about what we were discussing, it became apparent that she was not engaged, was retaining little information, and was in fact outright bored. In cases like these, I always think it is the job of the teacher to find ways to excite students like Candyce to want to participate, think, and learn. Many teachers do not agree with me and believe that students must come to class motivated to learn. I challenge that notion, and say what are we giving students to be motivated about? In Candyce's case, I noticed that whenever we discussed current events (e.g., abortion rights, capital punishment, immigration, climate change) she would always perk up, raise her hand, and participate verbally in class discussions with strong opinions about these topics. It became clear to me at that time that talking about issues of the day really interested Candyce. I would literally watch Candyce become a totally different student when we discussed current events. The takeaway is that engagement for students is often domain or subject matter specific. This comes back to my point about relevance. For many students, and Candyce shared this with me, they question the purpose of school, and they wonder why certain classes are so boring. And many students wonder why taking certain classes is required. Yet, Candyce, like many other students, became really captivated in class when she could think critically about things happening in the world. From that point forward, I always tried to bring in content about current issues into my classroom, and I was always amazed to see how engagement, interest, effort, and learning came alive.

The core ideals of student engagement and motivation center on responsive curriculum and pedagogy that allow students to make relevant connections to their own experiences and have positive relationships with the adults and peers in the learning environment. These same conditions that can lead to student engagement (and reduce student apathy) also contribute to a safe, positive, and creative school climate and culture. An increased focus on promoting engagement makes perfect sense, given the interrupted learning and consequent setbacks in academic achievement that many students endured due to COVID-19. Given the deleterious consequences of disengagement, teachers need to be equipped with effective strategies to ensure that all students are captivated by curricular content and eager to learn.

5. RIGOR

The word *rigor* is one of the more commonly used terms in education yet has various definitions. It is spoken about in high regard about something that we need in our schools, yet it remains elusive in far too many classrooms. Barbara R. Blackburn (2013) defines rigor as "creating an environment in which each student is expected to learn at high levels and is supported so that they can learn at high levels" (p. 13). Rigor does not mean giving students more, or excessively hard, work; nor does it mean busywork. When done best, rigorous instruction should have four components:

- **Critical thinking.** Are students analyzing information, asking questions, and creating work products that include unique ideas? Even young children can analyze, synthesize, and evaluate information that is centered on deeper and collaborative thoughts and ideas (Lindsay & Davis, 2013).

- **Applied problem solving.** Are students tackling realistic problems that can be solved in multiple ways, based on new information that they have acquired? Lessons must extend beyond classroom contexts so that students practice applying their critical thinking skills to real-world problems or to unfamiliar settings (Lombardi, 2007).

- **Productive struggle.** The National Council of Teachers of Mathematics (2023) defines productive struggle as "struggling at times with mathematics tasks but knowing that breakthroughs often emerge from confusion and struggle." Productive struggle entails communicating to students that making errors or failed attempts is "just another try." It also may entail reexamining our beliefs about scaffolding (e.g., do we scaffold and support not by giving answers but by asking probing questions, which requires students to think deeper and creatively?). Learning to persist when problem solving can also encourage students to explore and innovate, which can further strengthen students' problem-solving skills (Baker et al., 2020).

- **Interactivity.** Are students engaging with the teachers and their peers (small groups, think-pair-share, turn-and-talk), sharing their ideas, and getting feedback on them? Are there collaborative approaches for students to hear, learn, and process with their peers in interactive and supportive situations? (Pellegrino, 2014).

The ongoing efforts to make learning relational, relevant, and rigorous should always be at the forefront of educators' minds. As I have outlined throughout this book, the complexity of learning continues to increase as our student body becomes more diverse. To be clear, equity is about justice, and there is no more just act that teacher can engage in than providing students with a rigorous classroom environment every day. This is plain and simple the right thing to do and is one of the ways that educators can repair past harm students have incurred from less-than-ideal types of teaching. Teach students and teach them well; challenge their thinking, ask them to share their ideas and imagination, encourage them to take risks, and process their existing knowledge with new information they are introduced to in class. Teachers have the tall task of constantly thinking about how to reach, inspire, motivate, and challenge all students. To that end, the ability for teachers to constantly expand their instructional repertoire is essential. In Table 5.2, I lay out ways to think about classroom instruction through an equity lens as opposed to an approach that is steeped in traditional approaches that do not think about the sociopolitical and critical ways of engaging diverse learners.

TABLE 5.2 ● Classrooom Instruction Through an Equity vs. Traditional Lens

	EQUITY NOW	NO EQUITY
Beliefs About Students	High expectations	Unsure of student potential
Approach Toward Instruction	Daily rigorous instruction with cultural relevance	Busywork and no relevance
Pedagogy	Student-centered	Teacher-centered
Engagement	Explicit focus on skill development, synthesis, and applied problem solving	Exposure to content; disconnected from real-world issues and problems

LITERACY ACROSS THE CURRICULUM MATTERS

When thinking about instruction, engagement, and relevance for students, we must also consider the importance of literacy in the context of equity work. In short, we still struggle as a nation when it comes to having all students ready to learn, when reading proficiency is not where it should be, especially for our most vulnerable learners. Literacy proficiency is one of the biggest equity challenges that we face in schools today. Consider that a 2021 report from the National Assessment of Educational Progress (NAEP, 2022) discovered that more than 75% of fourth- and eighth-grade students from low-income backgrounds were not proficient in reading in 2019–2020. Moreover, the same report found that more than 75% of Native American, 77% of Latinx, and 79% of Black fourth- and eighth-grade public school students were not proficient in reading. So, while all subject matters are vital when it comes to student success and achieving equity, arguably there is no area more fundamental to students' academic success and life potential than literacy. More pointedly, reading is vital to closing equity gaps in schools and classrooms. Recently, we have seen increased attention placed on the question of the best approaches to teaching students how to read (Wyse & Bradbury, 2022). For the last few decades, balanced literacy has been deemed by many educators as the best approach. A balanced literacy approach is based on guided reading, asks students to look for contextual cues such as pictures in context, and then asks them to take informed guesses about what words might be. However, now a more robust data set is revealing that most students excel at learning how to read when they have explicit, consistent, systematic instruction in how letters represent sounds, culturally relevant content, and phonics instruction (Bowers, 2020; Tatum, 2021). An equity approach to literacy development would ensure that students receive instruction in phonemic awareness, relying not merely on clues, pictures, and guesses but on letters, sounds, and decoding. Once students have a sound phonemic awareness, then a focus on fluency is essential to reading, which can help students build robust vocabulary. Subsequently, students can then build comprehension strategies. More than half the states (30) in the country have passed legislation or policies mandating what is now referred to as a "science of reading" approach to early literacy, which has a profound impact on literacy development—in particular, that fluency, motivation, comprehension, instruction, knowledge development, language acquisition, and systematic phonics all play a vital role in developing proficient readers. Anything less than this for our most vulnerable students will do them a disservice. Literacy is justice. Teachers as thinkers and scholars are frequently looking to merge the best scientific research and evidence-based instructional approaches with the expertise and interests of their students. When it comes to literacy, many teachers believe that foundational literacy must be taught using an explicit and systematic approach to phonics. A strong phonetic approach is vital to build comprehension, vocabulary, language skills, and fluency, which are all equally important. Thus, teachers should look to personalize instruction based on each student's individual needs and circumstances, and providing high-quality, engaging reading materials is critical to effective early literacy instruction—along with a structured approach to phonics that prioritizes decoding and phonemic awareness. While there are many positive aspects of foundational reading skills being taught to emerging readers, some have questioned if such approaches are best for multilingual learners (O. García et al., 2017; Olsen, 2020). The concern that many multilingual learner experts raise is that a single approach or one-size-fits-all approach to teaching reading does not consider the need for many multilingual learners who may like and need the ability to express themselves through spoken language, conversation and their ability to understand what others are saying to them, and their vocabulary. Moreover, recognizing the connection between receptive and productive language and between reading, writing, and oracy is critical for many bilingual learners. Thus, while identifying words, sounds, and symbols is crucial for many emergent readers, discussion and the layers involved in hearing and listening to language are important as well and need to be part of a comprehensive literacy framework (Escamilla et al., 2022).

Thus, while identifying words, sounds, and symbols is crucial for many emergent readers, discussion and the layers involved in hearing and listening to language are important as well and need to be part of a comprehensive literacy framework

---

TEACHER REFLECTION AND EQUITY

A significant amount of information has been covered in this chapter that speaks to the way classroom-based equity can occur. To be clear, teachers must remember that there is no magic bullet and what works in one classroom may not be as effective in another. However, the key equity principles that should remain consistent across schools and classrooms are justice, recognition and repair of past harms, and belonging. Each of these principles must be centered within a framework of who our students are, being mindful of racial, gender, social class, and ability identities and status matters at all times. Educators must remain in continuous reflection about their beliefs, attitudes, and actions with respect to their students. Simply stated, our words, thoughts, and actions can have a profound impact on how students see themselves, their learning potential, their peers, and school in general. Hence, we must be sensitive to everything that we say and do in the course of our work, and one of the ways we can do that is through ongoing reflection about our work. T. C. Howard (2003) calls for "critical reflection" for teachers, a concept that, he states, "requires one to seek deeper levels of self-knowledge, and to acknowledge how one's own worldview can shape students' conceptions of self" (p. 198). Moreover, he offers key questions that teachers can ask themselves in this process:

- How frequently and what types of interactions did I have with individuals from racial backgrounds different from my own growing up?

- Who were the primary persons that helped to shape my perspectives of individuals from different racial groups? How were their opinions formed?

- Have I ever harbored prejudiced thoughts toward people from different racial backgrounds?

- If I do harbor prejudiced thoughts, what effects do such thoughts have on students who come from those backgrounds?

- Do I create negative profiles of individuals who come from different racial backgrounds?

Each of the preceding questions must be rooted in honesty and needs to be persistent about other student identities as well. While these questions are centered on racial identities, just as important is for teachers to think about students who come from different socioeconomic backgrounds, whose gender identities are different from those of teachers, and whose sexual orientation is different from theirs as well. Remember that two of the key principles of equity that have been stressed throughout this book are being inclusive and recognizing and repairing past harms. Students of color, students from low-income backgrounds, LGBTQ+ students, and gender-nonconforming students have been among the most excluded and harmed students in schools; therefore, intentional steps can and need to be taken to reverse past wrongs to these student groups.

Equity Now Chart

JUSTICE	REPAIR	BELONGING
• Recognizing and acting on the idea that powerful classroom instruction is the single most important way to enhance student learning	• Providing a curriculum and instruction that has rigor, depth, and complexity, even for struggling learners	• Using words of affirmation, encouraging productive struggle, and offering ongoing supports for struggling learners
• Holding high, yet reasonable, expectations for all students regardless of their race, ethnicity, language, gender identity, or socioeconomic status	• Not focusing excessively on discipline • Moving away from punishment to relationship building • Not remaining overly focused on students' areas of growth, but seeing their areas of strength	• Leader moving beyond "self-care" talk for teachers • Providing opportunities for school staff to get to know families in social settings • Banking relationship time at the start of the year • Getting to know students and their families and identifying similarities in interests, hobbies, and background between staff and students
• Ensuring that all students see themselves reflected somewhere in class curriculum (cultural responsiveness matters)	• Assessing classroom environments, and thinking about what pictures, posters, and people are most prominently displayed • Incorporating histories of people, neighborhoods, and stories most familiar to students' identities	• Remaining mindful of the obstacles that language learners can face in school • Offering constant support and encouragement • Partnering language learners with students who are multilingual to create a sense of connection

Questions for Teachers to Consider

1. What types of relationships do I have with my students?

2. What are strategies that I use to engage learners?

3. How relevant is my content to my students' identities?

4. How do I support my students as readers?

5. What do I reflect on most as a teacher?

6. How do I try to engage reluctant learners?

7. How rigorous is my instruction?

Recommendations for Readings and Resources

1. Muhammad, G. (2023). *Unearthing joy: A guide to culturally and historically responsive teaching and learning*. Scholastic.

2. Banks, J. A. (2016). *Cultural diversity and education* (6th ed.). Routledge.

3. Pollock, M. (2017). *Schooltalk: Rethinking what we say about and to students every day*. The New Press.

4. Turner Nash, K., Polite, C., & Polson, B. (2020). *Toward culturally sustaining teaching: Early childhood educators honor children with practices for equity and change*. Routledge.

5. Seda, P., & Brown, K. (2021). *Choosing to see: A framework for equity in the math classroom*. Burgess Consulting.

6. Bryan, N. (2021). *Toward a blackboycrit pedagogy: Black boys, male teachers, and early childhood classroom practices*. Routledge.

7. Gay, G. (2020). *Culturally responsive teaching* (3rd ed.). Teachers College Press.

CHAPTER 6

Parent/Caregiver Engagement and Equity

Sometimes it is easy to lose sight of a fundamental truth: Learning is not limited to what takes place inside the schoolhouse walls. Our brains are wired to learn throughout our lifetimes, and the learning that takes place in the early years of a child's life is significant. Learning takes place in schools, yes, but it also takes place in neighborhoods, in communities, and in our homes. From this, it stands to reason that families play a vital role in their children's education. In fact, a growing body of professional literature has examined the important role that parents/caregivers play in the educational outcomes of their children (P. A. Edwards, 2009, 2016). In short, parents and caregivers matter. Students' experiences and outcomes are vastly improved when they have access to caring and consistent adults at home. As professionals, we often are called upon to confront difficult questions—questions that call for some deep soul-searching. In this vein, ask yourself, *do we really want parents and caregivers involved in our schools? If so, what does that involvement look like?*

Much of the parent/caregiver literature on involvement has documented the important role that adults can play in enhancing the academic achievement and overall schooling experiences of their children through participation in school-sanctioned events such as Open House and Back-to-School Night, membership in organizations such as the parent–teacher organization or association (PTO/PTA), volunteering in classrooms, and the maintenance of a consistent level of involvement in students' academic progress such as the tracking of homework completion and accuracy (Bachman & Boone, 2022; Dugan, 2022). The implication is that responsibility for such forms of involvement rests entirely with parents/caregivers. In contrast, Jamila Dugan (2022) states that "true family partnership is concerned with building reciprocal relationships, shared responsibility, and joint work across settings, and focused on benefitting the learning and development of children" (p. 22). Education scholar Patricia A. Edwards (2016) defines parent involvement as "the participation in every facet of children's education and development through adulthood, accompanied by the recognition that parents are the primary influence in children's lives" (p. 8). Current language from the Every Student Succeeds Act (ESSA, 2015) provides a more comprehensive definition that puts a greater emphasis on schools when it states that

> local educational agencies (LEAs) conduct outreach to all parents and family members and implement programs, activities, and procedures for the involvement of parents and family members. Such programs, activities, and procedures shall be planned and implemented with meaningful consultation with parents of participating children. (Section 1116[a][1])

Parental involvement has garnered additional attention since the No Child Left Behind Act of 2001, which mandated parent participation as a condition for Title I funding. This particular caveat has been significant because issues of race and class come to the forefront when examining schools that receive Title I funding and the roles that schools play to solicit greater parent/caregiver involvement and participation. Issues of race and class are always at play when it comes to parent/caregiver engagement because in many communities of color, issues of mistrust with school officials have been ongoing for decades. In the case of many Black and Latinx families, schools have often been antagonistic toward families and students, where the best interests of students have not been served, thus causing acrimonious relationships at best. Students of color are far more likely than their more affluent and white peers to attend schools that receive Title I funding. Given the importance of parental involvement as well as the imperative for Title I schools to create opportunities for such involvement, I have chosen to devote a full chapter on identifying an equity-focused approach to parent/caregiver participation in schools. Rather than viewing such participation as "nice to have," equity-focused schools see family–school engagement as a *must* for student success and take active steps to create the type of ecosystem that parents/caregivers feel welcome to be part of. With this in mind, I focus on an approach that recognizes the diversity of families as well as the variety of ways of participating in schools beyond the traditional opportunities such as PTA meetings. Throughout this investigation, I ask readers to return to the question posed earlier: Do you really want such participation?

You may be asking yourself why I keep doubling down on this question. In many of my professional learning sessions with teachers, one of the most common questions I hear from teachers is, "Well, what about the parents? Where are they?" This is often followed by judgmental statements along the lines of "Parents need to do their job better so that I can do mine better!" Needless to say, I have encountered a lot of parent blaming in schools in the form of commentary that contends that if parents/caregivers only did their jobs, teaching would be a much easier endeavor. I will address that issue in this chapter. There is also another side of the "blame parents" coin, which is some parents/caregivers are overly involved in the manner that many refer to as helicopter parents. This form of "participation" includes overseeing, critiquing, second-guessing, and challenging everything that teachers attempt to do. I will address this matter as well in this chapter.

THE BARRIERS TO PARTICIPATION

Before concluding that there is something wrong with the parents/caregivers, let's consider the reasons why many do not participate in school-sanctioned activities in the first place. I want to stress that most parents/caregivers who do not participate in school-sanctioned activities are every bit as concerned about their children's education as those who do. Hence, the lack of visibility of parents/caregivers should not be seen as a lack of concern or indifference toward a student's education. To the contrary, overwhelmingly most parents/caregivers are doing their absolute best to help their students succeed. But what cannot be underestimated is the multitude of reasons why parents/caregivers do not attend school-sanctioned events. Remember, the goal of equity is to reach people where they are, and this includes parents and caregivers. To that end, here are some of the reasons that parents/caregivers may not attend school-sanctioned events:

- Many adults had less-than-ideal experiences with schools when they were students and have little or no desire to be present in schools.

- Many parents/caregivers never saw their parents/caregivers attend school-sanctioned events; therefore, they may think it is not necessary.

- Many parents/caregivers do not trust schools or school personnel.

- Many parents/caregivers believe the job of educating students is solely the job of school.

- Many parents/caregivers cannot attend school-sanctioned events due to work schedules (or multiple jobs) that do not allow them to attend.

- Some parents/caregivers cannot attend school-sanctioned events because of lack of caregiving for younger children.

- Some parents/caregivers cannot attend school-sanctioned events because of lack of transportation.

- Some parents/caregivers believe that all school matters are to be handled and managed by their children and relinquish all decision making to students (more common for secondary than elementary students).

I want to stress that most parents/caregivers who do not participate in school-sanctioned activities are every bit as concerned about their children's education as those who do. Hence, the lack of visibility of parents/caregivers should not be seen as a lack of concern or indifference toward a student's education.

Given these as well as other barriers to parental participation, the need for schools and educators to adopt equity-centered approaches "beyond the bake sale" (Grossman, 2012) that elicit family participation is clear. In this context, equity-centered approaches envision parents and caregivers to be engaged as active partners with schools. Education scholar Angela Cabrese Barton and her colleagues (2004), who coined the term *Ecologies of Parental Engagement* (EPE), intentionally use the word *engagement* rather than *involvement* to reflect a more authentic relationship between parents/caregivers and schools. In an EPE framework, parent engagement is situated as a relational phenomenon, built on trust, reciprocity, and respect, that relies on authentic communication. Frameworks for family and caregiver engagement assume that one of the reasons parents/caregivers do not participate at the school site can be attributed to the perception of differences in practices and beliefs held by the parents and the school. Moreover, as stated previously, many parents/caregivers may have had less-than-ideal experiences when they were in schools, and thus school is not seen as a welcoming or hospitable place for them, especially for adults who grew up in poverty or who come from racially, culturally, and linguistically diverse backgrounds. To shift the paradigm, "parent engagement" is seen as a dynamic, interactive process in which parents draw on multiple experiences and resources to define their interactions with schools and among school actors. Based on this definition of parent/caregiver roles comes power to impact decisions made on behalf of their children. This conceptualization is important to note when variables such as race, language, and class are introduced to the discourse. Many working-class parents and parents of color who suffered negative school experiences carry beliefs that influence how they define their own terms of involvement or engagement as parents and caregivers. Currently, parents/caregivers' roles and involvement in schools have been understood in terms of "what they do" and how that fits or does not fit with the goals of the school. Frequently, this approach to understanding parent involvement has relied upon the deficit model, especially in discussions of parent involvement in high-poverty communities (Gutman & McLoyd, 2000). To further underscore the point about parent/caregiver engagement, Mapp and Bergman (2021) offer an important analysis of what they refer to as equity-focused, transformative collaborations to family engagement. They offer the following questions for schools to ask when it comes to engaging parents/caregivers:

1. What is the range of beliefs educators hold about the purposes of our school's current family engagement practices?

2. What is the range of beliefs families hold about the purposes of our school's current family engagement practices?

3. Are our current identified purposes for engaging families intended to make schooling more equitable or to transform it in any way?

The work of equity-informed school–family partnerships must also operate from an asset-based perspective where school personnel see families, parents, and caregivers as possessing essential knowledge about how to best support their children. One of the key ideas stressed throughout this book is to recognize and repair past harm. Many parents/caregivers have experienced multiple generations of harm by way of exclusion of them as students and as parents. Schools have played a role in that harm and can play a role in repairing that harm. Asset-based approaches also recognize the types of capital that parents and caregivers possess, which are vital to problem solving, addressing complex situations, and advocating for their students. I am reminded of a school that I worked with in Ohio where the principal was determined to find ways for her staff to see the various types of assets that parents/caregivers possess that are often not seen by schools. She asked her staff to ask parents/caregivers to conduct a "Day in the Life/Week" activity, where they provided an overview of their tasks on a given day. In addition, the activity sheet asked for parents/caregivers to provide their duties and responsibilities at work. A number of educators were surprised to learn that many of the parents/caregivers in this low-income school were supervisors or case managers and were responsible for significant inventory counts of products at work. Many oversaw personnel, dealt with conflict resolution matters, and had levels of responsibility that educators did not know about. Moreover, the staff were surprised to learn how many parents/caregivers were caregivers for their parents, grandparents, and other family members for whom they handled affairs ranging from medication and social services appointments to power of attorney and financial matters. Therefore, schools must go beyond the typical parent volunteer chaperoning field trips, attending open houses, and participating in back-to-school events and recognize the complexity of the lives of most parents/caregivers. A more robust level of engagement invites parents/caregivers to play a more participatory role in how schools operate, seeks their input in crucial decision making, and truly sees them as equal partners in the education of students. Areas in which schools should consider parent engagement include the following:

- Budget decision making (schoolwide spending allocations)
- Input on staff and teacher hiring
- Input on school- and districtwide discipline policies
- Roles in schoolwide assemblies and extracurricular events
- Curricular/textbook adoption and decision making
- Regular access to principals
- Parents/caregivers as guest speakers/community experts

Moreover, just as we ask educators to rethink preconceived notions about students and who they are, the same considerations should be given to parents/caregivers. What we do not know about our students' home lives should not be subjected to stereotyping or biased perceptions that are not rooted in reality. Thus, to that end, we need to make a conscious effort to resist commonly held tropes about parents/caregivers as in the following examples:

- Not seeing parents/caregivers at school-sanctioned events does not mean they are not involved with or do not care about their students' education.

- Not all parents/caregivers in low-income communities are uneducated. Many have college degrees, and many have some college experience.

- Parents/caregivers in many low-income communities are often among the hardest-working people.

- Not all low-income families are single-parent households.

- Not all immigrant families are lacking in navigational and social capital.

- Parents/caregivers of students with disabilities are keenly aware of the needs of their students.

- Not all affluent households have engaged parents/caregivers.

- Most parents/caregivers of color are not colorblind.

- Parents/caregivers' anger with schools is often rooted in a deep-seated belief about how injustice has affected their students.

Finally, I want to strongly state that *family disposition is more important than family composition*. What this essentially means is that the makeup of a family does not always equate to family support. I have seen students come from two-parent households, in highly affluent neighborhoods, where student support is absent and the household is highly dysfunctional, leaving a lot to be desired about the social, emotional, and academic well-being of the children. Conversely, I have witnessed households being led by a single grandparent in a low-income community that are highly functional, where students' academic achievement is a high priority and the lines of communication and support between home and school are strong, which produces favorable outcomes for the students. In short, educators must work hard to avoid placing families and caregivers in a box based on demographic characteristics that do not align with the realities of families. To restate the point, *family disposition is more important than family composition*.

The makeup of a family does not always equate to family support.

When implementing an engagement-based framework, I strongly encourage faculty and staff members to listen to parents/caregivers, learn from them, suspend judgment about them, and commit themselves to doing the important (and at times hard) work of becoming partners in educating students. Parents/caregivers are our students' first teachers; thus, they possess a tremendous amount of knowledge about who our students are, what they can do, their areas of growth, and what can be done to spark learning. Again, equity-focused schools see family–school engagement as a must for student success. One of the approaches that many schools use is to send home surveys during the first weeks of school so that parents/caregivers can share more about their children/students. Among the questions that surveys can include are these:

- When does your child learn best?
- What are three words that best describe your child?
- What about your home do you think the school should know?
- What gets your child really frustrated?
- What is something that is misunderstood about your child?
- What is the best way to contact you as a parent/caregiver?
- What are your child's biggest strengths as a learner?
- What are the areas of growth for your child?
- What is something that is important for the school to know about your child?

A parent/caregiver engagement approach also rests on the idea that not all students are raised by their biological parents. An asset-based approach sees, understands, and affirms the diversity of family arrangements that have been common for years in our nation. For this reason, I intentionally use the terms *parents* and *caregivers* because the makeup of families is diverse in many ways, and an equity-centered approach recognizes and celebrates this fact. As of 2019, there were 423,997 children placed in the foster system within the United States (U.S. Department of Health and Human Services, 2020), and half will never reunite with their biological families. There are approximately 2.5 million children raised by grandparents (U.S. Census Bureau, 2021), as well as countless other students raised by older siblings, aunts, uncles, cousins, and family friends. To be clear, an asset-based, equity-centered perspective recognizes that these caregivers provide the same type of love, safety, shelter, food, security, attachment, and care to youth in ways that are akin to what biological parents provide. These students should never be led to feel less about their family structure because it is different than the traditional nuclear family arrangement. The same can be said for students whose families are comprised of same-sex couples and blended families. Recently, several protests have erupted across the country with protestors contending that celebrations such as Pride Month, LGBTQ+ recognition, and family diversity should not be celebrated at schools. In short, these messages are deeply divisive and destructive because they essentially are telling students that their families, if they include same-sex parents, do not matter, should not be seen, and are less important than heterosexual families. Honoring and recognizing family diversity is important. One of the goals of equity is to recognize harm when it affects students and their families. School staff need to be bold to stand up for family diversity and speak out against any effort to minimize, disrespect, or render invisible loving and caring adults who are raising children. Remaining silent on these matters, in many ways, is a form of complicity. Students are watching and listening to where teachers stand during these moments of hostility toward certain people and groups. It is in these moments where students will assess if teachers are allies and supporters of them and their families or if they are part of the problem. Teacher–student relationships are forged or broken during moments of conflict. Being an equity-minded educator requires individuals to do the right thing where matters of children and their families are concerned. It is not always popular, but it is the right thing to do. As I mentioned at the outset of this chapter, schools say that they want parents involved, but do they really want *all* parents involved? In an equity-based framework, schools and districts must double down to let students, staff, and the wider community know that all families matter and that any form of hatred, exclusion, or violence toward LGBTQ+ families and individuals will not be tolerated on any level.

WHEN PARENTS/CAREGIVERS ARE TOO INVOLVED

Is there such a thing as overinvolvement in a child's formal education? In keeping with our assets lens, consider the following: Parents/caregivers who might be perceived as overinvolved are, more often than not, motivated by deep-seated love, care, and desire to see their child(ren) get the best education possible. Rather than succumbing to the "helicopter mom" trope, shouldn't we see these parents/caregivers as conveying a genuine desire to be engaged in their children's learning? Again, we want parents involved, but do we really want them all involved, or only the ones who participate the way that we want them to participate? Engagement can take multiple forms from being present and volunteering in schools to serving on schoolwide committees, engaging in fundraising efforts, and being an active participant at home by monitoring a student's homework, class assignments, and grades. Moreover, there has been a wealth of evidence that consistently talking to their children daily about school and what they are learning, their homework and school assignments, peers, and extracurricular activities is just as important (if not more) for parents/caregivers as attending school-sanctioned events (Winthrop et al., 2022). So, for the parents who are overly involved, we must do our best to hear their concerns, affirm their worry and commitment for their students' well-being and achievement, and then co-construct a way to help achieve those goals. This can be done by defining what tasks and activities can be done at home that can complement and support the tasks and activities that the teacher will do at school. While many teachers may feel as if parents/caregivers are questioning their abilities to do their jobs, remember the concern comes from a place of wanting the best for the student. If such queries become too excessive, a one-on-one conversation may be warranted to let the parent/caregiver know that the teacher is doing everything in their power to ensure success, and to ask for space to do their jobs. If such a step does not work, then perhaps a meeting with an administrator will be helpful. Moreover, some schools take the step of requiring parents who want to be active in schools to play a role in classrooms other than their children's classroom to ensure that teachers are not being second-guessed or favoritism is not being shown to the child of the parent volunteering in a classroom. In Table 6.1, I highlight some of the distinctions between traditional parent involvement and equity-centered parent/caregiver/family engagement.

TABLE 6.1 ● Traditional Parent Involvement vs. Equity-Centered Parent/Caregiver/Family Engagement

TRADITIONAL PARENT INVOLVEMENT	EQUITY-CENTERED PARENT/ CAREGIVER/FAMILY ENGAGEMENT
Back-to-School Night	Introductory letters, webinars, and e-blasts communicating with families
Open House	Open access to schools at any time
Parent–Teacher Conference	Frequent and ongoing communication via email, text, or Zoom phone call
Parent Volunteer	Parent contribution list (tissue/paper towels, hand sanitizer, sticky notes, classroom supplies, etc.)
Parent–Teacher Association/ Organization; Parent Advisory Councils	School Site Council/School Governance Organization, School Budget Committee, Search Committee

PARENTS/CAREGIVERS AND SCHOOL BOARD PROTESTS: A MOVEMENT OR A MOMENT?

In the summer of 2020, we witnessed the largest social protest ever, demanding that Black Lives Matter in response to the deaths of George Floyd and Breonna Taylor. The unfortunate deaths led to significant movements for social change, including a call to do better around meeting the needs of Black students and other racially marginalized students. While such efforts would appear to be benevolent and much needed in schools, the backlash that has surfaced in schools and districts, in response, has been rapid and extreme. I want to be clear that schools need to recognize the highly political terrain that we are living through at this time. Some of the fiercest backlash has been in response to what has been characterized as an overreach of a focus on race, racism, sexual orientation, and gender identity in school curriculum. Over the past few years, at least 44 states have either introduced or passed legislation banning the teaching of critical race theory (CRT) or discussions around race and racism in schools. CRT is a theory originated by legal scholars to examine how racism has intersected with the law and American institutions. Parents/caregivers have shown up en masse at school board meetings, angry, threatening, and mobilizing around the elimination of CRT, despite the fact that there is little evidence that it is even being taught in PK–12 schools. It should not be lost that many of these protestors do not live in the vicinity of the districts that they were protesting, but were often serving as provocateurs. One can only surmise why such a response has become a staple nationwide in the absence of any evidence that CRT is even being taught in schools. So why the furor? Plain and simple, it is what some have called our country's "third rail," race. We have a race problem, but we do not want to talk about it, and we do not want our children to learn about it. James Baldwin once stated that "Not everything that is faced can be changed, but nothing can be changed until it is faced." Why are we not willing to face the role that race has always played in our society? As we become more racially diverse as a nation, we consistently choose to ignore our demographic realities. At this precarious moment in time, it is especially vital for schools to engage families, parents, and caregivers about what is, and is not, being taught in schools. Moreover, parents/caregivers need to recognize that any discussion of U.S. history includes discussions around the mistreatment of Indigenous populations, the institution of slavery, Jim Crow, racial segregation, Japanese internment, redlining, and many other ugly episodes of U.S. history. Silencing teachers from engaging in conversations about these aspects of U.S. history is a deliberate effort to conceal students from the full story of our nation. Much of the resistance to discussions around race and LGBTQ+ experiences has led to a disturbing trend of what many consider to be censorship of teachers or what PEN America—an organization dedicated to protecting free expression—calls "Educational Gag Orders." In 2022, PEN America issued a report titled *Banned in the USA: Rising School Book Bans Threaten Free Expression and Students' First Amendment Rights*, which covered the first nine months of the school year (July 2021 to March 2022). This report helped shed light on the role of organized efforts to drive many of the bans. The report highlighted that

- from July 2021 to June 2022, PEN America's Index of School Book Bans lists 2,532 instances of individual books being banned, affecting 1,648 unique book titles; and

- the 1,648 titles are by 1,261 different authors, 290 illustrators, and 18 translators, impacting the literary, scholarly, and creative work of 1,553 people altogether.

As we become more racially diverse as a nation, we consistently choose to ignore our demographic realities. At this precarious moment in time, it is especially vital for schools to engage families, parents, and caregivers about what is, and is not, being taught in schools.

Some of the additional findings from PEN America also revealed that among the 1,648 unique banned book titles in the Index,

- 674 banned book titles (41%) explicitly address LGBTQ+ themes or have protagonists or prominent secondary characters who are LGBTQ+ (this includes a specific subset of titles for transgender characters or stories— 145 titles, or 9%);

- 659 banned book titles (40%) contain protagonists or prominent secondary characters of color; and

- 338 banned book titles (21%) directly address issues of race and racism.

To be clear, issues around race, racism, and LGBTQ+ themes are raising levels of concern for many adults nationwide. Book bans that focus on removing titles that address race, racism, sexual orientation, and gender identity are frequently framed as matters of "parental rights." I would argue that it is important for parents/caregivers to understand that diversity of all types exists in our society, and students who are comfortable interacting with people from diverse backgrounds will be at an advantage in an increasingly diverse society. While parents may feel that shielding their children from some of the ugly episodes in American history is the right thing to do, the occurrence of such episodes, including discrimination, prejudice, hate, violence, and even murder, simply cannot be erased. Think of it this way: The more students learn about history, the less likely they are to repeat it. Educators must impress upon parents/caregivers that schools can go a long way toward reducing prejudice, eliminating stereotypes, and rooting out hate by adopting curriculum, literature, and assignments that require students to engage in age-appropriate and thoughtful dialogue, inquiry, and multiple perspective taking. The bottom line is that banning books is not a solution to avoid topics that are the reality for many, but uncomfortable for some. Moreover, my experience has been that the more things that we try to keep from students, the more that many will make efforts to find out about those topics. After all, curiosity is a natural, human trait!

Finally, it is always important that these discussions be age appropriate, and in some cases, it may be helpful for teachers to notify parents/caregivers about topics that will be discussed in advance. I know one of my eye-opening moments occurred years ago when I was a first-grade teacher, and we discussed our families. What would appear to be an innocent conversation took an unexpected turn when a student shared with the class that she had "two mommies." What could have been an awkward moment was avoided when I told the class that it is okay for some people to have two moms or two dads, after a student told the student that she could not have two mommies. Remember, a key pillar to equity is belonging, and no student deserves to be told that their family is not legitimate, not as loving, or not as important as anyone else's. It is vital for schools to honor students' family composition, as well as students' identities. Many parents/caregivers may not understand or agree with such stances, but again, schools must make it clear that absolutely no type of discrimination, mistreatment, or exclusion of any student because of their identities or family structure will be tolerated. This is a core pillar upon which equity rests. Upon having the discussion around family diversity, I was shocked to find an irate parent waiting for me at my classroom door the following day. This mom shared that her son told her that I told the students that it was okay to have two moms, which she fervently disagreed with, she stated. Moreover, this mom proceeded to tell me quite angrily that it was not my place to "promote homosexuality to first graders." After hearing out the mother in shock and dismay, I conveyed to her what was discussed the previous day, and that in no way was I "promoting homosexuality," but that I was and will always continue to honor family diversity and the humanity and equality of same-sex couples. My retort fell on deaf ears and resulted in this mother telling me that she would be having her son removed from my class because did not like my "agenda." I share this story to help educators know that a big part of equity is doing the right thing in the face of hostility and untruth. I have thought about that exchange over the years and have wondered what, if anything, I would have said or done differently in that situation, and the answer remains the same: nothing!

Remember, a key pillar to equity is belonging, and no student deserves to be told that their family is not legitimate, not as loving, or not as important as anyone else's. It is vital for schools to honor students' family composition, as well as students' identities.

I want to reiterate that parent/caregiver participation can and *should* be a focal point in school reform. However, that reform must be mindful of the experiences and backgrounds of *all* students. Again, the research is clear: When parents/caregivers are involved in their children's formal education, math and reading scores increase, truancy rates and disciplinary issues decrease, and college success is more likely (Pondiscio, 2022). "One-way involvement" is characterized in many schools by the idea of "send me parents, but not *all* parents"—meaning that schools value parents who will comply with school rules, will never challenge practices or certain teachers, will not hover over schools, and will not constantly question teachers' and leaders' decisions. In many ways, schools want rubber-stamp parents—parents who will not question, challenge, or disrupt what they see as harmful practice to their children or other people's children. They essentially rubber-stamp everything that is happening at the school. The stance of not wanting all parents involved is often punitive toward parents who do not fit traditional models of parental participation and those who are critical of school policies and practices. Parents/caregivers are an afterthought until there is a problem—typically with their child. Then parents/caregivers are ushered into the conversation as a centerpiece for blame, and such approaches plant seeds of anger, mistrust, and resistance that many parents/caregivers have about schools and school personnel.

RELATIONAL TRUST

Teachers can play a foundational role in building healthy parent/caregiver–school partnerships, since they are often the initial point of contact for families. As the "face" of the school or classroom, their initial goal should be establishing relational trust, which recognizes the family/caregivers' humanity, honors their differences, and builds bonds based on equal status. In doing so, teachers apply an assets-based mindset by recognizing that the adults are doing their best to raise and support students despite life challenges and obstacles. The idea of relational trust is built on the idea that practices, policies, and pedagogies are done at the school that have the best interest of students in mind.

Bryk et al. (2010) describe the relational trust they observed as

> forged in day-to-day social exchanges. Through their actions, school participants articulate their sense of obligation toward others, and others in turn reciprocated. Trust grows over time through exchanges in which the expectation held by others are validated by actions. (p. 139)

Thus, relational trust is built through daily interactions and shared accountabilities and requires cultural humility and vulnerability of all parties. Moreover, relational trust asks both parties to consider new practices and different roles when it comes to supporting students' educational experiences and outcomes. Practices can include the following:

- **Authentic respect**—Listening and learning about the basic, day-to-day realities of youth and their families, and not passing judgement on these realities

- **Care**—Conveying an authentic sense of concern and well-being for others in a manner that is received and felt by the receiver

- **Compassion**—Being empathetic when learning about parents/caregivers' situations and seeing the best in them despite what may be challenges and difficulties

- **Cultural humility**—Recognizing that cultural differences and complexities exist across groups and knowing that we do not always know or understand how people navigate life, child-rearing, problem solving, and communication styles

Furthermore, relational trust is built through day-to-day social exchanges in a school community that are centered on trust, reciprocity, respect, and reflexivity, which can include some of the following characteristics:

- **Respect**—Understanding that there is a level of decency, courtesy, and consideration that all parties are given, which requires listening to and valuing others' opinions

- **Consistency**—The ability to reliably do what is asked over a period of time, or the act of being dependable and reliable in a persistent fashion
- **Regard for others**—An empathy-oriented approach that asks individuals to extend themselves beyond what their role might be
- **Reliability**—Ability to be depended on for delivery of support, service, or ask
- **Competence**—The ability to carry out given tasks with success
- **Integrity**—Consistency between what a person says and what one does

Establishing relational trust also connects to a central component of our equity framework—repairing past harms. As previously stated, many parents/caregivers have fractured relationships with schools that date back to their youth, wherein they experienced less-than-ideal circumstances between their own parents/caregivers and the schools they attended. As adults, they have retained those painful memories and frequently convey to their own children the mistrust, harm, and deep animosity that they have toward schools and school personnel. In many ways for some parents/caregivers, coming back to schools is akin to coming back to the scene of the crime. The mere presence of being in schools, seeing teachers, and hearing about punitive practices can be a trigger for adults who experienced deep hurt when they were younger. Hence, educators have important work to do in repairing broken relationships, instilling trust, and addressing harm that they most likely were not directly responsible for. It is a tall order and takes time, but it is a process that our students and their families deserve.

LEADERS MATTER TOO

School leaders play an important role in setting expectations for school personnel in the interest of establishing healthy dynamics between schools and homes. To that end, leaders must lead by example here. The way school leaders are accessible, cordial, respectful, and engaging with parents/caregivers sends a message to the school community that families matter. School leaders can take practical steps to make sure that the ideals of justice, recognizing and repairing harm, and inclusivity are in place when interacting with families. Equity-minded leaders take the time and effort to get to know families, remember names, and ask about family members' backgrounds and interests. Families need to know that they are welcomed in the school community. Leaders play a major role in creating the sense of belonging that is essential to creating equitable schools. If the school leader has established a sound relationship with the parent/caregiver, the connection with the student can soon follow. Leaders need to be present in the mornings when the school day starts, greeting families/parents/caregivers, engaging students, talking to the bus drivers, and having an overall presence that says that students' safe arrival matters, that they are in our care, and that we will do well by them. School leaders must also know that the job of connecting to parents/caregivers also means knowing and connecting to the communities where they live. Leaders who can be present and frequent local businesses, local parks, after-school programs, and sporting events, and even be a member of the local church, mosque, or synagogue, can also make valuable connections. But the act of being present must also be authentic, meaning that the leader is committed to do all that can be done to make the school the best it can be for every student. This commitment is driven not only by a moral imperative but also in the interest of sustainability and, frankly, self-preservation. In our current environment, parents/caregivers have more choices of schools than ever before including charter, magnet, private, independent, and parochial schools. The stakes are high for public schools, and it behooves leaders to also become marketers or promoters for their schools. In this case, their "clients" are the parents/caregivers who have the final say in where their children attend school. While this role isn't necessarily one that building principals signed up for, they should be prepared to offer a realistic message of what families and students can experience at their school. Some questions to help shape the content of such messaging follow:

- Is there a particular focus on arts, language, math/science, or college readiness?
- Does our school have teachers with experience and expertise that sets it apart?
- How does our school support multilingual students?
- Will our students have access to dual-language instruction?
- Do we have a particular expertise around science, technology, engineering, and mathematics (STEM) that other schools do not?
- Does our school have an emphasis on computer science that is the best in the city or district?
- How does our school support students with special needs?
- Are students college and career ready when they graduate from our school?

- What types of extracurricular activities are available for our students?

- How is safety assured for our students?

- Does our school offer culturally relevant and sustaining practices across grade levels and subject matters?

- How does our school show support for LGBTQ+ students, staff, and families?

- How does our school address matters tied to anti-Blackness and other forms of racial discrimination and hate?

- What types of restorative practices are used in lieu of excessive punishment and discipline?

- Does our focus on exploration and environment provide students a well-rounded education?

In short, leaders have to be able to communicate to the larger community why parents/caregivers should choose their school over other available options. In addition to the questions raised earlier, leaders should think about their school motto, the quality of their staff, the way educators demonstrate concern and care for all students, and a firm and sincere commitment to helping students develop academically, socially, emotionally, and culturally. In this moment, parents/caregivers are empowered (justifiably so) with the ability to speak with their feet and disenroll students if they are unsatisfied, knowing that there can be more viable options within a given community. Therefore, it is vital now for school leaders to recruit and retain families, and the best way to do that is to offer high-quality schools that will provide safety, security, inclusivity, and sustained learning.

Leaders can prioritize the formation of family–school partnerships by providing professional learning on strategies that staff can use to foster better relationships with parents and caregivers. In some instances, schools have parent centers on the school campus so that a parent liaison can be the point person to help connect other parents and caregivers to share essential information about the school. A more transformative approach can include having virtual centers that could allow more parents/caregivers to participate. We learned during the pandemic that Zoom meetings work for many parents/caregivers who might not otherwise have the opportunity to participate. Some schools experimented with webinars and other recorded messages to help families feel connected to schools even if they could not have face-to-face contact. Leaders can reinforce the importance of recognizing and repairing harm by impressing upon staff that parents/caregivers may not always show up in the way and at the times that we want them to show up, but they are still showing up on their terms and on their own time. Such awareness can be amplified by cultivating an understanding of why some parents/caregivers are upset, disengaged, tardy, or unwilling to accept responsibility for students' behaviors or outcomes. Recognizing past harm for parents/caregivers may mean understanding that the effects of racism, sexism, misogyny, homophobia, chronic poverty, antisemitism, Islamophobia, and other isms continue to influence how parents/caregivers' parent, how they raise their children, how they see schools, and the way they show up for their children. Part of recognizing and repairing past harms is showing cultural humility and an understanding of the harm, injury, and trauma that many adults live with every day in their efforts to rear families. While leaders are not always able to repair those harms, an acknowledgement (when known) of people's stories, struggles, and setbacks is a first step in the right direction. Lastly, exhibiting the human decency, respect, positive regard, and empathy that all people want, need, and deserve can go a long way to building healthy parent/caregiver–school relationships.

> *Part of recognizing and repairing past harms is showing cultural humility and an understanding of the harm, injury, and trauma that many adults live with every day in their efforts to rear families.*

Equity Now Chart

JUSTICE	REPAIR	BELONGING
• Engaging parents/caregivers on an ongoing basis in the teaching, learning, and overall development of students	• Acknowledging that the overwhelming number of parents/caregivers are doing the absolute best to raise and support their children, given their circumstances • Not judging or assessing students based on "what my parents did"	• Engaging in constant communication • Providing compliments to parents/caregivers about positive attributes of their student • Seeking engagement over involvement • Identifying multiple ways for parents/caregivers to participate in school functions

(Continued)

(Continued)

JUSTICE	REPAIR	BELONGING
• Recognizing the diversity of families • Honoring same-sex parents, single parents, foster parents, and grandparents as primary caregivers in the same way that two-parent heterosexual families are seen and honored	• Talking and teaching about family diversity • Recognizing that family disposition is more vital than family composition • Speaking out against any language, comments, or jokes that criticize same-sex parents, foster parents, or students being raised in "nontraditional" households	• Regularly inviting parents/caregivers into the school and classroom if they are interested and able • Having grandparents' days at schools, feasting with families in schools, and encouraging parents/caregivers to share ideas about how to garner greater engagement for families
• Having constant communication in multiple formats (email, text messages, websites, paper posts) to families about what is happening in schools and encouraging their participation • Seeing parents/caregivers as partners in the education of students	• Conducting informative workshops on child development for parents/caregivers of elementary school students • Sharing valuable resources, tools, and reading materials • Collaborating with community partners and organizations on specialized programs	• Regularly communicating with families through surveys to acquire feedback, ideas, and suggestions • Recognizing and appreciating families' contributions and support • Consistently asking for parent/caregiver input on how schools can serve their students better
• Recognizing that trust matters when it comes to families • Speaking up and standing up for families in the midst of attacks from those who want topics around race, racism, sexual orientation, and gender identity excluded from schools	• Showing up at board meetings to show support for diverse families • Organizing and partnering with parents/caregivers to demonstrate care and concern for those who feel silenced and excluded	• Building partnerships that seek parents/caregivers' ideas about how to talk across differences with families who have different beliefs and thoughts about current issues • Leaders being present and accessible • Knowing students and their parents/caregivers by name

Questions Regarding Parents/Caregivers

1. How does our school invite parents/caregivers to engage in schools?

2. How would I describe my relationship with most parents/caregivers?

3. How do I respond to parents/caregivers who are not engaged?

4. How do I handle matters that parents/caregivers think should not be discussed around race and LGBTQ+ matters?

5. How do I respond to parents/caregivers who are too involved?

6. How do I typically communicate with most of my parents/caregivers?

7. What were my parents/caregivers' involvement in schools when I was young?

Recommendations for Reading and Resources

1. Edwards, P. A. (2016). *New ways to engage parents: Strategies and tools for teachers and leaders, K–12*. Teachers College Press.

2. Mapp, K. L., & Bergman, E. (2021). *Embracing a new normal: Toward a more liberatory approach to family engagement*. Carnegie Corporation.

3. Ishimaru, A. M. (2020). *Just schools: Building equitable collaborations with families and communities*. Teachers College Press.

4. Reynolds, R., & Howard, T. C. (2013). Chapter 20. Sharing responsibility: A case for real parent-school partnerships. In M. B. Katz & M. Rose (Eds.), *Public education under siege* (pp. 201–206). University of Pennsylvania Press. https://doi.org/10.9783/9780812208320.201

5. McCarthy Foubert, J. L. (2022). *Reckoning with racism in family–school partnerships: Centering Black parents' school engagement*. Teachers College Press.

6. Cuevas, S. (2021). *Apoyo sacrificial, sacrificial support: How undocumented Latinx parents get their children to college*. Teachers College Press.

7. Morgan, N. S. (2017). *Engaging families in schools: Practical strategies to improve parental involvement*. Routledge.

CHAPTER 7

Data and Equity

Ask any seasoned educator how much schools have changed since they first entered the profession. Chances are, they will tell you that they have changed a great deal and not only because of changing student demographics. As noted in previous chapters, the needs of today's students are vast and complex, and what may have "worked" in classrooms during the 1980s may no longer be effective in our present reality. At the same time, an equally important shift in American society is our full-blown transition to an information age.

For schools, this shift has been characterized by increased availability of multiple forms of data. In brief, we no longer need to guess or surmise what is happening in our schools; consequently, our decisions and actions should be informed by our data. And this includes the decisions we make and actions we take in pursuit of more equitable classrooms and schools.

The concept of teacher as researcher is not new. Even before the widespread availability of "big data," teachers have been called upon to collect, organize, analyze, and evaluate data from their students and classrooms on a minute-by-minute basis every day. In many ways, teachers are the ultimate researchers because from the start of the day to the end, good practice is centered on watching, observing, listening, questioning, interpreting, documenting, describing, evaluating, and deciphering data from all the students that they teach. In so many ways, teachers are data miners.

Remember the goal of equity is creating conditions in which each child receives what they need to develop to their full academic and social potential. Equity is not a destination, but a journey that we are constantly in pursuit of attaining. Equity is centered on an approach with a commitment to being fair, recognizing and repairing past harms, and being inclusive. So how do our data help us to reach those aims?

FORMS OF DATA

In this moment, education professionals have a dizzying array of data from which to draw. How does one begin to navigate such complexity? To begin, it is vital to recognize that data can come in many forms. Data can come in the form of texts, documents, observations, anecdotes, emails, reports, comments, body language, stories, figures, images, words, numbers, graphs, charts, or symbols. For example, data might include the more traditional metrics such as students' grades, test scores, attendance rates, addresses, ages, names, educational histories, and individualized education plans (IEPs). Data are also a matter of justice. When we gather the right information, we can take the steps necessary to repair harm and create belonging that all students deserve. In this chapter, I will lay out ways that we can engage with more robust and nontraditional data sets that are all around us, if we are to create more equitable schools.

If we are operating from the understanding that data are a collection of facts, such as numbers, words, measurements, observations, or descriptions of things, try thinking about data collection in two large categories: *quantitative* and *qualitative*. Both data categories provide us with useful information about how to best understand our schools, our students, our staffs, and even how we can be better leaders or practitioners.

QUANTITATIVE DATA

Think of quantitative data as measurable information or numbers. Quantitative data are used when someone needs to quantify a problem, and they answer questions like "what number," "how many," and "how often." This type of data is frequently used in math calculations, algorithms, or statistical analysis. In schools, common questions may include "How many days of school has a student missed?" Or "How much growth have we seen with a student's math proficiency?" These numerical data provide us with a snapshot in time of a particular phenomenon. Quantitative data typically fall into two categories: discrete and continuous. Discrete data refer to numbers that are fixed. Examples of discrete data include the following:

- The number of students at a school
- The number of staff in a district
- The number of students who are picked up and dropped off by buses in a day
- The number of lunches served in a day
- How much money can be dedicated to tutoring

These figures are indisputable because they tend to be a finite number that is usually fixed at a given day and time. Discrete data are important because they provide us with a snapshot or picture of a specific focus. Typically using charts, graphs, or labels, we can numerically see where we are with respect to a particular reality. The equity challenge is that schools often use discrete data to make huge overstatements and generalizations about particular students, which can be quite harmful. Equity is about undoing, and not contributing to, harm. Continuous data, on the other hand, are equally relevant to schools in that they can take any value and usually change over time. This type of data can be infinitely and meaningfully broken down into smaller and smaller parts. The following are some classroom examples:

- The number of right and wrong questions on quizzes from week to week
- The number of missed assignments over a monthlong period
- A student's grade in each class over the course of a semester

The third example is one in which the data can be useful to students as well as teachers. Students frequently ask questions about how they can get a particular grade in a class. Many will go through the process of calculating their current grade over the course of a semester. In such instances, the student might look at continuous data to arrive at an understanding of where they stand and what they need to get a desired grade. Continuous data are typically fluid and can change from moment to moment, from class to class, or over a longer period. Examples of continuous data that are relevant at the building and district levels include the following:

- District enrollment over a three-to-five-year span
- Per-pupil expenditure from year to year in a district
- Number of substitute teachers needed in the building from day to day
- Numbers of parents/caregivers who show up at parent–teacher conferences over the course of the year

We typically see quantitative data collected by surveys, experimental designs, log-in sheets, big data sets with numerical values, polls, and structured observations. One potential downside to quantitative data is that they often lack context. In other words, these data tell you *what* something is but not always *why* it is. This is an important distinction to remember when it comes to equity, because frequently we look at student behaviors, test scores, or performance in isolation, and to be clear, when applying an equity lens, context matters. It is also important to note that conclusions drawn from quantitative research are only applicable to the particular case studied, and any generalized conclusions are only hypotheses.

One potential downside to quantitative data is that they often lack context. In other words, these data tell you what something is but not always why it is. This is an important distinction to remember when it comes to equity, because frequently we look at student behaviors, test scores, or performance in isolation, and to be clear, when applying an equity lens, context matters.

QUALITATIVE DATA

Qualitative data, on the other hand, are descriptive data that are usually expressed in words or visuals. So, where quantitative data are used for statistical analysis, qualitative data are categorized according to themes or patterns. Qualitative data are defined as non-numerical data such as language, stories, testimonials, anecdotes, text, video, audio recordings, and photographs (Seidman, 2019). Qualitative data can be collected through methods such as interviews, open-ended survey questions, observations, focus groups, or writing reflections and diary accounts. One of the more frequent criticisms of qualitative data is sample size. The same damage that was mentioned in quantitative data can also occur with qualitative data. Making an inference or decision about what to do for a large group of students, based off data from one student, can be misleading and dangerous. There are typically small accounts of a particular phenomenon that cannot be generalized to a larger body of people's feelings, thoughts, or experiences. Some might explain qualitative data as the touchy-feely aspect of research because it seeks to capture people's thoughts, opinions, emotions, and feelings about a particular situation in their own words. Collecting qualitative data is an approach that encourages participants to elaborate on their likes or dislikes about something that has happened. What is important to note when it comes to quantitative and qualitative data where equity is concerned is that historically speaking the quantitative data would tell us the *what*, and the qualitative data would usually tell us the *why*. However, in school contexts we have often placed more emphasis on the what and not done a deeper dive into the why. The why is important because it often provides us with context, a root cause, a deeper explanation, or an insight into why we might be seeing certain behaviors or phenomena. One of the key pillars of equity used in this book has been recognizing and repairing past harms. If we learn from parents/caregivers of immigrant students that their children may not have been provided access to schooling in their native homeland, that might explain why students are struggling with reading, and therefore our approach moving forward is being mindful of that reality. Another example: If a student has taken five different quizzes in their math class and has failed all five of them, a quantitative lens will only reveal the obvious—a student failing. The why behind repeatedly failed quizzes often remains unexamined. Rather than succumb to deficit-laden beliefs about this student, our mission to repair past harm should motivate us to collect qualitative data, beginning with asking the student several questions. Those questions could include these:

- Can you tell me why you think you have not been doing well on your quizzes?
- Are there certain concepts that you are not understanding?
- Is everything okay at home?
- Am I not explaining the content in a way that you can comprehend?
- How can I help you do better for the next quiz?

Each of these questions can provide important qualitative data that when paired with quantitative data can provide a more complete picture of what may explain a student's performance. Most importantly, when quantitative data go unexamined within a contextual framework, the all-too-common outcome is a deficit-laden interpretation that can be quite damaging. For example, the student does not care about their education; the student does not study at all; or the teacher assumes that the student is not motivated to do well. The history of various types of research has often used pseudoscience to create, and reinforce, harmful depictions of people of color, women, people living in poverty, certain immigrants, people with disabilities, and members of the LGBTQ+ community (Selden, 1999). In contrast, equity-centered data are anti-racist, disrupt homophobia, challenge xenophobia, are pro students with disabilities, and are anti-misogynistic. In short, equity-centered data always seek to disrupt surface interpretations that operate from deficit and pathological standpoints, and always need to be questioned.

WHAT DATA SHOULD WE BE COLLECTING?

Many school leaders and practitioners often struggle to understand what data are most important to collect. From an equity standpoint, it is always important to collect data about our students. The more we know about our students, the better. I do not think that we can adequately teach students that we do not know. In fact, I would contend that the students who typically fare well in school are those that we know best through the data we collect about them. In Chapter 5, I outlined various student surveys that schools may send home to parents/caregivers about their student, which are always helpful. In the classroom context, we are receiving data from students daily when they enter our classrooms. This is the type of informal data that can be crucial in creating more equitable schools. Collecting informal data is often an intuitive evaluation method, where a teacher assesses students without measuring their behavior or performance against some standard or formal rubric or metric. The structure of informal evaluation methods allows teachers to observe a student's progress at different points in the learning period. Informal data can be derived from questions such as the following:

- Does a student arrive on time?
- Does the student participate in class? If so, how often?
- What do the student's nonverbal cues seem to be communicating?
- Is the student prepared to learn?
- How does the student interact with peers?
- What is the level of engagement that the student demonstrates?

Each of these data points informs how students may be perceiving our learning community. What is important from an equity standpoint is to not rely solely on the traditional, formal data points that have defined students for years: grades and test scores. This is not to say that we should discard grades and testing. Rather, we recognize that the value of such metrics is limited for depicting student growth, development, learning, and potential. Equity challenges us to think beyond grades and test scores, and not to reduce students to numbers but to imagine ways of assessing students' learning in more dynamic and comprehensive ways. Many students show tremendous growth and uncanny intellect in schools yet can have dismal test scores. Some of our most brilliant students have the worst grades. What does that say about our education system? Equity, in its efforts to recognize and repair past harms, sees student learning in a variety of ways that traditional forms of assessment do not fully capture. An equity-based approach would challenge many of the traditional mechanisms that have been used to define achievement because they often do not provide context or flexibility.

In short, we should be thinking of multiple ways to create learning spaces and providing multiple pathways for students to demonstrate learning and mastery of content, such as these:

- Development of learning portfolios (various pieces of student work over time)
- Multimodal evidence of learning and growth such as visual and performance-based tasks
- Observing student effort
- Students' use of academic language
- Multilingualism
- Student effort and growth
- Project-based assignments
- Problem-based assignments
- Demonstration of leadership skills
- Individual and group presentations
- Artistic representation
- Oral reports
- Reflective pieces
- Concept maps
- Critical analyses
- Case-based scenarios

Each of these nontraditional methods of evaluating students is a data point and can give us a fuller picture of how well a student may be comprehending content. Moreover, what cannot be overlooked is that student learning manifests in a diversity of ways. One of the goals of equity is to meet students where they are to get them where we want them to be. The increasing body of research on Universal Design for Learning (UDL) has helped us to understand the diversity in student learning (Al-Azawei et al., 2016; Smith, 2019). The goal of UDL is to use a variety of teaching methods to remove any barriers to learning and give all students equal opportunities to succeed. UDL is about designing flexibility in the learning environments that can be adjusted for every student's strengths and academic, social, and emotional needs. UDL is a framework for how to develop lesson plans and assessments that is based on four main principles:

- **Representation:** UDL recommends offering information in more than one format—for example, textbooks that are primarily visual.

- **Action and expression:** UDL suggests giving students more than one way to interact with the material and to show what they have learned.

- **Engagement:** UDL encourages teachers to look for multiple ways to motivate students. Allowing students to make choices and giving them assignments that feel relevant to their lives are some examples of how teachers can sustain students' interest.

- **Voice and Choice:** UDL prioritizes empowering students by having them feel like they have some ownership in their learning. Allowing students to offer input and providing feedback about assignments and tasks can generate greater buy-in for many students. Providing students with options for various learning formats can also increase interest.

In line with one of equity's key pillars, belonging, UDL recognizes that students learn in a variety of ways, and from a data standpoint, collecting information about where students may thrive, and where some are frustrated, gives us insight into how classrooms can be malleable. UDL suggests that there is a cultural context to learning that is often missing in traditional pedagogy; and the utility of posted lesson goals, assignment options, flexible learning spaces, regular feedback, and digital and audio text can all be used to help diverse learners (Waitoller & King Thorius, 2016). Education scholar Donna Ford (2021) has long argued that one of the reasons why there is such an underrepresentation of Black students in gifted and talented education (GATE) programs across the country is because the traditional metrics of how schools and districts define "gifted" do not tap into the cultural proclivities of diverse learners.

INFORMAL ASSESSMENTS AS DATA EQUITY

Data points can be informal assessments of student learning, wherein nonstandardized measures that are often personalized to the student are part of the learning ecosystem. Assignments can be given flexibly throughout the school year to provide a snapshot of a student's skill in a specific area at any given time. The challenge of standardized tests is that they provide us with one data point, at one point in time. In contrast, teachers have access to students over the course of an entire year and collect data throughout 180 days in most states. Informal assessments, which many teachers use regularly, are often spontaneous forms of assessments that can easily be incorporated in day-to-day classroom activities (think about quick writes, question of the day, homework reviews, problem of the day, etc.) and measure students' understanding and progress. They are often used as quick observational tools to provide low-stakes feedback about where students are with their understanding of a particular concept or skill. Informal assessments can assist teachers in identifying students' strengths and areas of growth—invaluable data points for planning future lessons.

To further underscore the need to think about data in a more equity-based manner, education scholars Shane Safir and Jamila Dugan (2021) offer a transformative approach to how we should think about data in what they call "street data," which they define as

> the qualitative and experiential data that emerges at eye level and on lower frequencies when we train our brains to discern it. These data are asset based, . . . helping educators look for what's *right* in our students, schools, and communities instead of seeking out what's *wrong*. (p. 57)

They make a compelling argument that schools often rely on narrow slices of data that are not informed by an equity-focused lens. Rather than basing critical education decisions on the typical indicators (what Safir and Dugan call "satellite data") such as high-stakes test scores, the street data method looks at data from the ground up. Their methodology calls upon educators and school leaders to act as ethnographers to gather stories, artifacts, and observations with an emphasis on centering those at the margins: in particular children and families of color, students living in poverty and/or unhoused families, LGBTQ+ children/families, students with disabilities, and students whose first language is not English. Borrowing from Safir and Dugan (2021), an asset-based approach would start from the point of collecting data from key stakeholders asking key questions such as the following:

- How can we best support your child(ren)?
- What does our school need to do to best support diverse learners?
- What have been your best experiences with schools?
- What would you like to see the school do better to support your student?

Another area where we can collect data is to give students a voice in what they think about their teachers and schools.

As college professors, we are required by university bylaws to do an end-of-semester course evaluation for every course that we teach. Teacher evaluations are instruments that offer students the anonymous opportunity to provide both quantitative and qualitative data about their impressions of and experiences in a course. I always look forward to reading what my students have thought about our time together, because it helps me reflect on my own practice. The process can be humbling. At times, when I thought that a course has gone well, I have had students say that the course did not meet their goals and objectives. Conversely, there have been times where I have thought my course was okay at best, but students have spoken favorably about the course. I have often asked why we do not give high school students the opportunity to complete anonymous course evaluations of their teachers at the end of the semester. I think it can be instructive for teachers. One of the challenges with course evaluations is that they are at the end of a class, and while helpful for my next class, it does not give me the opportunity to support the students who have provided me the feedback. Thus, I now use an approach with my classes where when I am halfway through the course, I ask students to take out a piece of paper and to anonymously respond to three questions:

1. What do you like about the class so far?

2. What do you dislike about the class so far?

3. What would you like to see, or do more or less of, the rest of the class to best support your learning?

These three simple questions have been transformative for my teaching, because they have provided me with real-time data in the middle of a quarter or semester about how to best meet my students' needs. Upon receiving these data points, I have rethought assignments, eliminated certain lessons, made sure to check for understanding, reduced course readings, and introduced more group projects all based on what students said would contribute most to their learning. I encourage secondary teachers to try a similar approach. Some take the advice to heart, while others think that students are not able to articulate their learning needs in a thoughtful way—something with which I wholeheartedly disagree. Data collection is about equity in student voice. Students know what they like and do not like when it comes to teaching and learning. I think students provide us with data every day on what they think about our classrooms. The data are not always positive, but even that can be beneficial to us as practitioners. Student data can include not showing up to class, refusing to participate in class, not doing the work, being disruptive or defiant, and even ignoring teachers. Or, to the contrary, some students will arrive to class early or stay late, and others might express joy in discussing the content with a teacher. For some teachers, students will come to their classrooms before school, after school, or at lunch. Once again, these are all data points that communicate to us that students find enjoyment, support, affirmation, or learning in our classrooms. All these types of behavior are data points from students, which reveal what they think about us or our classrooms. With that said, I am also aware of concerns about the use of student-centered feedback in high schools that have been voiced by teacher unions. Some teachers believe that students' comments could be used against them, could work against them receiving tenure, or could be deemed evaluative and harm their formal evaluations (Sawchuk, 2015). I would challenge this sentiment as well. Our goal is to become better teachers; therefore, the more data that we receive, the better, and who better to receive that feedback from than students? We formally evaluate students every day in their role as learners, yet we provide them with no formal mechanism to evaluate us as teachers.

Our goal is to become better teachers; therefore, the more data that we receive, the better, and who better to receive that feedback from than students?

STUDENT VOICES AS DATA

Equity now is anchored on an idea that students' voices matter. If we listen to our students, they will tell us precisely what they need, but they might tell us things that we may not want to hear. Listening to students can be a valuable data point. There will be no need to guess or hypothesize about how we can best support them; we can go directly to the source. But we must be prepared to hear the honest, insightful, surprising, critical, and at times angry perceptions that young people can offer. I recently worked with a school district that has been focused on improving the experiences and outcomes of Black students. I was brought in to help the district "do better" by its Black students. The district asked me if I could help to create a plan of action or set of professional learnings to help improve Black student outcomes across the district. The first question I asked was "Have you talked to the Black students yet?" After receiving a negative to that question, that was my first data point to collect. How can we figure out how to support and serve Black students without first talking to Black students? In response, I was part of a team that did just that; over the course of a three-month period, we held "listen and learn" sessions with hundreds of Black high school students about their likes and dislikes of their schools, what they wish teachers knew about them, how to make schools better, what contributes most to their learning, and their experiences with their peers. These data (which were collected anonymously) were powerful, sad, infuriating, and enlightening. As follows, you will see some of the comments (data) that came from Black students about their experiences in school. Students were provided several prompts and then asked to respond on sticky notes. The prompts are followed by a sampling of responses.

What should teachers/staff know about Black students that they don't already know?

- "We are humans just like everyone else; we are not angrier or criminals just because we are Black."

- "I feel like they should know Black students aren't all the same or act the same."

- "I want them to know that we do care to be something and be successful in life. I want them to care and put the same amount of effort they put in other students to us."

- "I feel like teachers and staff should know that Black students aren't as strong and tough as some may appear. We do have feelings, and some stuff really does hurt."

- "Teachers should know that skin color does not equal the way somebody learns, and we are all here for the same reason."

What would you like to see in the curriculum that would better support you as a student?

- "I would like to see more real-life application of the curriculum, and I would like to see more teachers encourage Black and Brown students to take Advanced Placement/Honors."

- "I would like about three minutes to ask how we as students are doing, especially if it is an elective. Three minutes to do a mental check-in won't hurt our instruction time."

- "I want to see teachers trying as hard as the students, and I want more time to study."

- "To help me out when I need it and stop guessing I am a dumb person."

- "I would like to see more talk about our heritage as Black people. There are a lot of things about Black culture and history that get overlooked."

- "Stop expecting very little/too much from me. I know that I am an intelligent Black student, but it should not be surprising. I want to succeed like everyone else. Don't put me in the spotlight."

All these responses are part of a large data set that highlights how Black students see school, but the comments highlight some of the raw, unedited, and direct views that Black students have about their teachers and schools, which need to be taken seriously by school personnel if there is a real commitment to support Black students under an equity framework. Data can be compelling and insightful, but at times it can be sad and discouraging yet informative about the work that needs to be done. If one of our key goals is to recognize and repair harm for students, asking them in what ways they believe they have been harmed is the most authentic way to capture those injuries. Our students are brilliant, insightful, and highly intelligent. They are more than capable of letting us know what they think, feel, and need. The equity issue is whether we are willing to listen. And, if not, why?

EXAMINING DATA THROUGH A DISPROPORTIONALITY LENS

An important data indicator is the concept of disproportionality, which refers to a group's representation in a particular category that exceeds expectations for that group or differs substantially from the representation of others in that category. For example, special education has been deemed an area where students of color are represented in higher numbers than they are in the general population (Harry & Klinger, 2014). Disciplinary disproportionality is another area that encompasses the significantly high rates at which students of color are subjected to discipline referrals, suspensions, expulsion, and school arrests. School leaders and practitioners should always be assessing school-wide data and individual data to determine if certain groups of students are being subjected to differential or unfair treatment. At the school or district level, leaders might ask the following questions:

- What is the racial/ethnic breakdown of students who are suspended and expelled?
- What is the racial/ethnic breakdown of students who are in GATE courses?
- What is the racial/ethnic breakdown of students who are in Advanced Placement/Honors and International Baccalaureate courses?

- What is the gender breakdown of students in leadership positions?
- How many students whose first language is not English are in advanced courses?
- How many students with disabilities are in advanced classes?
- What is the graduation rate for non-white students?

For classroom teachers, similar types of reflective data points should be occurring that help them think about their own practice and ensure that some students are being recognized and affirmed, while others are being rendered invisible, surveilled, or punished. Questions to think about for practitioners could include these:

- Do I call on the same students consistently?
- Do I try to offer affirming comments to all my students?
- Whose name have I not called today?
- How have I made sure to recognize my quiet students?
- What are the types of comments that students have heard from me today?
- Who have I recommended for leadership opportunities, and why?
- What has the racial/ethnic/gender breakdown been of students who I have disciplined or sent to the office?

DISAGGREGATED DATA

By now, it should be clear that student data can be quite revealing, but only when we are willing to take a deeper dive into what the data are really telling us. The disaggregation of data involves data that have been divided into detailed subcategories. It can reveal inequalities between different subcategories that aggregated (large) databases cannot. Often, larger data sets can paint a positive picture of something such as district achievement rates, but a more analytical look at the data can highlight disturbing outcomes. Most disaggregated data are numerical, but it is possible to have categorical disaggregated data as well. For example, many schools will boast about a high school graduation rate that may be close to 90%–95%, which is an impressive feat. However, the disaggregated data would ask, What are the graduation rates for students with IEPs? How many students who are multilingual learners graduated? What are the graduation rates for Black or Indigenous students? A close look at disaggregated data reveals that, in some cases, the graduates for those subgroups are only in the 60%–65% rate, which is completely unacceptable. While the numbers might be low, the percentage is still important. Losing one student is one too many. At the classroom level, a teacher may have taught a lesson, and it appears that most of the students understood the concept being taught. Only after disaggregating data across all students do teachers recognize that of the 30 students in a class, 6 failed to understand the concept. The disaggregating of data allows the teacher to see where there is a need for additional support for certain students to bring them up to par. One of the areas that also helps us to disaggregate data is when we look at big subject areas like reading or literacy.

The National Reading Panel has identified five key concepts at the core of every effective reading instruction program: phonemic awareness, phonics, fluency, vocabulary, and comprehension. According to the National Assessment of Educational Progress, or NAEP, evaluating reading for students in Grade 4 covers three key areas:

- **Reading for literary experience:** Readers explore events, characters, themes, settings, plots, actions, and the language of literary works by reading novels, short stories, poems, plays, legends, biographies, myths, and folktales.

- **Reading for information:** Readers gain information to understand the world by reading materials such as magazines, newspapers, textbooks, essays, and speeches.

- **Reading to perform a task:** Readers apply what they learn from reading materials such as bus or train schedules, directions for repairs or games, classroom procedures, tax forms (Grade 12), maps, and so on.

Yet often schools will get a general (aggregated) reading score for students, but this amorphous score does not provide educators—nor does it provide the students and parents/caregivers—with an accurate assessment of where a student may not have been taught well. Is the student strong in phonemic awareness, but needs more support in reading comprehension? Does that student show strong ability to identify characteristics, sequence, and plot of a text, but struggle with reading to perform a particular task? Disaggregation of test scores gives a better glimpse into where there is need for additional support and avoids a generalizing of what needs a student has or does not have in a particular subject area.

If schools and districts want to keep an open eye on becoming equity focused, understanding data and creating more data-informed decision-making processes are a must. However, in a number of my interactions with teachers, I have been told that many do not understand much of the data that are given to them from their schools. Having data is important, and understanding data is vital, but using data to inform decision making around curriculum, instruction, assessment, and policies can be transformative. To that end, district and school leaders bear a major responsibility to make data accessible, understandable, and usable for school personnel, students, and parents/caregivers. Among the steps that can be taken are the following:

CREATION OF DATA TEAMS. The purpose of data teams is to create a collaborative community of stakeholders who can discuss data, identify important trends, and serve as the conduit to the rest of the school or district. These teams can help ensure that multiple voices and perspectives are honored when interpreting data and share a consistent message with members of the school community. While each school is responsible for determining the composition of their data teams, a diverse representation of school personnel across grade levels and years of experience is highly recommended to ensure that multiple perspectives (and analyses) are honored.

OFFER ONGOING PROFESSIONAL DEVELOPMENT ON DATA. Most schools offer professional development on a multitude of topics. However, what is often missing are ongoing learning sessions that explain to teachers and staff what data are being collected and how to interpret these data. Having someone with expertise who can go over data, address any questions, and be a resource for those seeking greater clarity can help to increase awareness around data. The more valuable professional learning sessions occur when teachers can demonstrate how they use data in their classrooms to inform instruction and student learning. Moreover, teacher training that has an explicit focus on equity-driven data is largely absent in most school districts.

IDENTIFY USER-FRIENDLY DATA PLATFORMS. A step that can be useful for building data literacy is the incorporation of user-friendly data formats. Many districts have platforms that allow parents/caregivers and students to track student progress. Using learning management systems that allow users to track student performance can be a game changer for parents/caregivers and students. Many find these formats quite useful to monitor daily, weekly, and monthly progress. Identifying a format that teachers, staff, students, and parents/caregivers find beneficial can go a long way in creating more transparent and user-friendly ways to track student work and progress. There are also lots of platforms that allow school personnel to see trends, patterns, and areas of concern for students. Each district should be diligent in identifying the platform that works best for them.

TALKING TO PARENTS/CAREGIVERS ABOUT DATA. One of the ways that equity comes to fruition is when all stakeholders feel as if they are seen, are valued, and have a voice. Belonging matters. To that end, as I discussed in Chapter 6, schools should strive toward finding ways to get parents/caregivers engaged in school-related matters. Schools can make major strides to be inclusive by offering seminars, webinars, and learning sessions that are specifically for parents/caregivers about how to navigate data platforms about their schools, their students' performance, and various resources that are available to support learners. In the spirit of transparency and openness, such endeavors send a clear message to parents/caregivers: *We want you to be informed and knowledgeable about what we are doing as a school community, how your child is doing academically, identifying supports for your child, and offering concrete ways about how best to access your child's teachers.* Such efforts can go a long way to invite parents/caregivers into the learning process. Examples of such forms of parental engagement may be more popular at the primary grades but could be strongly encouraged at the middle and high school grades as well.

DATA TO INFORM INSTRUCTION

One of the areas where we can learn a lot about data use is by studying how schools serve students in special education. Since the inception of the Individuals with Disabilities Education Act (IDEA) in 1965, educators are required to monitor student progress often by way of IEP mandates. In many instances, IDEA may have been our nation's first equity-based policy. IDEA designation requires that instruction be adapted in a manner that meets a student's unique needs and provides the student with access to the general education curriculum to meet the educational standards of the state or district (U.S. Department of Education, Office of Special Education Programs, 2021). Differentiated instruction is often the key to meeting this goal of access to the curriculum. As mentioned in Chapter 1, there are over 7 million students in special education, and supporting their diverse needs is certainly a major equity issue. Moreover, data on students in special education have raised serious concerns about the overrepresentation of students of color in special education, many of whom have been misdiagnosed (Harry & Klinger, 2014). But using data to inform instruction can be a powerful approach to meet students where they are and provide supports on where we want to see growth. When using data to individualize instruction, it is important to focus on various forms of assessment. When teachers use formative and summative assessments with digital tools to collect data on student performance, progress, and comprehension of core skills, they can increase instructional efficiency, alter certain interventions, reduce testing bias, and share outcome information quickly and in a useful and accessible format. While a key use of such data is informing instruction, it is also critical to have in-the-moment, reliable, and relevant information in a format that is readily understood by teachers who may be less familiar with formal data analysis. In this way, teachers can make modifications during a particular lesson, alter a task or assignment, or reteach a particular concept because students may not have understood it.

I discussed Universal Design for Learning (UDL) earlier, and it is important to note that it is different from differentiated instruction (DI). UDL is a function of instructional *design*, while DI is a function of instructional *delivery*. DI is an instructional approach that is centered on developing an understanding of how each student learns best and then tailoring instruction to meet students' individual needs (Tomlinson & Moon, 2015). DI is centered on three key ideas: *content*—the knowledge and skills students need to master, *process*—the activities students use to master the content, and *product*—the method students use to demonstrate learning. Each is tracked by different data points to inform how instruction is delivered. When considering content through an equity lens, the data that teachers should be mindful of are what prior knowledge students have and whether the material is culturally relevant. From a process standpoint, the key data point might be how diverse are the instructional strategies, and whether they tap into a diverse way of students knowing, processing, and communicating. And finally, from a product standpoint, does the classroom allow for a multitude of ways for students to express how they have come to understand the content? Table 7.1 provides additional ways of thinking about how data mining across content, process, and product can be helpful in teaching diverse learners.

TABLE 7.1 ● Differentiated Instruction: Data Mining Across Content, Process, and Product

CONTENT (Data points to consider)	PROCESS (Data points to consider)	PRODUCT (Data points to consider)
What prior knowledge and skills do students already possess?	Are varied instructional strategies being used?	Are there multiple ways to express comprehension?
Is curriculum content culturally relevant?	Is there individual, pair-share, or group time for students to engage in content?	Are students given choice and voice with expression of comprehension?
Are there explicit statements or discussion of learning goals and expectations?	Are students given spaces to engage in productive struggle?	Does assessment provide equal weight to diverse ways of knowing and expression?

Data can and should be one of our most consistent allies when doing equity work. Data, whether quantitative, qualitative, summative, formal, or informal, provides us with a picture of how we are doing with our students. Data should inform our decision making and influence what policies, practices, and procedures are part of the school day. School leaders need to take the lead to ensure that they can help their personnel demystify data and help them become better teachers. In many instances, people think of data as large intimidating numerical banks. Schools must break out of traditional ways of thinking about what data count, and whose data count. Far too often, the data that are most essential to achieve equity are overlooked, underexplained, or used as a tool to create further inequities. Much of our data will tell us how we allow anti-Black racism to persist in schools, how we do not create supportive spaces for trans students, or how we lower expectations and have no rigor in classrooms for language learners. These truths must be faced if we are to better serve our students. Remember, equity is about justice and doing what is right for students. In this chapter, I have laid out the variety of ways that multiple points of data are in our midst. The question is, will we listen? Will we be willing to reflect on our practices and policies? Or will we remain silent, which usually leads to inaction and maintenance of the status quo, which causes even further discomfort, hurt, and pain for marginalized students in schools and classrooms where adults say that they value equity and diversity? Commitments to equity must not limit the ways that we come to understand our schools, our classrooms, or our students' needs and concerns. Knips et al. (2022) lament the fact that in many schools, equity conversations happen in one place, and data conversations happen in another. Such an approach is not sufficient. Data are about equity, and equity should be about data. If equity is our goal, we must provide multiple pathways of making meaning of data; offer suggestions for how data can inform our instruction, programming, and engagement with students and families; and continuously seek ways from teachers and other school personnel for how best to document their efficiency as professionals.

Schools must break out of traditional ways of thinking about what data count, and whose data count. Far too often, the data that are most essential to achieve equity are overlooked, underexplained, or used as a tool to create further inequities.

Equity Now Chart

JUSTICE	REPAIR	BELONGING
• Knowing and understanding the multiple types of data that are present in schools	• Recognizing that generalizing data from a small sample size can cause harm • Moving away from excessive testing to assess if students are learning	• Asking students what the best ways are to capture student learning • Engaging parents/caregivers in how to track student data at school
• Recognizing the diversity in ways of knowing, expressing, comprehending, and learning	• Incorporating Universal Design for Learning principles • Utilizing differentiated instruction strategies centered on content, process, and product	• Consistently communicating to students that there are multiple ways to decipher, analyze, and learn new information • Celebrating diversity of expression, comprehension, and cognition

JUSTICE	REPAIR	BELONGING
• Using data to create asset-based learning environments	• Looking for what's *right* in our students, their efforts, schools, and communities instead of seeking out what's *wrong*	• Creating data teams for all stakeholders to be involved in discussing data points • Asking students what would make their learning environments better
• Eliminating all forms of racism, misogyny, homophobia, and discrimination	• Having "listen and learn" sessions with marginalized groups, asking them what they experience in schools because of their identities	• Believing students when they share the pain, frustration, anger, and exclusion that many experience in schools • Taking steps to incorporate the suggestions that students offer to improve schools

Questions Regarding Data

1. What data systems does my school or district have in place to help me best understand trends of students?

2. Do I rely primarily on formal data to make assessments of student learning, or do I take note of informal data as well?

3. What are ways that I collect data to understand how students are learning in my class (or not)?

4. Does my school or district have racial disproportionality when it comes to discipline? If so, how are we addressing the issue?

5. In what ways do I disaggregate data to best support my students who may need additional support?

6. What data sources do I find most beneficial to help me as a teacher or leader?

7. What data systems do I wish my school or district had in place?

Recommendations for Reading and Resources

1. Safir, S., & Dugan, J. (2021). *Street data: A next-generation model for equity, pedagogy, and school transformation.* Corwin.

2. Martinez-Alvarez, P. (2023). *Teaching emergent bilingual students with dis/abilities: Humanizing pedagogies to engage learners and eliminate labels.* Teachers College Press.

3. Hernandez, M. G., Lopez, D. M., & Swier, R. (2022). *Dismantling disproportionality: A culturally responsive and sustaining systems approach.* Teachers College Press.

4. Knips, A., Lopez, S., Savoy, M., & LaParo, K. (2022). *Equity in data: A framework for what counts in schools.* Association for Supervision and Curriculum Development.

5. Feldman, J. (2019). *Grading for equity: What it is, why it matters, and how it can transform schools and classrooms.* Corwin.

6. Bernhardt, V. L. (2017). *Equity in data: A framework for what counts in schools.* Association for Supervision and Curriculum Development.

7. Schulten, K. (2020). *Student voice: 100 argument essays by teens on issues that matter to them.* Norton.

References

Abdelfatah, R., & Arablouei, R. (Hosts). (2020, September 17). James Baldwin's fire [Audio podcast episode]. In *Throughline*. https://www.npr.org/transcripts/912769283

Abraham, A. (2019). *Queer intentions: A (personal) journey through LGBTQ+ culture.* Pan Macmillan.

Al-Azawei, A., Serenelli, F., & Lundqvist, K. (2016). Universal Design for Learning (UDL): A content analysis of peer reviewed journals from 2012 to 2015. *Journal of the Scholarship of Teaching and Learning, 16*(3), 39–56.

Allen, B., & Vacca, J. S. (2010). Frequent moving has a negative affect on the school achievement of foster children makes the case for reform. *Children and Youth Services Review, 32,* 829–832.

Anda, R. F., Felitti, V. J., Bremner, J. D., Walker, J. D., Whitfield, C., Perry, B. D., & Giles, W. H. (2006). The enduring effects of abuse and related adverse experiences in childhood: A convergence of evidence from neurobiology and epidemiology. *European Archives of Psychiatry and Clinical Neuroscience, 256,* 174–186. https://doi.org/10.1007/s00406-005-0624-4

Atteberry, A., & McEachin, A. (2016). School's out: Summer learning loss across grade levels and school contexts in the United States today. In K. Alexander, S. Pitcock, & M. Boulay (Eds.), *Summer learning and summer loss* (pp. 35–54). Teachers College Press.

Aviles de Bradley, A. M. (2015). *From charity to equity—Race, homelessness, and urban schools.* Teachers College Press.

Bachman, H. F., & Boone, B. J. (2022). A multi-tiered approach to family engagement. *Educational Leadership, 80*(1), 58–63.

Baker, K., Jessup, N. A., Jacobs, V. R., Empson, S. B., & Case, J. (2020). Productive struggle in action. *Mathematics Teacher: Learning and Teaching PK–12, 113*(5), 361–367.

Banaji, M. R., & Greenwald, A. G. (2013). *Blindspot: Hidden biases of good people.* Random House.

Banks, J. A. (2004). Multicultural education: Historical development, dimensions, and practice. In J. A. Banks & C. A. M. Banks (Eds.), *Handbook of research in multicultural education* (2nd ed., pp. 2–29). Jossey-Bass.

Banks, J. A. (2006). *Race, culture, and education: The selected works of James A. Banks.* Routledge.

Banks, J. A. (2016). *Cultural diversity and education* (6th ed.). Routledge.

Banks, J. A. (2019). *An introduction to multicultural education* (6th ed.). Pearson.

Barton, A. C., Drake, C., Perez, J. G., St. Louis, K., & George, M. (2004). Ecologies of parental engagement in urban education. *Educational Researcher, 33*(4), 3–12.

Battistich, V., Schaps, E., & Wilson, N. (2004). Effects of an elementary school intervention on students' "connectedness" to school and social adjustment during middle school. *The Journal of Primary Prevention, 24*(3), 243–262.

Beal, S. J., Nause, K., Crosby, I., & Greiner, M. V. (2018). Understanding health risks for adolescents in protective custody. *Journal of Applied Research on Children: Informing Policy for Children at Risk, 9*(1), Article 2. https://digitalcommons.library.tmc.edu/childrenatrisk/vol9/iss1/2

Bell, D. (2004). *Silent covenants: Brown v. Board of Education and the unfulfilled hopes for racial reform.* Oxford University Press.

Benjamin, R. (2022). *Viral justice: How we grow the world we want.* Princeton University Press.

Bernhardt, V. L. (2017). *Equity in data: A framework for what counts in schools.*

Association for Supervision and Curriculum Development.

Berson, I. R., & Baggerly, J. (2012). Building resilience to trauma: Creating a safe and supportive early childhood classroom. *Childhood Education*, 85(6), 375–379. https://doi.org/10.1080/00094056.2009.10521404

Bîrneanu, A. (2014). The resilience of foster children: The influence and the importance of their attachment. *Revista de Asistenta Sociala*, 13(4), 85–100.

Bitsko, R. H., Claussen, A. H., Lichstein, J., Black, L. I., Jones, S. E., Danielson, M. L., Hoenig, J. M., Davis Jack, S. P., Brody, D. J., Gyawali, S., Maenner, M. J., Warner, M., Holland, K. M., Perou, R., Crosby, A. E., Blumberg, S. J., Avenevoli, S., Kaminski, J. W., & Ghandour, R. M. (2022). Mental health surveillance among children—United States, 2013-2019. *Morbidity and Mortality Weekly Report—Supplements*, 71(Suppl. 2), 1–42. http://doi.org/10.15585/mmwr.su7102a1

Blackburn, B. R. (2013). *Rigor is not a four letter word*. Routledge.

Blankstein, A. M., & Noguera, P. (2015). *Excellence through equity: Five principles of courageous leadership to guide achievement for every student*. Association for Supervision and Curriculum Development.

Borman, G. D., & Overman, L. T. (2004). Academic resilience in mathematics among poor and minority students. *Elementary School Journal*, 104(3), 177–195.

Bowers, J. (2020). Reconsidering the evidence that systematic phonics is more effective than alternative methods of reading instruction. *Educational Psychology Review*, 32(3), 681–705. http://doi.org/10.1007/s10648-019-09515-y

Brown, B. (2018). *Dare to lead: Brave work. Tough conversations. Whole hearts*. Random House.

Bryan, N. (2021). *Toward a blackboycrit pedagogy: Black boys, male teachers, and early childhood classroom practices*. Routledge.

Bryk, A. S., Bender Sebring, P., Allensworth, E., Luppecscu, S., & Easton, J. Q. (2010). *Organizing schools for improvement: Lessons from Chicago*. University of Chicago Press.

Bubrick, K., Goodman, J., & Whitlock, J. (2015). *Non-suicidal self-injury in schools: Developing and implementing school protocol*. Cornell Research Program on Self-Injury and Recovery. https://www.selfinjury.bctr.cornell.edu/perch/resources/non-suicidal-self-injury-in-schools-1.pdf

Burgess, S., & Greaves, E. (2013). Test scores, subjective assessment, and stereotyping of ethnic minorities. *Journal of Labor Economics*, 31(3), 535–576.

Burks, N. (2018). *The deepest well: Healing long-term effect of childhood adversity*. Houghton Mifflin Harcourt.

Camangian, P. R. (2019). "It's not so much . . . for a grade": Humanization as real social and emotional learning. In T. C. Howard, P. Camangian, E. J. Edwards, M. Howard, A. C. Minkoff, T. Orange, J. D. Tunstall, & K. T. Watson (Eds.), *All students must thrive: Transforming schools to combat toxic stressors and cultivate critical wellness* (pp. 125–147). International Center for Leadership in Education.

Chetty, R., Friedman, J. N., Saez, E., Turner, N., & Yagan, D. (2020). *The determinants of income segregation and intergenerational mobility: Using test scores to measure undermatching* (No. w26748). National Bureau of Economic Research.

Chetty, R., Hendren, N., & Katz, L. F. (2016). The effects of exposure to better neighborhoods on children: New evidence from the moving to opportunity experiment. *American Economic Review*, 106(4), 855–902.

Child Welfare Information Gateway. (2021). *Child maltreatment 2019: Summary of key findings*. U.S. Department of Health and Human Services, Administration for Children and Families, Children's Bureau. https://www.childwelfare.gov/pubs/factsheets/canstats/

Cole, S. F., O'Brien, J. G., Gadd, M. G., Ristuccia, J., Wallace, D. L., & Gregory, M. (2005). *Helping traumatized children learn*. Massachusetts Advocates for Children.

Collins, P. H. (1990). *Black feminist thought: Consciousness and the politics of empowerment*. Hyman.

Comer, J. P. (1995). Lecture given at Education Service Center, Region IV, Houston, TX.

Costello, E. J., Erkanli, A., Fairbank, J. A., & Angold, A. (2002). The prevalence of potentially traumatic events in childhood and adolescence. *Journal of Traumatic Stress*, 15, 99–112. https://doi.org/10.1023/A:1014851823163

Craig, S. (2016). *Trauma informed schools*. Teachers College Press.

Craig, S. (2018). *Trauma-sensitive schools for the adolescent years: Promoting resiliency and healing, grades 6–12*. Teachers College Press.

Craig, S. E., & Sporleder, J. (2017). *Trauma-sensitive schools for the adolescent years: Promoting resiliency and healing, grades 6–12*. Teachers College Press.

Creamer, J., Shrider, E. A., Burns, K., & Chen, F. (2022, September). *Poverty in the United States: 2021* (Current Population Reports. P60-277). U.S. Census Bureau. U.S. Government Publishing Office.

Crenshaw, K. W. (1991). Mapping the margins: Intersectionality, identity politics and violence against women of color. *Stanford Law Review*, 43(6), 1241–1299.

Crosby, S. D. (2015). An ecological perspective on emerging trauma-informed teaching practices. *Children & Schools*, 37, 223–230.

Cuevas, S. (2021). *Apoyo sacrificial, sacrificial support: How undocumented Latinx parents get their children to college*. Teachers College Press.

Curby, T. W., Rimm-Kaufman, S. E., & Ponitz, C. C. (2009). Teacher–child interactions and children's achievement trajectories across kindergarten and first grade. *Journal of Educational Psychology*, 101(4), 912–925. https://doi.org/10.1037/a0016647

Czeisler, M. É., Lane, R. I., Petrosky, E., Wiley, J. F., Christensen, A., Njai, R., Weaver, M. D., Robbins, R., Facer-Childs, E. R., Barger, L. K., Czeisler, C. A., Howard, M. E., & Rajaratnam, S. M. W. (2020). Mental health, substance use, and suicidal ideation during COVID-19 pandemic—United States, June 24–30, 2020. *Morbidity and Mortality Weekly Report*, 69, 1049–1047.

Darling-Hammond, L., Hyler, M. E., & Gardner, M. (2017). *Effective teacher professional development*. Learning Policy Institute.

Darling-Hammond, L., Schachner, A., & Edgerton, A. K. (with Badrinarayan, A., Cardichon, J., Cookson, P. W., Jr., Griffith, M., Klevan, S., Maier, A., Martinez, M., Melnick, H., Truong, N., & Wojcikiewicz, S.). (2021). *Restarting and reinventing school: Learning in the time of COVID and beyond*. Learning Policy Institute.

Davis, D. J., Chaney, C., & BeLue, R. (2020). Why "we can't breathe" during COVID-19. *Journal of Comparative Family Studies*, 51(3–4), 417–428.

Davis, P. C. (1998). *Neglected stories*. Macmillan.

Day, A. G., Somers, C. L., Baroni, B. A., West, S. D., Sanders, L., & Peterson, C. D. (2015). Evaluation of a trauma-informed school intervention with girls in a residential facility school: Student perceptions of school environment. *Journal of Aggression, Maltreatment & Trauma*, 24(10), 1086–1105. https://doi.org/10.1080/10926771.2015.1079279

Decker, D. M., Dona, D. P., & Christenson, S. L. (2007). Behaviorally at-risk African American students: The importance of student-teacher relationships for student outcomes. *Journal of School Psychology*, 45(1), 83–109.

Dee, T. S. (2005). A teacher like me: Does race, ethnicity, or gender matter? *American Economic Review*, 95(2), 158–165.

Dee, T. S. (2007). Teachers and the gender gaps in student achievement. *Journal of Human Resources*, 42(3), 528–554.

Dettlaff, A. J., Weber, K., Pendleton, M., Boyd, R., Bettencourt, B., & Burton, L. (2020). It is not a broken system, it is a system that needs to be broken: The upEND movement to abolish the child welfare system. *Journal of Public Child Welfare*, 14(5), 500–517. https://doi.org/10.1080/15548732.2020.1814542

DiAngelo, R. (2018). *White fragility: Why it's so hard for white people to talk about racism*. Beacon Press.

Dietrichson, J. (2017). Academic interventions for elementary and middle school students with low socioeconomic status: A systematic review and meta-analysis. *Review of Educational Research*, 87(2), 243–282. https://doi.org/10.3102/0034654316687036

Douglass, S. (2011). *Learning in a burning house: Educational inequality, ideology, and (dis)integration*. Teachers College Press.

Duckworth, A. (2016). *Grit: The power of passion and perseverance*. Simon & Schuster.

Dugan, J. (2021). Beware of equity traps and tropes. *Educational Leadership*, 78(6), 35–40.

Dugan, J. (2022). Radical dreaming for education now. *Educational Leadership*, 80(2), 56–61.

Duncan-Andrade, J. M. R. (2022). *Equality or equity: Toward a model of community-responsive education*. Harvard Education Press.

Dweck, C. (2006). *Growth: The new psychology of success*. Random House.

Edwards, E. (2019). Helping the unseen: Providing educational equity for students experiencing homelessness. In T. C. Howard, P. Camangian, E. J. Edwards, M. Howard, A. C. Minkoff, T. Orange, J. D. Tunstall, & K. T. Watson (Eds.), *All students must thrive: Transforming schools to combat toxic stressors and cultivate critical wellness* (pp. 148–170). International Center for Leadership in Education.

Edwards, P. A. (2009). *Tapping the potential of parents: A strategic guide to boosting student achievement through family involvement*. Scholastic.

Edwards, P. A. (2016). *New ways to engage parents: Strategies and tools for teachers and leaders K–12*. Teachers College Press.

Elliott, A. (2022). *Invisible child: Poverty, survival, and hope in an American city*. Random House.

Emerson, J., & Lovitt, T. (2003). The educational plight of foster children in schools and what can be done about it. *Remedial and Special Education*, 24(4), 199.

Escamilla, K., Olsen, L., & Slavik, J. (2022). *Toward comprehensive effective literacy policy for English learners and emergent bilingual students*. National Committee for Effective Literacy for Emergent Bilingual Students.Every Student Succeeds Act, 20 U.S.C. § 6301 (2015). https://www.congress.gov/bill/114th-congress/senate-bill/1177

Ewing, A. R., & Taylor, A. R. (2009). The role of child gender and ethnicity in teacher-child relationship quality and children's behavioral adjustment in preschool. *Early Childhood Research Quarterly*, 24(1), 92–105.

Feldman, J. (2019). *Grading for equity: What it is, why is matters, and how it can transform schools and classrooms*. Corwin.

Felitti, V. J., Anda, R. F., Nordenberg, D., Williamson, D. F., Spitz, A. M., Edwards, V., & Marks, J. S. (1998). Relationship of childhood abuse and household dysfunction to many of the leading cause of deaths in adults. *American Journal of Preventive Medicine*, 14, 245–258.

Ferguson, R. F. (2003). Teachers' perceptions and expectations and the Black-white test score gap. *Urban Education*, 38(4), 460–507.

Ford, D. Y. (2021). *Multicultural gifted education*. Routledge.

Francois, A., & Quartz, K. H. (2022). *Preparing and sustaining social justice educators*. Harvard Education Press.

Fredricks, J. A., Blumenfeld, P. C., & Paris, A. H. (2004). School engagement: Potential of the concept, state of the evidence. *Review of Educational Research*, 74(1), 59–109. https://doi.org/10.3102/00346543074001059

Frey, W. H. (2018). *Diversity explosion: How new racial demographics are remaking America*. Brookings Institution.

Fryer, R. G. (2016, March). *The production of human capital in developed countries: Evidence from 196 randomized field experiments* (NBER Working Paper No. 22130). National Bureau of Economic Research.

Fullan, M., & Quinn, J. (2016). *Coherence: The right drivers in action for schools, districts, and systems*. Corwin.

Gallagher, H. A., & Cottingham, B. (2020, August). *Improving the quality of distance and blended learning*. EdResearch for Recovery No. 8. Policy Analysis for California Education, Stanford University.

Galperin, H., & Le, T. (2021). *CETF-USC statewide broadband adoption survey*. https://assets.uscannenberg.org/docs/CETF-USC_Statewide_Broadband_Adoption_Survey.pdf

Gandolfi, E., Ferdig, R. E., & Kratcoski, A. (2021). A new educational normal an intersectionality-led exploration of education, learning technologies, and diversity during COVID-19. *Technology in Society*, 66, 101637.

Garcia, A. R., Pecora, P. J., Harachi, T., & Aisenberg, E. (2012). Institutional predictors of developmental outcomes among racially diverse foster care alumni. *American Journal of Orthopsychiatry*, 82(4), 573–584. https://doi.org/10.1111/j.1939-0025.2012.01181.x

García, O., Johnson, S. I., Seltzer, K., & Valdés, G. (2017). *The translanguaging classroom: Leveraging student bilingualism for learning*. Caslon.

Gay, G. (2000). *Culturally responsive teaching*. Teachers College Press.

Gay, G. (2020). *Culturally responsive teaching* (3rd ed.). Teachers College Press.

Gersheson, S., Holt, S. B., & Papageorge, N. W. (2016). Who believes in me? The effect of student–teacher demographic match on teacher expectations. *Economics of Education Review*, 52, 109–224.

Goldhaber, D., Kane, T., McEachin, A., Morton, E., Patterson, T., & Staiger, D. (2022). *The consequences of remote and hybrid instruction during the pandemic* (Research report). Center for Education Policy Research, Harvard University.

Gorski, P. (2018). *Reaching and teaching students in poverty: Strategies for erasing the opportunity gaps* (2nd ed.). Teachers College Press.

Gorski, P. (2019). Avoiding racial equity detours. *Educational Leadership*, 76(7), 56–61.

Gross, B., & Opalka, A. (2020, June). *Too many schools leave learning to chance during the pandemic*. Center on Reinventing Public Education. https://crpe.org/too-many-schools-leave-learning-to-chance-during-the-pandemic/

Grossman, P. (2012). *Beyond the bake sale: The essential guide to family-school partnerships* by Anne T. Henderson, Karen L. Mapp, Vivian R. Johnson, and Don Davies. *Journal of School Choice*, 6(3), 427–430. https://doi.org/10.1080/15582159.2012.702045

Gruenert, S., & Whitaker, T. (2015). *School culture rewired: How to define, assess, and transform it*. ASCD.

Gutman, L. M., & McLoyd, V. C. (2000). Parents' management of their children's education within the home, at school, and in the community: An examination of African-American families living in poverty. *The Urban Review*, 32, 1–24. https://doi.org/10.1023/A:1005112300726

Haberman, M. (2018). What stars think they're doing. In M. Haberman, M. Gillette, & D. A. Hill (Eds.), *Star teachers of children in poverty* (2nd ed., pp. 38–55). Routledge.

Haberman, M., Gillette, M. D., & Hill, D. A. (2018). *Star teachers of children in poverty* (2nd ed.). Routledge.

Hannah-Jones, N. (2019–present). The 1619 project. *The New York Times Magazine*. https://www.nytimes.com/interactive/2019/08/14/magazine/1619-america-slavery.html

Harry, B., & Klinger, J. (2014). *Why are so many minority students in special education? Understanding race & disability in schools* (2nd ed.). Teachers College Press.

Harvey, B. (2023). *Defying carceral entrapment: Black foster youth narratives of subversion, survival and liberation* [Doctoral dissertation]. University of California, Los Angeles.

Harvey, B., Gupta-Kagan, J., & Church, C. (2021). Reimagining schools' role outside the family regulation system. *Columbia Journal of Race and Law*, 11(3), 575–610.

Harvey, B., & Whitman, K. L. (2020, July 8). Child welfare and a just future: From a moment to a movement. *The Imprint.* https://imprintnews.org/child-welfare-2/from-moment-to-movement-envisioning-child-welfare-system-we-have-yet-see/45035

Hattie, J. (2005). The paradox of reducing class size and improving learning outcomes. *International Journal of Educational Research, 43*(6), 387–425.

Hattie, J. (2008). *Visible learning: A synthesis of over 800 meta-analyses relating to achievement.* Routledge.

Hernandez, M. G., Lopez, D. M., & Swier, R. (2022). *Dismantling disproportionality: A culturally responsive and sustaining systems approach.* Teachers College Press.

Hill, L., & Artiga, S. (2022). *COVID-19 cases and deaths by race/ethnicity: Current data and changes over time.* Kaiser Family Foundation.

Holt, S. B., & Gershenson, S. (2015). *The impact of teacher demographic representation on student attendance and suspensions* (IZA Discussion Paper No. 9554). Institute for the Study of Labor (IZA).

hooks, b. (2000). *Feminism is for everybody.* South End Press.

Horsford, S. D., Cabral, L., Touloukian, C., Parks, S., Smith, P. A., McGhee, C., Qadir, F., Lester, D., & Jacobs, J. (2021). *Black education in the wake of COVID-19 and systemic racism: Toward a theory of change and action.* Black Education Research Collective. Teachers College, Columbia University.

Howard, J. R. (2023). Empathetic approaches for supporting Black students during remote learning. *Urban Education.* Advance online publication. https://doi.org/10.1177/00420859231153416

Howard, J. R., McCall, T., & Howard, T. C. (2019). *No more teaching without without positive relationships.* Heinemann.

Howard, M. (2019). How to create a trauma-aware learning environment. In T. C. Howard, P. Camangian, E. J. Edwards, M. Howard, A. C. Minkoff, T. Orange, J. D. Tunstall, & K. T. Watson (Eds.), *All students must thrive: Transforming schools to combat toxic stressors and cultivate critical wellness* (pp. 19–44). International Center for Leadership in Education.

Howard, T. C. (2003). Culturally relevant pedagogy: Ingredients for critical teacher reflection. *Theory Into Practice, 42*(3), 195–202.

Howard, T. C. (2016). Why Black lives (and minds) matter: Race, Freedom Schools and the quest for educational equity. *Journal of Negro Education, 85*(2), 101–113.

Howard, T. C. (2020). *Why race and culture matter in schools* (2nd ed.). Teachers College Press.

Howard, T. C., Camangian, P., Edwards, E. J., Howard, M., Minkoff, A., Orange, T., Tunstall, J. D., & Watson, K. T. (2019). *All students must thrive: Transforming schools to combat toxic stressors and cultivate critical wellness.* International Center for Leadership in Education.

Howard, T. C., & Terry, C. L. (2011). Culturally responsive pedagogy for African American students: Promising programs and practices for enhanced academic performance. *Teaching Education, 22*(4), 345–362.

Huff, B. L. (2015). *Shared accountability to improve educational outcomes of foster youth: Examining the conditions that influence evidence-based decision making* (Order No. 3712447). Dissertations & Theses @ University of California; ProQuest Dissertations & Theses A&I: Social Sciences; ProQuest Dissertations & Theses Global: Social Sciences (1704383932). https://search.proquest.com/docview/1704383932?accountid=14512

Irvine, J. J., & Fraser, J. W. (1998). Warm demanders. *Education Week, 17*(35), 56.

Ishimaru, A. M. (2020). *Just schools: Building equitable collaborations with families and communities.* Teachers College Press.

Ivey-Stephenson, A. Z., Demissie, Z., Crosby, A. E., Stone, D. M., Gaylor, E., Wilkins, N., Lowry, R., & Brown, M. (2020). Suicidal ideation and behaviors among high school students—Youth Risk Behavior Survey, United States, 2019. *Morbidity and Mortality Weekly Report—Supplements, 69*(Suppl. 1), 47–55.

J-PAL Evidence Review. (2020). *The transformative potential of tutoring for preK–12 learning outcomes: Lessons from randomized evaluations.* Abdul Latif Jameel Poverty Action Lab. https://www.povertyaction lab.org/sites/default/files/publication/Evidence-Review_The-Transformative-Potential-of-Tutoring.pdf

Johnson, S. L., Jr., Bishop, J. P., Howard, T. C., James, A., Rivera, E., & Noguera, P. A. (2021). *Beyond the schoolhouse, digging deeper: COVID-19 & reopening schools for Black students in Los Angeles.* Center for the Transformation of Schools, School of Education & Information Studies, University of California, Los Angeles.

Johnson, S. M. (2019). *Where teachers thrive: Organizing schools for success.* Harvard Education Press.

Johnson, S. M., Kraft, M. A., & Papay, J. P. (2012). How context matters in high need schools: The effects of teachers' working conditions on their professional satisfaction and their students' achievement. *Teachers College Record*, 114(10), 1–39.

Joseph, N. (2022). *Making Black girls count in math education: A Black feminist vision for transformative teaching.* Harvard Education Press.

Kafele, B. K. (2021). *The principal 50: Critical leadership questions for inspiring schoolwide excellence.* Better World Books.

Kahn, J. (2017). *Race on the brain: What implicit bias gets wrong about the struggle for racial justice.* Columbia University Press.

Kendi, I. X. (2019). *How to be an antiracist.* One World.

Kennedy, R. L. (2000). Who can say "nigger"? And other considerations. *The Journal of Blacks in Higher Education*, 26, 86–96.

Khalifa, M. (2018). *Culturally responsive school leadership.* Harvard Education Press.

Kids Count Data Center. (2020, September). *Child population by race in the United States.* https://perma.cc/N3CA-S6YP

Kim, H., Wildeman, C., Jonson-Reid, M., & Drake, B. (2017). Lifetime prevalence of investigating child maltreatment among US children. *American Journal of Public Health*, 107(2), 274–280.

Kirwan Institute for the Study of Race and Ethnicity. (2013). *Implicit bias module series.* https://kirwaninstitute.osu.edu/implicit-bias-module-series

Kirzinger, A., Hamel, L., Muñana, C., Kearney, C., & Brodie, M. (2020, April 24). *KFF health tracking poll—Late April 2020: Coronavirus, social distancing, and contact tracing.* Henry J. Kaiser Family Foundation. https://www.kff.org/corona virus-covid-19/issue-brief/kff-health-tracking-poll-late-april-2020/

Kleinfeld, J. (1975). Effective teachers of Eskimo and Indian students. *The School Review*, 83(2), 301–344.

Klem, A. M., & Connell, J. P. (2004). Relationships matter: Linking teacher support to student engagement and achievement. *Journal of School Health*, 74(7), 262–273.

Knips, A., Lopez, S., Savoy, M., & LaParo, K. (2022). *Equity in data: A framework for what counts in schools.* Association for Supervision and Curriculum Development.

Ladson-Billings, G. (1994). *Dreamkeepers.* Jossey-Bass.

Ladson-Billings, G. (2006). From the achievement gap to the education debt: Understanding achievement in US schools. *Educational Researcher*, 35(7), 3–12.

Lindsay, J., & Davis, V. (2013). *Flattening classrooms to global collaboration one step at a time.* Pearson.

Lomawaima, K., & Ostler, J. (2018). Reconsidering Richard Henry Pratt: Cultural genocide and native liberation in an era of racial oppression. *Journal of American Indian Education*, 57(1), 82.

Lombardi, M. (2007, January 1). *Authentic learning for the 21st century: An overview.* EDUCAUSE Learning Initiative. https://library.educause.edu/resources/2007/1/authentic-learning-for-the-21st-century-an-overview

Lorde, A. (1984). *Sister outsider: Essays and speeches.* Crossing Press.

Loury, G. C. (2009). *The anatomy of racial inequality.* Harvard University Press.

Love, B. (2023). *Punished for dreaming: How school reform harms Black children and how we heal.* Beacon Press.

Lynch, K., An, L., & Mancenido, Z. (2022). The impact of summer programs on student mathematics achievement: A meta-analysis. *Review of Educational Research, 93*(2). https://doi.org/10.3102/00346543221105543

Maier, A., Daniel, J., Oakes, J., & Lam, L. (2017). *Community schools as an effective school improvement strategy: A review of the evidence.* Learning Policy Institute.

Mapp, K. L., & Bergman, E. (2021). *Embracing a new normal: Toward a more liberatory approach to gamily engagement.* Carnegie Corporation.

Martinez, R. A. (2018). Beyond the English learner label: Recognizing the richness of bi/multilingual students' linguistic repertoires. *Reading Teacher, 71*(5), 515–522.

Martinez-Alvarez, P. (2023). *Teaching emergent bilingual students with dis/abilities: Humanizing pedagogies to engage learners and eliminate labels.* Teachers College Press.

Maslow, A. H. (1943). A theory of human motivation. *Psychological Review, 50*(4), 370–396.

Massinga, R., & Pecora, P. J. (2004). Providing better opportunities for older children in the child welfare system. *The Future of Children, 14*(1), 151–175. https://doi.org/10.2307/1602759

Mathews, K. (2022). *Voices from the classroom: Developing a strategy for teacher retention and recruitment. Key findings from a survey of TK–12 teachers in California and in-depth interviews with aspiring and former teachers in California.* UCLA Center for the Transformation of Schools. https://transformschools.ucla.edu/research/voices-from-the-classroom/

Matthews, M. L. (2019). *Urban ACEs: How to reach and teach students traumatized by adverse childhood experiences.* Koelerbooks.

McCarthy Foubert, J. L. (2022). *Reckoning with racism in family–school partnerships: Centering black parents' school engagement.* Teachers College Press.

McCormack, L., & Issaakidis, G. I. (2018). Complex trauma in childhood; psychological growth in adulthood: Making sense of the "lived" experience of out-of-home care. *Traumatology, 24*(2), 131–139.

McGhee, H. (2022). *The sum of us: What racism costs everyone and how we can prospect together.* One World.

McKee, G., Sims, K. R. E., & Rivkin, S. G. (2015). Disruption, learning, and the heterogeneous benefits of smaller classes. *Empirical Economics, 48,* 1267–1286. https://doi.org/10.1007/s00181-014-0810-1

Meadow, T. (2018). *Trans kids: Being gendered in the twenty-first century.* University of California Press.

Mickelson, R. A. (1990). The attitude-achievement paradox among Black adolescents. *Sociology of Education, 63*(1), 44–61.

Milner, H. R. (2015). *Rac(e)ing to class: Confronting poverty and race in schools and classrooms.* Harvard Education Press.

Milner, H. R. (2020). *Start where you are, but don't stay there.* Harvard Education Press.

Milner, H. R. (2023). *Play the race card.* Corwin.

Milner, H. R., Cunningham, B. H., Delale-O'Connor, L., & Gold Kestenberg, E. (2019). *"These kids are out of control": Why we must reimagine "classroom management" for equity.* Corwin.

Monte, L. M., & Perez-Lopez, D. J. (2021). *COVID-19 pandemic hit Black households harder than white households, even when pre-pandemic socioeconomic disparities are taken into account.* U.S. Census Bureau.

Morgan, N. S. (2017). *Engaging families in schools: Practical strategies to improve parental involvement.* Routledge.

Morris, M. W. (2016). *Pushout: The criminalization of Black girls in schools.* The New Press.

Morris, M. (2018). *Pushout: The criminalization of Black girls in schools.* New Press.

Morton, B. M. (2012). *Foster youth and post-secondary education: A study of the barriers and supports that led to academic achievement* (Order No. 3515009). ProQuest Dissertations & Theses A&I; ProQuest Dissertations & Theses Global (1019241356). https://search.proquest.com/docview/1019241356?accountid=14512

Mueller, D. (2023). *A kids book about gender.* Penguin Random House.

Muhammad, G. (2020). *Cultivating genius: An equity framework for culturally and historically responsive literacy.* Scholastic.

Muñoz, R. T., Hanks, H., & Hellman, C. M. (2019). Hope and resilience as distinct contributors to psychological flourishing among childhood trauma survivors. *Traumatology.* National Foster Youth Institute. https://www.nfyi.org/issues/education/

Muñoz, S. M. (2021). Historical and contemporary articulations of white supremacist, anti-immigrant and racist rhetoric. In L. Perez & S. Muñoz (Eds.), *Why they hate us: How racist rhetoric impacts education* (pp. 27–48). Teachers College Press.

Nasir, N. (2011). *Racialized identities racialized identities: Race and achievement among African American youth.* Stanford University Press.

National Alliance on Mental Illness. (2023, April). *Mental health by the numbers.* https://www.nami.org/mhstats

National Assessment for Education Progress (NAEP). (2022). https://www.nationsreportcard.gov/

National Center for Education Statistics (NCES). (2022). *Fast facts: Back-to-school statistics.* https://nces.ed.gov/fastfacts/display.asp?id=372#

National Child Traumatic Stress Network. (2018). *Impact of complex trauma.* https://www.nctsn.org/sites/default/files/resources//impact_of_complex_trauma.pdf

National Council of Teachers of Mathematics. (2023). *Professional services: Supporting students' productive struggle (grades PK–12).* https://www.nctm.org/Conferences-and-Professional-Development/Professional-Services/Productive-Struggle/

Nelson, K., & England, A. (2023, May 9). *These are the US states allowing mental health days.* Verywell Mind. https://www.verywellmind.com/us-states-allowing-student-mental-health-days-5270047

Nieto, S. (2018). *Language, culture, and teaching: Critical perspectives* (3rd ed.). Routledge.

Noguera, P., Bishop, J., Howard, T., & Johnson, S. (2019). *Beyond the schoolhouse: Overcoming challenges and expanding opportunities for Black youth in Los Angeles County.* Center for the Transformation of Schools, Black Male Institute, Graduate School of Education & Information Studies, University of California, Los Angeles.

Noguera, P., Darling-Hammond, L., & Friedlaender, D. (2015). Equal opportunity for deeper learning. Deeper Learning Research Series. *Jobs for the Future.*

Novoa, C., & Jessen-Howard, S. (2020, March 24). *The U.S. coronavirus response must meet health workers' child care needs.* Center for American Progress. https://www.americanprogress.org/issues/early-childhood/news/2020/03/24/482086/u-s-coronavirus-response-must-meet-health-workers-child-care-needs/

Oehlberg, B. (2008). Why schools need to be trauma-informed. *Trauma and Loss: Research and Interventions, 8*(2), 1–4. http://www.traumainformedcareproject.org/resources/WhySchoolsNeedToBeTraumaInformed(2).pdf

Olsen, L. (with Martinez, M., Herrera, C. B., & Skiggins, H.). (2020). Multilingual programs and pedagogy: What teachers and administrators need to know and do. In California Department of Education (Ed.), *Improving multilingual and English learner education: From research to practice* (pp. 115–188). https://www.cde.ca.gov/sp/el/er/documents/mleleducation.pdf

Oluo, I. (2018). *So you want to talk about race.* Seal Press.

Orfield, G. (2022). *The walls around opportunity.* Princeton University Press.

Pellegrino, J. W. (2014). *Assessment as a positive influence on 21st century teaching and learning: A systems approach to progress.* International Association for Educational Assessment. p. 1.

Pember, M. A. (2019, March 8). Death by civilization. *The Atlantic.* https://www.theatlantic.com/education/archive/2019/03/traumatic-legacy-indian-boarding-schools/584293/

PEN America. (2022). *Banned in the USA: Rising school book bans threaten free expression and students' first amendment rights.* https://pen.org/banned-in-the-usa/

Pérez Huber, L., & Muñoz, S. (2021). *Why they hate us: How racist rhetoric impacts education.* Teachers College Press.

Perfect, M., Turley, M., Carlson, J., Yohanna, J., & Saint Gilles, M. (2016). School-related outcomes of traumatic event exposure and traumatic stress symptoms in students: A systematic review of research from 1990 to 2015. *School Mental Health, 8*(1), 7–43. https://doi.org/10.1007/s12310-016-9175-2

Pollock, M. (Ed.). (2008). *Everyday antiracism: Getting real about race in school.* The New Press.

Pollock, M. (2017). *Schooltalk. Rethinking what we say about and to students every day.* The New Press.

Pondiscio, R. (2022). Schools must rebuild trust. *Educational Leadership, 80*(1), 64–67.

Putnam-Hornstein, E., Ahn, E., Prindle, J., Magruder, J., Webster, D., & Wildeman, C. (2021). Cumulative rates of child protection involvement and terminations of parental rights in a California birth cohort, 1999–2017. *American Journal of Public Health, 111,* 1157–1163. https://doi.org/10.2105/AJPH.2021.306214

Radd, S., Generett, G. G., Gooden, M. A., & Theoharis, G. (2021). *Five practices for equity-focused school leadership.* ASCD.

Reynolds, R., & Howard, T. C. (2013). Chapter 20. Sharing responsibility: A case for real parent-school partnerships. In M. B. Katz & M. Rose (Eds.), *Public education under siege* (pp. 201–206). University of Pennsylvania Press. https://doi.org/10.9783/9780812208320.201

Roberts, D. E. (2009). *Shattered bonds: The color of child welfare.* Civitas Books.

Roberts, D. E. (2011). Prison, foster care, and the systemic punishment of Black mothers. *UCLA Law Review, 59,* 1474.

Roberts, D. E. (2022). *Torn apart: How the child "welfare" system destroys Black families—and how abolition can build a safer world.* Basic Books.

Rudasill, K. M., Reio, T. G., Jr., Stipanovic, N., & Taylor, J. E. (2010). A longitudinal study of student-teacher relationship quality, difficult temperament, and risky behavior from childhood to early adolescence. *Journal of School Psychology, 48*(5), 389–412.

Safir, S. (2017). *The listening leader: Creating the conditions for equitable school conditions.* Jossey-Bass.

Safir, S., & Dugan, J. (2021). *Street data: A next-generation model for equity, pedagogy, and school transformation.* Corwin.

Saunders, M., Tieu, D., Vega, R., Jimenez, R., Yarnes, Y., & Alvarado, N. (2021, Fall). Community teachers: Taking ownership of whole child educational practices. *Community Schooling, 1.* UCLA Center for Community Schooling.

Sawchuk, S. (2015, September 3). Teacher evaluation: An issue overview. *Education Week.* https://www.edweek.org/teaching-learning/teacher-evaluation-an-issue-overview/2015/09

Schulten, K. (2020). *Student voice: 100 argument essays by teens on issues that matter to them.* W.W. Norton.

Seda, P., & Brown, K. (2021). *Choosing to see. A framework for equity in the math classroom.* Burgess Consulting.

Seidman, I. (2019). *Interviewing as qualitative research: A guide for researchers in education and the social sciences.* Teachers College Press.

Selden, S. (1999). *Inheriting shame: The story of eugenics and racism in America.* Teachers College Press.

Shalaby, C. (2017). *Troublemakers: Lessons in freedom from young children at school.* The New Press.

Shujaa, M. (1994). *Too much schooling, too little education: A paradox of Black life in white societies.* Africa World Press.

Sinek, S. (2009). *Start with why: How great leaders inspire everyone to take action.* Penguin Press.

Smith, J. (2019). Making assessment equitable for learners on an alternate curriculum. *Allies for Education, 2*(2). https://journals.calstate.edu/afe/article/view/3292

Sparks, S. D. (2016, April 26). Emotions help steer students' learning, studies find.

Education Week. https://www.edweek.org/leadership/emotions-help-steer-students-learning-studies-find/2016/04

Spring, J. (2016). *Deculturalization and the struggle for equality* (8th ed.). Routledge.

Spring, J. (2022). *Deculturalization and the struggle for equability* (9th ed.). Routledge.

Steele, C. M. (1997). A threat in the air: How stereotypes shape intellectual identity and performance. *American Psychologist, 52*(6), 613–629.

Stephens, T. (2020, June 24). Supporting families of color: How racial and complex trauma affect parents of color navigating family court during the time of COVID and beyond. *Rise.* https://www.risemagazine.org/2020/06/supporting-families-of-color/

Stevenson, H. (2014). *Promoting racial literacy in schools: Differences that make a difference*. Teachers College Press.

Suarez-Orozco, M. M., & Michikiyan, M. (2016). Introduction: Education for citizenship in the age of globalization and mass migration. In J. A. Banks, M. M. Suárez-Orozco, & M. Ben-Peretz (Eds.), *Global migration, diversity and civic education: Improving policy and practice* (pp. 1–28). Teachers College Press.

Substance Abuse and Mental Health Services Administration (SAMHSA). (2014). *SAMHSA's concept of trauma and guidance for a trauma-informed approach.* SAMHSA.

Szilagyi, M. A., Rosen, D. S., Rubin, D., & Zlotnik, S. (2015). Health care issues for children and adolescents in foster care and kinship care. *Pediatrics Digest, 136*(4), 1–25.

Tatum, A. W. (2021). *Teaching Black boys in the elementary grades: Advanced disciplinary reading and writing to secure their futures.* Teachers College Press.

Tomlinson, C. A., & Moon, T. R. (2015). *Differentiated instruction: The differentiated classroom* (2nd ed.). Association for Supervision and Curriculum Development.

Turner Nash, K., Polite, C., & Polson, B. (2020). *Toward culturally sustaining teaching: Early childhood educators honor children with practices for equity and change.* Routledge.

U.S. Department of Education, Institute of Education Sciences, National Center for Education Statistics, National Assessment of Educational Progress (NAEP). *Various years, 1992-2022 Reading Assessments.*

U.S. Department of Education Office for Civil Rights. (2021, June). *Education in a pandemic: The disparate impacts of COVID-19 on America's students.* https://www2.ed.gov/about/offices/list/ocr/docs/20210608-impacts-of-covid19.pdf

U.S. Department of Education, Office of Special Education Programs. (2021, September). *Annual report to congress on the implementation of the Individuals with Disabilities Education Act, selected years, 1979 through 2019.* https://www2.ed.gov/about/reports/annual/osep/index.html

U.S. Department of Health and Human Services. (2020). *The AFCARS report: Preliminary FY 2019 estimates as of June 23, 2020—No. 27.* Children's Bureau.

U.S. Department of Health and Human Services, Administration for Children and Families, Administration on Children, Youth and Families, Children's Bureau. (2023, February 9). *Child maltreatment 2021.* https://www.acf.hhs.gov/sites/default/files/documents/cb/cm2021.pdf

U.S. Census Bureau. (2021). *Population Reference Bureau analysis of data from the U.S. Census Bureau, 2005 through 2019, 2021.* American Community Survey.

Valencia, R. R. (Ed.). (1997). *The evolution of deficit thinking: Educational thought and practice.* The Falmer Press.

Waitoller, F. R., & King Thorius, K. A. (2016). Cross-pollinating culturally sustaining pedagogy and universal design for learning: Toward an inclusive pedagogy that accounts for dis/ability. *Harvard Educational Review, 86*(3), 366–389.

Walker, T. (2020). *Average teacher salary lower today than 10 years ago, NEA report finds.* NEA Today.

Watson, K. T. (2019). Confronting implicit bias and microaggressions in the classroom: Distinguishing intent from impact. In T. C. Howard, P. Camangian, E. J. Edwards, M. Howard, A. Minkoff, T. Orange, J. D. Tunstall, & K. T. Watson. *All students must thrive: Transforming schools to combat toxic stressors and cultivate critical wellness* (pp. 45–68). International Center for Leadership in Education.

West, C. (2008). *Hope on a tightrope: Words and wisdom.* Greenworld Books.

Williams-Butler, A. (2018). Reducing delinquency among African American youth in foster care: Does gender make a difference in crossover prevention? *Children and Youth Services Review, 94,* 563–571.

Willis, D. J., & Fensterwald, J. (2021, May 5). Over half of California public school students remain in distance learning. *EdSource.* edsource.org/2021/new-data-55-of-california-public-school-students-remain-in-distance-learning/653848

Winn, M. T. (2018). *Justice on both sides: Transforming education through restorative justice.* Harvard Education Press.

Winn, M. T., & Winn, L. T. (2021). *Restorative justice in education: Transforming teaching and learning through the disciplines.* Harvard Education Press.

Winthrop, R., Barton, A., Ershadi, M., & Ziegler, L. (2022, October 21). *Collaborating to transform and improve education systems: A playbook for family-school engagement.* Brookings. https://www.brookings.edu/essay/collaborating-to-transform-and-improve-education-systems-a-playbook-for-family-school-engagement/

Wolpow, R., Johnson, M. M., Hertel, R., & Kincaid, S. O. (2009). *The heart of learning and teaching: Compassion, resiliency, and academic success.* Washington State Office of Superintendent of Public Instruction Compassionate Schools.

Wood, J. L., Harris, F., III, & Howard, T. C. (2016). *Get out! Black male suspensions in California public schools* [Policy report]. Community College Equity Assessment Lab and the UCLA Black Male Institute.

Wyse, D., & Bradbury, A. (2022). Reading wars or reading reconciliation? A critical examination of robust research evidence, curriculum policy and teachers' practices for teaching phonics and reading. *Review of Education, 10,* e3314. https://doi.org/10.1002/rev3.3314

Zamarro, G., & Camp, A. (2021, April 20). Returning to in person learning might be more complex than simply reopening schools for minority families. *The Evidence Base.* University of Southern California Dornslife Center for Economic and Social Research. https://healthpolicy.usc.edu/evidence-base/returning-to-in-person-learning-might-be-more-complex-than-simply-re-opening-schools-for-minority-families/

Index

A Sage Company

CORWIN HAS ONE MISSION: to enhance education through intentional professional learning.

We build long-term relationships with our authors, educators, clients, and associations who partner with us to develop and continuously improve the best evidence-based practices that establish and support lifelong learning.